Psychic
JUNKIE

Psychic

JUNKIE

A Memoir

Sarah Lassez
with Gian Sardar

SIMON SPOTLIGHT ENTERTAINMENT
New York · London · Toronto · Sydney

SIMON SPOTLIGHT ENTERTAINMENT

An imprint of Simon & Schuster

1230 Avenue of the Americas, New York, New York 10020

Copyright © 2006 by Sarah Lassez

SIMON SPOTLIGHT ENTERTAINMENT and related logo are trademarks of Simon & Schuster, Inc.

Designed by Steve Kennedy

Manufactured in the United States of America

First Edition 10 9 8 7 6 5 4 3 2 1

Library of Congress Cataloging-in-Publication Data

Lassez, Sarah.

Psychic junkie : a memoir / Sarah Lassez with Gian Sardar.—1st ed.

p. cm.

ISBN-13: 978-1-4169-1838-7

ISBN-10: 1-4169-1838-8

1. Lassez, Sarah. 2. Actors—France—Biography. I. Sardar, Gian. II. Title.

PN2638.L29A3 2006

792.02'8092–dc22

2006005130

For Jean-Louis and Catherine

Acknowledgments

THE INSPIRATION FOR THIS BOOK CAME DURING A conversation over a cup of Café du Monde coffee and chicory with the magical Grace Zabriskie. Thank you, Grace, for urging me to start writing down my stories and for lighting my creative fires.

I'd always hoped to say this while accepting an Oscar, but I'll say it now: I'd like to thank my manager, Beth Holden-Garland, for believing in me through all these years and for her undying loyalty. She is a rarity in Hollywood: a dolphin among sharks.

In September 2004, thanks to accidentally running into Beth at a Broadway show, I ended up at a Paris Hilton book signing party. I'd like to thank God for making it occur to me, *Hey! I'm at a book signing party! I'm writing a book! There might be a* book *agent here!!!*

Thank you to Alissa Vradenburg for introducing me to the great literary agent Dan Strone at said party.

Thanks to Dan for not laughing in the face of the girl with the crazy glint in her eye, rambling on about being addicted to psychics. Dan, laughing or not, you promised to read the book proposal and then, being a man of your word, you actually read it! Lucky me, finding the best book agent in the biz! (I finally get the whole "networking" concept.)

Big thanks to our editor, Patrick Price, for championing the book. Patrick, you rock and rule!

Thank you to David Koth at Untitled Entertainment for keeping me afloat during the woebegone years, and many thanks to his father for praying on my behalf.

Thanks to my family in France, especially to my cousins, Nathalie and Anne, who helped me through some of the more difficult moments.

I want to thank my friends—some old, some new, all loved and appreciated—for being an integral part of the prismatic patchwork of my life: Anastasia, Kearie, Jimmy, Felicia, Silenn, Devon, Andrea, Komal, Erika, Liz, Merle, Steven, Abraham, J.P., Jaason, Alex, Trish, Pina, Rawea, Felicity, Jill, Reverge, and Sondra.

Lastly, and most important, my deepest gratitude goes to my friend and collaborator, Gian Sardar, for coming aboard and lending her literary magic to my screwy saga. Gian, I remain your biggest fan.

A few additional thanks from Gian: First I'd like to thank Sarah, whose endearing craziness has been so much fun. I'm thrilled to have been a part of this, and am honored to be your friend. I'd also like to thank those who've encouraged and inspired me to write. Though I've seen one too many sunrises and have guzzled far too much coffee, it's been worth it and I'm grateful to each and every one of you. And last—but certainly not least—I'd like to thank Joe, just for being who he is.

PROLOGUE

For Entertainment Purposes Only

I'VE JUST BEEN TOLD MY RELATIONSHIP IS CELERY.
For two weeks I've been hiding in my room, which looks as though it has suffered a raid from a *very* disrespectful FBI team. I'm flat broke, unemployed, and rarely showered. And now I'm dating produce. Or was dating produce. Or *am* produce? I'm trying to figure that out—are you what your relationship is, and hence *I'm* celery?—when I realize I'm paying for silence. The word "celery" has thrown me. In the past, psychics have called Wilhelm many things (my favorite to this point being a hippopotamus; a deceivingly sedate plant eater one would, it turns out, be wise to fear), and I'd always rebounded quickly. But celery? Celery takes the man I love, aching green eyes and high German cheekbones, and replaces him with something that is, let's face it, tasteless unless dipped in ranch.

I press the phone closer to my ear. I have to say something. "Celery?" I say. *Brilliant, Sarah. Great response. Well worth the long expensive pause.*

"Yes. Celery." The psychic now sounds irritated, as if everyone should be aware there's a good chance their relationship is celery. Clearly I'm a troublemaker. "Celery that's been snapped in two. You know those stringy things at the end? That's what's holding you together. Those stringy things. So you're not completely separated, because the two pieces, you and him, are being held together by those stringy things, which are essentially—"

"Yeah, okay," I say, interrupting her monologue on the workings and philosophical implications of celery. "I get it. So, do you see us getting back together?"

She takes a long, deep, punishing breath. I'm not kidding that it's punishing—at $7.99 a minute, I think I just paid $1.30 for her to inhale and exhale.

"Yes," she says eventually. "I do. But it's gonna take a while. He's a turtle right now. Moving verr-rry slowwww-ly. Picture a turtle—"

Great. I can't afford groceries, but I just paid a bitchy psychic to tell me my relationship is celery and the man I love is a turtle. I hang up. At least Wilhelm and I are getting back together. On to the next one. Redial.

"Welcome to Psychicdom. Please hold while we connect you with your adviser."

"Hello, this is Glenda."

Now, Glenda has one of those sultry voices that sounds slick with brandy and primed for a smoke, as if she spends her afternoons reclining languidly in ivory silk, wrist bent just so, exotic eyes lending an impression of eternal boredom that causes men to trip and stutter. Though this is what she *sounds* like, if I had to put money on it, I'd say she's actually wearing sweatpants, is stuffing her face with bonbons, and has just put her game of video poker on pause. I cross my fingers. *Make me happy, Glenda.* "HithisisSarahandIwannaknowwhat'sgonnahappenwithWilhelm."

If you spread out those words, maybe slowed down while speaking so they are each on their own (as, technically, words should be), they would look like this: "Hi, this is Sarah and I want to know what's going to happen with Wilhelm." At one point they *did* look like that, but as my addiction to psychics advanced (and my credit card debt increased), I developed an issue with paying to hear my own voice, and those words sped up, eventually taking permanent residence at the tip of my tongue, a tightly banded cluster ready to hurl itself out at whoever might be within earshot. So trained is my mouth to form these words that I've actually verged on answering the phone this way. "Hello?" is traditional and expected, but answering with "HithisisSarahandIwannaknowwhat'sgonnahappenwithWilhelm" would be much more true to who I am and what's on my mind. Sadly, anyone who knows me well enough to be calling would not be thrown by this.

"Ah, Wilhelm," Glenda says, as if he's a new toy who's just stumbled into her boudoir. "Wilhelm. Willllllhelmmmm . . ."

I hear the shuffling of tarot cards, that all-too-familiar repetitive flutter, the flutter that stalks me in my sleep the way the jangling bells of slot machines stalk those over-oxygenated empty-pocketed souls who've spent too much time in Vegas. I also hear a lawn mower starting up next door, and for a second I'm reminded that an entire world exists outside that I am in no way a part of. Apparently people still have lawns. This upsets me. How can people care about grass when Wilhelm isn't calling me? How can grass even *exist* if Wilhelm doesn't love me?

Glenda begins to tsk–tsk, as if she doesn't care for the cards she's seeing, though in truth I bet she just looked back up at her game of video poker and realized she was one spade away from a flush. Meanwhile, I accidentally glimpse the unruly stack of envelopes on my nightstand, each with plastic address windows (*Look away! Those are bills!*), and my heart speeds up. Depending on what Glenda says about Wilhelm, I may have to ask her if I'll be rich soon. Of course, I haven't had an audition in weeks . . . but then again, I never found out what happened with that last audition, so there is a chance they haven't chosen anyone and they could still cast me. I should hang up and call my agent. I eye the phone. I *really* don't want to talk to my agent. She's always so rushed and annoyed, as if somehow she's perpetually boarding a plane, and often I wonder if that's because she has no clue who I am. Besides, it's not as if she'd really know what the producers thought. Much better to just ask Glenda how the audition went.

"I sense distance," Glenda says finally. "Emotional or physical or mental. But I also see sudden communication. Things will be full of *hope*! He's very sorry for what he's done, and you'll be back in each other's arms in three to ten days."

I shove wadded up Kleenex off my laptop, about to add her name to my "Psychics I Like and Why" document, when she continues.

"But then the cycle will repeat itself, and this time the break is permanent. Darling, he's not the one for you. And I—"

I hang up without saying good–bye, just like they do on TV. That always used to bug me. I mean, how much extra effort does it take to say good–bye? But they don't. They hold the phone in their glossy-nailed grips and without warning place it in the cradle so they can stare off, contemplatively, at nothing. I always wanted to scream, "Say good-bye!" But now I understand. At some point in TV history there was an editor who realized that the two seconds it took to say that word were costly—and "good-bye" was forever banished. I understand because I myself now know the cost of good-bye.

Who's next? I search the Web site, studying pictures of psychics, trying to find one who looks kind and open. I bet most of these psychics are bitter, that's the problem. Wilhelm and I aren't over; I just need to find someone who still believes in true love, that's all. My eyes scan to the bottom of the page, and I see it: the disclaimer. I've never noticed this before. I read through a snarl of legal-sounding words that ends with the proclamation that these readings are "for entertainment purposes only." I reread that phrase. I start to laugh.

This, this stupid disclaimer, is the *only* thing I've found to be entertaining on this site. Everything else is purely evil, creating a tormented agony similar to—I would imagine—that of a sugar-craving diabetic locked inside a chocolate factory. They must have been confused when they chose their words. Maybe what they really meant to say, in claiming the site was for entertainment purposes only, was this: "You, like countless others, will not take these readings lightly. You will use this site as a tool to destroy your life, and you will have no fun doing it. What you are embarking on will lead to overwhelming debt, debilitating self-doubt, and an addiction that will rule your every thought. This will not be entertaining at all. At least not to you, it won't be. To others it will be hysterical. Your silly little existence is now for entertainment purposes only. Good luck, and don't forget to leave feedback."

If only people came with disclaimers. Mine would be written in graceful lavender-colored scroll, revealed with a flick of my bangs: "Sarah is a wonderful person who is capable of immense love and caring—as well as psychotic and obsessive behavior. Be warned that should you not provide an engagement ring within a year, the real Sarah will crack through her marriage-isn't-all-that-important facade and you will find yourself scared and in jewelry stores. Proceed with caution." And of course Wilhelm's disclaimer would reflect his difficulties with the English language: "Thinks declaring 'I intend to marry you' to a thirty-year-old woman is just harmless conversation that would never be taken seriously. Ultimately claims no responsibility for his words, may periodically develop amnesia, and believes saying 'I meant the marriage thing at the time' is acceptable and would never cause said thirty-year-old woman to spontaneously combust."

Of course no one listens to warnings. Especially not me, and especially not about psychics. After all, I've amassed far too much debt calling these psychics, and made countless decisions based on their readings, and now I'm being told this is just for *fun?* Are they kidding? On to the next one!

"Welcome to Psychicdom. Please hold while we connect you with your adviser."

"Hi, you've got Andre."

I've got Andre? Is it curable? *No, Sarah, don't mock the psychic, just speak.* "HithisisSarahandIwannaknowwhat'sgonnahappenwithWil-helm."

"There's a vibration between the two of you," he says, jumping right in without pause, as if he'd actually been thinking of our relationship before I called and was just dying to tell someone his theories. "I see shaky streams of red and purple, these throbbing colors between you."

Fabulous. Andre's voice is light and airy as if his entire body is filled with happy helium and more than anything he longs to float away, to just float away and join seagulls and stars and nestle inside a cloud. I hate people like this—they can talk for hours and still you have no clue what they're saying. This call settles it; I'm having a bad psychic day.

"You need to detach from him," he continues. "Reliance on him is painful. Take back your power! You need to become more *like* him for him to become more like *you*."

Oh, for the love of God, won't someone just give me a straight answer? I can't afford this! With as much dignity as a girl who's been wearing the same 1980s B.U.M. Equipment sweatshirt for two weeks can muster, I shriek, "But will we get back together? Does he love me?"

This does not throw Andre. I can only begin to imagine the things people have shrieked at him, and yet, being the professional that he is, he remains calm. "Yes, he loves you. Be patient. You should feel *very* confident that you'll be together again, because I *do* see it *very* clearly."

Andre is the man! I love Andre! Now I'll ask The Big Question. The Big Question is only ever asked when I feel certain the answer will be yes. "Will we get married?"

He doesn't miss a beat. "The proposal's in August. Marriage in a year and a half to two years. I see peonies in your bouquet. Just lovely."

My heart soars, my face stretches into a grin that would

frighten children and threaten animals. At the moment, Wilhelm considers us over and thinks he's moving on, but clearly that's because he hasn't realized we're getting married. Poor unaware Wilhelm. Of course *I've* always known we'd get back together. We've gone through too much for our relationship to have just been some transitory fling. In this case especially, good–bye is not something I'm willing to say.

Beep. "One minute remaining."

"Do you see anything else?"

"Changes will be very positive for the two of you. Your relationship will be an offshoot of what it was. But I *feel* his fear of getting close. You need to be patient. Does he have green eyes?"

My breath catches. "Yes." Beautiful green eyes. Green eyes like lucky clovers, like a secret tropical lagoon, like grass after a rain, like . . . celery?

"I see him walking toward you holding out a—"

Beep!

No! "Holding what, holding *what*!"

"Holding—"

"Hello. Sorry to interrupt your call. To continue your conversation at the rate of $4.99 a minute, you will need to add to your account. To add twenty-nine dollars, press one. To add fifty-nine dollars, press two. To add a dollar amount of your choice, press three. To end this call, press four."

No! Don't end this call! I'm pressing three, I'll enter thirty bucks! Here, take it! Float back to me, Andre! Don't nestle in a cloud! Come back!

"Don't forget to leave feedback at the end of your call."

Of course! I love Andre—put him back on the line!

"I'm sorry, but your credit card has been declined. Please hold for an operator."

1

How It All Started: The Beginning of the End

THIS WAS MY AFTERNOON: AT TWO O'CLOCK MY CAR wouldn't start; at two fifteen I found out my boyfriend was a sex fiend drug addict who'd cheated on me with a *Baywatch* babe. It'd just been one of those days. The way I saw it, my first mistake was waking up, and my second mistake was not going back to sleep.

Somehow I made it through the rest of the day—a bout with AAA (bastards had a theory about membership fees being required for membership); an audition (I certainly won't be getting *that* part); and what seemed like hours of L.A. traffic as I sat in my car, trapped in one of those numb visionless states where an alien could drop from the sky and knit me a sweater and I'd not blink an eye.

Finally home, I flopped onto the bed, arm flung across my eyes in an effort to make the world go away. Life outside my apartment was dangerous, and the events of the day were proof that I was not equipped to handle it. I'm much more cut out for island living—resort island living, I should say, not *Survivor* island living. Actually, I realized a piña colada could seriously be the answer. I wondered if I could have one (fine, five or six) delivered, and tried to remember what menus people had so thoughtfully crammed beneath my windshield wipers. A place called "Foo Chung's Heartbreak Express—We Deliver Booze and Chocolate, No Questions Asked!" would be ideal right about now.

I was about to journey to the kitchen, when I saw it above me: the water stain from hell. Just this morning it had been a little yellow dot, and yet somehow, in the course of my day, it had been fed a million other little dots and was now the size of a small child. I lay back down, hypnotized by the blistering mustard yellow stain. *Hmmm*, I thought, *it looks familiar.* I tilted my head, studying the mark. *Oh my God. An Oscar. It looks exactly like an Oscar! It's a sign I'm going to win an Academy Award!*

But then, as quickly as the hope shot through me, it was gone. I'd have to tell my landlord about this. The ceiling could collapse and kill me in my sleep.

I started to cry.

Here I'd just found out that the man I thought I'd loved was a sex fiend drug addict who'd cheated on me with a *Baywatch* babe (okay, she had just a brief stint on the show, but she *was* in a bikini, and I think that counts), but it was the water stain on my ceiling that made me lose it. I loved my little apartment: a 1940s-style studio apartment with a view of the Hollywood sign and a charming black-and-white checkered kitchen floor that made me want to wear white gloves and full skirts, and set pies in windowsills to cool.

Sarah Lassez

But my landlord was the not-so-wonderful aspect of my apartment. A rotund and prickly man, he acted as if I'd been sent from hell to personally orchestrate his downfall. This, I knew, was because I was a woman, as the men in the building could do no wrong. I swear the guy downstairs could douse his kitchen in gasoline, drop a match, and walk away—yet my landlord would simply study the charred remains, shrug, and proceed to talk about football or basketball or one of the many sports I do not pretend to understand. If I, however, so much as let a *strand* of my hair *touch* the bathtub, he'd fly into a tantrum about drains and clogs and exploding pipes and women and their hair.

To cope with this annoying chauvinism I'd usually enlist whatever boyfriend I had at the time to deal with said fat landlord. But now I was alone. The water stain had waited to emerge (no one lived above me, and I swear it hadn't rained in months) until I was freshly wounded and newly single, hence illustrating yet another reason why it sucks to be alone.

Just call, my logical side said. *Call and report the ceiling! Get it over with! Be responsible!* I was about to reach for the phone, but the image of my landlord standing in my apartment with a scowl stopped me. "Obviously you were on the roof with a jackhammer," he'd say, shaking his fat head. No, I had no choice. My only option was to forget about my landlord, brave death by falling ceiling, call my friend Gina, and get drunk.

Gina and I met when she was nineteen and I was twenty-two and her father was dating a friend of mine. No stranger to dysfunctional relationships, she'd always maintained there were a few lines she wouldn't cross, one being dating an actor.

According to her theory, actors are essentially trained liars, and dating one is the same as having a dangerously high fever: You can't think straight, no one makes sense, you start seeing things, you lose your appetite, and you think you might die. Tom, the sex fiend, drug addicted, *Baywatch*-babe-chasing cheat, also had the honor of being an actor—though my take on dating him had obviously been different. The way I saw it, Tom was employed as a waiter, not an actor, so clearly he wasn't a *good* liar, or at least not a successful one. Besides, I myself am an actress, so wouldn't I be prepared to handle a fellow thespian?

The answer is no. I was not, and most likely never will be. In a city where there are egotistical issue-riddled actors and musicians everywhere you turn, and the egomaniacal issue-riddled people (producers, agents, directors, whatever) who made the aforementioned famous, odds are you won't escape unscathed. However, even worse than that group is the one that resides many ranks below: the struggling souls who *want* to be famous actors and musicians, and so on. As far as issues and egos are concerned, this group is essentially the same as their successful counterparts, the way a shadow resembles a form . . . only they're broke. Tom, bless his twisted evil little heart, was a member of the latter category.

The key, Gina insisted, was to meet a "normal person," that rare individual who's not in the entertainment industry at all. This, alas, is a near impossibility, practically a pipe dream. But for a chosen few it happens. Gina herself, for instance, dated an accountant for one month, and yet told the story for years, as if she'd been fishing in a stream and found gold. "A tad on the boring side," she'd say, though I got the distinct impression he was more than a tad boring, as on their dates she'd call me from restaurant bathrooms just to chat. "Still, they're out there," she'd remind me. "The normal people are out there!" "Really?" I liked to ask her incredulously. "And after a date do you remember anything, or has time gone missing? Tell me about their ship!"

I knew calling her and admitting that Tom had indeed lived up to his trained-liar status would elicit a big fat "I told you so," but I took the risk. That damn water stain above me still looked like an Oscar, but now it looked like a laughing Oscar, a mocking, spiteful, cruel Oscar. "Who do you think you are? You'll never make it as an actress! Give up! Move back to Kansas!" Granted, I've never even been to Kansas, yet still the idea upset me. I reached for the phone.

Calm, I thought as her answering machine beeped. *Calm and rational.*

"It's me. Just calling to say hi." I paused and took a deep breath, and as I exhaled, anything that was once calm and rational escaped. "I must have been Jack the Ripper in a past life. That's the only reason my love life would suck so bad! He was cheating on me with that slut hostess at his restaurant, that *Baywatch* chick! And he was a drug addict and a sex fiend! Pick up the phone! I've had a bad day! *Pick up the phone!*"

Gina finally answered and listened to my afternoon's saga with the perfect amount of cursing and comforting. At the end I paused, trying to get my heart rate to settle into a safer zone, and Gina took advantage of the silence to announce she'd be over in ten with wine. I thought of calling her back to utter the words "piña colada," but instead I simply stared at the door until she arrived.

We sat on the bed with full glasses of merlot. Stains already covered the comforter; what did I care? In a studio apartment you have very limited space, so I was very limited with furniture, and hence my bed served as just about everything: couch, chairs, coffee table, dining room table, et cetera. This tended to make dates difficult, as at the end of the evening my inviting a guy inside was the same as saying, "Please, welcome to my bed."

"I deserved it," I told Gina. "I should've known."

"Don't beat yourself up. We all get delusional. Actors look good. That's their job. They're like pretty shiny toys—they're hard to resist."

"You make us sound so bad. Remember, I'm an actor too."

"I know. And you couldn't *pay* me to date you, either."

"Thanks."

"No problem. Oh," she said as she lit a cigarette, "and I told you so."

Ah, there it was. I smiled. "Did you? I don't remember. Maybe that was the same day *I* told *you* not to take that job you know is going nowhere."

"Huh. Could've been."

I sniffled. "I hate *Baywatch*."

"*Baywatch* sucks. And Candy—"

"Cindy."

"Sorry, Cindy, whatever; she looks like a Candy. Fake boobs. And bad fake boobs. They're like shelves, they—"

"I hate fake boobs."

"I know you do. We all do."

"Tom doesn't."

Gina took a deep drag of her cigarette, her words smoky. "Tom sucks."

It was another night of reveling in our misery. I'd stopped crying and was now looking out my dark window at pretty much nothing. One solitary tear skittered down my cheek and rested on my lower lip. It dangled there, but I made no move to brush it away, as somewhere in my grief I was still a twisted actress aware that the combination of my pained silence and puffy eyes and that one single tear must have been heart-breakingly beautiful. So impressed was I with the vision I'd created of myself that I actually forgot about Tom long enough to wish Gina had a camera.

"It's seriously for the best," she continued. "Think 'normal person.' Wouldn't it be nice to be with someone responsible? Someone with a savings account? With a 401(k)? That accountant I dated—granted he was a tad boringish, but shit—he had a 401(k). A 401(k). I don't even know what those are really, something to do with retirement, but I know normal people have them. God, what would it be like to retire? I wanna retire."

Recently Gina had been promoted to manager at a clothing store she'd worked at during college, a job that had been fine during her student years but was now a reminder that she'd amassed tons of student loan debt to graduate and fold sweaters. Ever since then, she'd been obsessed with the idea of fleeing the country, running off to some place where people didn't use the phrase "career path"—a place where her high school newsletters, with their maddening updates on all her successful past friends, would never find her. Her dream, as she called it, was to move to Europe, live on an Alp, and make cheese. She really loved cheese—and I don't mean that she just loved eating it; she actually loved *looking* at it. How weird is that?

"You know," she continued, "that water stain on your ceiling is pretty bad. You should tell your fat landlord about that."

With the mention of my fat landlord the tears were no longer silently beautiful but full-force heaving ugly. I wasn't crying because I didn't have Tom; I was crying because I had no one. Again. Once more I'd be reduced to eating frozen dinners. (The only thing more depressing than cooking for just yourself is sitting down, alone, to eat the meal—so why fight it? Frozen meals are the answer. They say, "I'm single but still deserve a meal!") Once more I'd be doomed to sleep and wake in a bed that was just too tragically big. Saturday nights would again involve Gina and parties that always slightly horrified us, or evenings in sweatpants watching *Grease* for the hundredth time and eating blocks and blocks of Brie. (Some girls binge on ice cream. I binge on Brie. It's the one cheese I really like, and I blame it on being French. Gina loves this about me and claims it's a sign that her Move to Europe and Make Cheese plan is the answer.)

I was bawling and she was uttering reassuring sayings, a universal soundtrack of consolation with a few Gina originals in the mix: "It's okay. It'll be okay. This happened for a reason. Tom sucks. One day you'll laugh at this. Someone better is out there. Fuck that *Baywatch* bitch." Meanwhile, my cat, China, a snotty and obese Himalayan who seemed determined to live up to the size of her name and who had no interest in me unless I had a can opener in my hand, heaved herself onto the bed. The mattress springs moaned. I reached for her—it would have been so comforting to have her curled up and purring in my lap—but

Sarah Lassez

she shot me a dirty look and arranged her girth on, and over, a pillow.

All of a sudden I realized there was a third bottle of wine on the floor. My tears stopped. Now, Gina tends to be, for lack of a better word, psychic. It's not something she has much control over, and usually the things she predicts are fairly useless. (Did it help anyone that she dreamt a total stranger would tell her he stapled his finger?) But one thing we've learned is that when she gets drunk, she can be quite the oracle. There have actually been a few times when her predictions were scarily right on, and because of this I take what she says very seriously. Unfortunately, her opinion is that I take it too seriously, and she usually flat-out refuses to make predictions, since she's perfectly aware that revealing a vision of me at a party wearing a stunning pair of pink Manolo Blahnik shoes as I talk to a gorgeous guy who looks *very interested* will only send me scurrying off to Neiman Marcus, where I will blow my rent money on those shoes.

I eyed the wine bottles. "You're pretty drunk, huh?"

"Yeah, I didn't have dinner. I was too—" She stopped. Her eyes narrowed. "No."

"Please! Just tell me you see a man in my future. I need to know."

"I see a man in your future."

"No, come on, Gina. Look at me." I held my arms up, displaying myself as if I were the principal exhibit at a high school assembly meant to warn students of all things dangerous. "This," a woman with a tight bun and a gray pencil skirt would say as she pointed to me, "is what dating an actor can do to you." I concentrated a bit and forced tears to well in my eyes. "I need this. I need hope."

Gina laughed, as I figured she would. "You're pathetic. It's a good thing I love you." She downed the rest of her wine. "All right, fine. Here I go." She closed her eyes and was silent for a while. Then, all of a sudden, she was glaring at me.

"What? What? What do you see?"

She shook her head.

"Tell me!"

She sighed. "He's an actor."

I recoiled. "What? Why would I do that again?"

"I don't know, Sarah, why *did* you do it again? It's not like Tom was your first."

"Tell me what you see exactly. What does he look like?"

She closed her eyes again. "Dark hair, dark eyes. Not too tall—I mean, he's an actor."

Right there she'd described half the men in Los Angeles.

"Maybe you work with him?" she said, rubbing her temples. "It's horrible. You both look happy. Really happy. He's doing the whole gaze-into-your-eyes bit and holding your hand." Then she shrugged. "That's it. That's all I get."

It was enough. Just that sliver, that snapshot, gave me hope. That night I thought of my future dark-eyed man. I played with scenes, fiddled with settings. We were on a bench in a park, surrounded by majestic oaks, the moon slinking through branches as he leaned in close. No, we were on the beach at night, inky water slipping around our bare feet, an open bottle of wine awaiting us at our blanket. I stopped. I didn't need that. I didn't need any of that. What I really wanted, what I really craved in that way that actually hurt, could take place right here in my boring little studio apartment. Just him opening the door for me, then walking inside the cramped room with no couch and no coffee table and my fat furry mass of a cat hissing from the bed—just him smiling, smiling because it's my life he's seeing, my world he's a part of, me that he has.

God I *am* pathetic.

A couple months later and Tom was nothing more than a sex fiend drug-addicted dot in my rearview mirror. I'd moved on, partially healed by my acting career, which suddenly seemed on the rise. A movie I'd done was finally released, and my tormented performance (my character committed suicide) garnered an attention I'd only dreamt of. Strangely enough, that role was just the first of many suicides for me. Though my parents have always found it slightly horrifying, casting directors, producers, and directors alike all tended to see me as a natural when it came to committing suicide, being raped, or being murdered. Eventually I did break free from my snare of victim roles, though I was then hurled in the extreme opposite direction, going from playing innocents to being cast as whores— and not just your simple garden-variety whore, but a whole range of whores, my favorite being a ghostly whore from 1900. Evidently, anything that was whorish just screamed "Sarah!" And though I'm always thankful to be working, I'm still not quite sure how I feel about that.

The success truly hit home when I discovered myself in *Vogue*. Not featured, of course, but there I was, in the fashion section, right next to Madonna. Apparently our shared love for leopard-print handbags had catapulted me into the same league as the Material Girl—if only in terms of handbags, and I had to resist the urge to buy hundreds of copies of *Vogue* and mail them off to anyone who'd ever doubted me. "Just thought you might want to check out the latest in leopard-print hand-bags. . . . Oh, and yeah, that is me next to Madonna. Talk to you soon!" The only thing that stopped me was that TALKING FASHION was inconsiderately splashed across my face, though I believe the G brushed into my idol's picture as well—yet one more thing we had in common.

When another magazine decided to do a spread called "Twelve Actors to Watch," and they selected me—one of only six women—I could barely contain my glee. A bit nervous, I showed up on time for the photo shoot, dreaming of looking glamorous, until the coordinator stared at me—eyes wide and skittering from my face to the door—in a way that made me realize there'd been a huge mistake. They didn't want me. Somewhere out there was a different Sarah Lassez, and obvi-ously *she* was the one to watch. Her career was on the rise while I was anchored to the earth.

Finally the woman spoke. "You . . . you're here alone?"

I couldn't believe it. I'd been there for approximately sixty seconds and already she was pointing out how alone I was. "Yes. Why?"

She started laughing. "Oh, how cute!" And then she dis-appeared to select my outfit.

How odd, I thought. Sadly, it later made sense. As I eventually learned, the actresses before me had arrived with entourages, groups of people there for support and flattery . . . and, it turned out, protection. While everyone else got to look beautiful and glamorous, I was for some reason featured as a dour musician in electric blue hot pants, morosely meandering across a park with a guitar case. I don't even play the guitar.

Still, life was going well. I was receiving praise, my manager was still taking my calls, and I actually got a birthday present from my agent. I believe the present was an unscented candle, which may not be much, but my agency was so big and powerful that their remembering they even represented me was gift enough. Seriously. When I'd call to talk to my agent, I'd say my name and cross my fingers.

Even the water stain had been fixed, repaired by a man who'd stubbornly insisted it looked more like Elmo than Oscar. *Oh, well,* I thought. Everyone's got his own particular dream.

All I could really complain about was my lack of love and that my cat had started to stubbornly mistake my bathtub for her litter box. To anyone else the bathtub–litter box confusion would simply be an annoyance. But to me, a bath freak, it was beyond devastating. No longer was I able to gaze proudly at my vast array of bath products, as their view had been eclipsed by ugly bottles of Clorox, Tilex, Ajax, Comet, and a few others. (I tend to overreact.) Despite my dutifully cleaning the litter box and even hanging catnip on the wall above as a sort of temptation, nothing worked. She knew what I loved, and continued to go for the kill.

Then I was cast in another movie. Working again not only meant money, which tends to come in handy for that whole survival aspect of life, but also served to reinforce my agent's frail memory of who I was. Though I wouldn't be making bankloads of cash on the film, it was another great role (I played an inno-cent girl whom a psycho plots to kill), and the movie starred an ex-Brat-Packer whom I'd worshipped during some of my most formative/traumatized years—a chunk of time in the eighties when I'd failed to adjust from my old posh private school in Australia to my new tough high school in New York.

Yes, the ex-Brat-Packer and I would become best friends. We'd try on each other's lipstick, and laugh over the fact that during those high school years I'd endured the wrath of the most popular cliques, evil girls who used to insult my outfits loudly and cruelly, though sometimes they tired of speaking and simply hissed when they spotted me in the hallways. To me their picking on my thrift-store finery was a clear indication that my Australian hipness was just too avant-garde for them and their penchant for feathered hair and rhinestones. Though, I admit I did go through a dress-like-a-carrot stage, an unfor-tunate time when I insisted on wearing bright orange shoes, thick orange tights, a blaring orange miniskirt, and a fluorescent green top. But still, I thought I looked pretty darn cool.

It was when I hid in my room, pretending to be sick in order to evade the harassment, that I watched the ex-Brat-Packer's movies over and over, sometimes throwing *Grease* into the line-up—even though that movie was a harsh reminder that my powers of concentration and determination had failed, as upon *my* move to the states, John Travolta was nowhere to be found. At any rate, I'd known at the time that the then-Brat-Packer would see me as the cool fashionista I was, and I imagined that one day she'd be my best friend and after school would pick me up in her convertible, music blasting as we tore off to get an ice cream cone or go roller skating or partake in any number of ridiculous activities my fourteen-year-old mind could conjure. Then, of course, all the evil popular girls would be so jealous they'd spontaneously combust, the Aqua Net-juiced flames leaving nothing but piles of ashes and rhinestones on the sidewalk.

And now it was actually going to happen. The ex-Brat-Packer and I *would* be best friends! The only problem was that the movie in which I was cast was set to shoot in Detroit. Not that I had anything against Detroit. I mean, I'd never been there—though I'd heard they made lovely cars—but in my experience, going on location for months is a little like going off to summer camp: It could be great and you might make lots of friends, or you could be miserable and be praying nightly for someone to come save you. And usually when on location, I get stuffed away in a tiny brown-carpeted hovel, a place where the fake wood-paneled television (with its two maddeningly fuzzy channels) hovers in the upper corner of the room and some poor soul has undertaken the colossal challenge of bolting down everything that can be bolted, the only exception being the Bible in the nightstand drawer. If I'm lucky, I walk away with a bag full of horribly drying mini shampoo bottles that I will never use but take anyway so I can add them to the collection of hotel freebies I keep hidden in my bathroom.

An aside about the hotel freebies: There are a few motivations at play. First, I tend to collect. Doesn't matter what it is; I'll collect it. Second, I enjoy the sport of raiding a maid's unattended cart. Third, I'm an actress with no steady income, so my life is spent in constant preparation for Rock Bottom, a land where I could very possibly end up too poor to buy shampoo and where I would be forced to stand in a cold shower with wet and latherless hair. But now, thanks to my foresight, should that time come, I may not be able to eat, but damnit, I'll have clean hair and a couple dozen plastic disposable shower caps.

And one thing I've learned: The kind of freebies provided directly reflects the class of hotel you're staying in. Bottom rung would be a place that only provides an infuriatingly tiny wedge—alas, a splinter—of soap, and a sad little bottle of shampoo. A step up would involve conditioner, lotion, and a shower cap, sometimes even face soap. Higher still would be a place with mini sewing kits, as everyone knows that the finer establishments encourage their guests to mend their clothes. Above that I've yet to encounter, though in my fantasies there are free little bottles of Chanel products and those great oversized fluffy robes, which the hotel wouldn't charge you hundreds of dollars for, should one accidentally find its way into your suitcase.

At any rate, it's been a rare and lucky day when I've encountered the mini sewing kits—and even in those places, I was afraid to touch the bedspread and insisted on wearing flip-flops in the shower. So, getting ready to head off to Detroit, I packed my conditioner, lotion, face soap, and flip-flops. I was prepared for the worst and resigned to using their shampoo at least until I got my per diem, which would then be blown on one horribly expensive shampoo containing some inane ingredient like white truffles or crushed diamonds, something that would ultimately make *no* difference to my hair and leave me feeling so guilty it would be months till I bought another bottle.

But then something happened. I arrived in Detroit—during

what I swear was a monsoon—and was taken to a place that lacked a pulsating neon MOTEL! DISCOUNT ROOMS! sign. Utterly confused, I played along with what I knew was a cruel mistake and checked in to a beautiful hotel. We're talking crystal chandeliers, cherrywood-lined walls, and a lobby with a fireplace where continental breakfasts would never ever be served.

An actual bellboy led me down the hall and stepped out of the way once he'd opened the door to Room 611; he then waited for me to stride inside. But I couldn't. I couldn't because what I saw was dark walnut living room furniture, flowers on the coffee table *and* dining room table, and French doors that led to the bedroom. (A bedroom!) So naturally I assumed I'd been brought to meet the director, which pissed me off because the shirt I was wearing had fallen victim to the ill-fated combination of a Bloody Mary and turbulence, and I was quite certain the humidity and rain had caused my hair to grow taller. Taller hair is never a good thing. Where was this director who insisted on seeing me at my worst? I stood at the threshold and scanned the room. No one was there. In fact, I didn't see any luggage or signs of inhabitance. The bellboy was now watching me with concern. Tentatively I stepped inside. This couldn't be my room, could it? My suite?

It was. And it got better. In the large marble bathroom was a huge, gorgeous, cat-piss-free bathtub—with water pressure, I guessed, unlike my little apartment where if anyone in any part of the building flushed a toilet, your hopes of a relaxing bath would fizzle and you'd end up angry and attempting to make the best of a puddle. And, I spotted with unadulterated glee, lined alongside said gorgeous tub was an array of Crabtree & Evelyn bath products. I felt tears well in my eyes as I approached the dazzling tub, running my hand down its smooth porcelain side. *You and I,* I thought, *we will get to know each other.*

"Just down the street," the bellboy said, "is a bath store."

I looked back at him. He had a young face but was cute. Very cute. *No, Sarah, he's like twelve.* I quickly tipped him so he'd leave.

Left alone with my tub, I immediately understood my new mission in life: to never leave this porcelain vessel. Sure, I may have to be on-set part of the day, doing that whole acting thing, but everything else—eating dinner, learning my lines, talking on the phone—all other activities could be conducted while I was turning into a prune and breathing in the vapors of over-priced aromatherapy products. I was so excited.

And on top of all this, I realized the next morning, I never had to clean. As I left for the day, I glanced over my shoulder. The bed was in a severe state of disarray, not unlike the bed in *The Exorcist,* and yet I knew that when I returned it would have magically repaired itself and the down pillow would have somehow birthed another chocolate for my sweet-toothed, sex-deprived self.

I was in heaven.

But then, as tends to happen to me, I was plucked from the soft nest of my life and dropped into some thorny scorching lobby of hell.

Enter the man. There he was—my "Danger, danger!" radar homed in on him the second I arrived on-set—an actor. The not-too-tall, dark-haired, dark-eyed actor Gina had predicted.

The second I saw him I knew I was toast. For fun, let's just call him That Dickhead Actor.

The weeks progressed and I fell into a rather shocked state of bliss. I couldn't believe it: He was into me. Really into me. He was dangerously handsome with long dark lashes and warm mahogany eyes that somehow always looked as though they'd found a crack into my soul that all others before had ignored. All his professing and flattering and soulful gazes made me feel as though something inside me had come unhinged and was swinging wildly in the gust of his affection. So, naturally, I dove straight in and did my usual swim in the Denial River. *He's different. He's a working actor and in no way, shape, or form a waiter.* (As if in the past the waiter part had been the problem.)

That Dickhead Actor was promising, and thus my days were threaded with visions of our future life together. He was from New York, and in my free time, when he was working, I soaked in my tub and decorated our future brownstone. The interior, I decided, would be all dark wood and red velvet, and we'd have a big four-poster bed in which to eat chocolate-covered strawberries while lost in a tangle of our twelve-thousand-thread-count (I tend to aim high) ivory sheets. The decision, by the way, to have ivory sheets rather than white was difficult and time-consuming and did slightly interfere with my memorizing my lines—but how could I picture *us* in bed if I couldn't properly see the bed?

So impressed and convinced was I, that I actually braced myself for the scolding of the century and called Gina to share my joy. ("Why would you do that?" she wailed. "Why?!") I tried telling her he was the man she'd predicted—she should be proud!—but she didn't care. She informed me I was demented and begged me to date the grip, the gaffer, anyone but the actor.

Then one day That Dickhead Actor simply changed his mind about me. Just like that he changed his mind—as if I were a dinner he'd ordered and sent back just to piss off the chef. I was so confused by the complete turnaround that for a second I actually doubted myself. Had I made up an entire romance in my head? Maybe he was ignoring me because *nothing had ever happened*? He's probably scared because I keep planting myself around each corner so he can run into me! I'm a freak!

But no. It was real. It had happened. I was once again brokenhearted—and, sadly, that made perfect sense. To add to the fun, the ex-Brat-Packer and I had a blowout, an argument ill-timed, as it was during a scene where I was gagged, hysterically crying, and tied to a bed while she threatened to kill me with a knife. When she stormed off the set, everyone went after her, forgetting all about me as I continued to bawl and writhe in my ropes. After that, things between us were never the same.

I was miserable. My driver Karen saw it all unfold and tried to help. Knowing I had several days off with nothing to do but hide in my hotel room—curled into a fetal position and weeping—she'd made plans to introduce me to her friend Aurelia.

"You have nothing else to do."

My head was against the window. Everywhere I went I perfected a posture of defeat. "Yes, I do."

"You're not spending three days crying."

"I like crying."

"But you'll have *fun* with Aurelia. And guess what?" She smiled. "She's a psychic."

The way she said the word "psychic" was the way an adult says "ice cream" to a child who's about to have her tonsils ripped out. And it worked. I lifted my head from the window. Never before had I been to a real psychic. "She's a psychic?" I asked.

Like I said, it was the beginning of the end.

Frankly, I was disappointed when I met Aurelia. Karen had told me Aurelia was Hungarian, and I just knew she'd be my gypsy psychic; would open the door in a swirl of exotic smoke, jasmine, and patchouli; dressed in bright colors and flowing scarves and mystery; her voice deep and thick with an accent that would scare children. Instead, not only did she not have an accent, but she also had one of the smoothest, silkiest voices I'd ever heard. The girl could've made a fortune in radio. And scarves? Mystery? Nope. What she had was jeans, a sweatshirt from the Gap, and long blond hair swept up in a tight ponytail. For all intents and purposes she looked as though she'd just escaped from a local sorority. *This* was my gypsy psychic?

I'd also—and this is somewhat embarrassing to admit, but it appears I've lost all pride—harbored a secret fantasy that she'd take one look at me and gasp at the bright future she immediately saw. Yes, I'd had visions of her opening the door and being overcome by images of my success in a way that normally never happened to her.

"This," I imagined her gravelly voice saying as her kohl-lined eyes widened, "normally never happens to me. Usually I need to read cards to see the future, but with you I see it so clearly! It *exudes* from you! You will be a famous actress! Like Julia Roberts famous! People will give you free clothing and makeup. Success! I see it all! This is very exciting for me, that one day I can say I read your cards. Would you mind signing those napkins over there? I also see myself selling your autograph for a lot of money."

I know it's ridiculous, but I did hope for something like that when she opened the door. Just a fraction of it, maybe. So again, I was slightly disappointed when she simply introduced herself and asked me if I wanted a Coke. Though, actually, I did want a Coke.

As Aurelia fixed my drink, I took the opportunity to inspect her kitchen. It was a discerningly decorated room, save for the avocado–colored appliances, which immediately told me she was renting and the landlord was cheap. But other than the hideous green remnants of the 1970s, everything was cheerful and reassuring. White cotton curtains on the windows, colorful mixing bowls stacked on the counter, pot holders with smiling pigs, and something that must've been a pantry covered by a long red gingham curtain. Always into things I shouldn't be, I was immediately drawn to the secret room.

"Oh!" Aurelia gasped as I pulled the curtain aside.

I didn't know what to say. "It's a, uh, it's a uh, uh—"

"Altar."

"Right, it's an altar."

Because, yes, it was an altar. I mean, at some point it had been a normal breakfast table crammed inside a pantry, but now that table was something on which no one would ever expect to find a plate of bacon and eggs. Adorned with a dark purple velvet cloth, it was covered with crystals, silver candles, and dried rose petals, then creatively set off with a cauldron on the left and a carved wood pentagram in the center. Perched innocently next to a ceramic chalice was a double-edged dagger. I stared. This was no sorority girl. Aurelia, I was learning, was all about incongruity, like a millionaire who clips coupons or a lawyer not a fan of confrontation. With her, nothing was as it seemed.

I leaned in, examining a little copper-colored bowl filled with a dark powdery substance. "What's this?"

"My ex-boyfriend's blood."

"Oh, sure." *Holy shit.*

"I'm kidding. It's merlot, or it was merlot. I'm Wiccan. Wine's used to symbolize blood." She smiled and handed me my Coke. "Do you want a straw? I have those fun curly ones."

"No, thanks. So that's cool, you're a witch." What does one say to this? I could think of a few spell requests, but after that I was stumped for witch conversation. And the funny thing was that Aurelia looked remarkably like an *angel,* a doll-like porcelain angel with clear fair skin, striking blue eyes, and golden hair. Looking at her, one would actually expect to find her in a long white dress with a white satin ribbon, stuck on a doll stand and placed in a curio cabinet for old ladies to coo over—and yet here she was, in her Gap sweatshirt and actually a witch.

She tightened her ponytail. "Think Glinda the Good Witch, not the Wicked Witch of the West."

"Okay," I said, though my eyes flickered to her feet to check for striped socks.

We sat down at the table, and Aurelia lit a lavender-scented candle. Now, lavender is supposed to be relaxing, soothing, but my reaction was instead that of pure terror. There it was; the candle was lit. Soon I would know everything. What if she told me she didn't see me acting at all, but saw me as a very successful receptionist? Or that she saw me as a very contented never-been-married older woman with a family of cats that piss in the tub? "This is great!" she'd say. "I see you as very happy and not at all upset that no one loves you!" I pushed the image from my mind, frantically breathed in the lavender, and commanded myself to relax.

She placed three decks of tarot cards on the table, closed her eyes briefly, and breathed in deeply. "I'd like you to pick one."

The pressure. In one of those decks would be my future. Well, I suppose my future would be in all of them, but I could already see that each would have its own unique method of delivery. The first seemed determined to announce the future with detailed disturbing and bleak drawings, images of people suffering, bent beneath the weight of stones, skewered by swords, tied up and blindfolded beneath gray and menacing skies. Even if that deck told me my future held happiness and love, I'd be scared. The second deck was less detailed but equally as frightening. But then there was the last one, and this deck immediately radiated a pleasing nonhostile feel; the cards were round, and the pictures were pretty and done in soft pastels. I tapped that deck, and Aurelia smiled. Clearly I wasn't the only one who'd requested a pretty pastel future.

"Now for a quick prayer." She closed her eyes. "I call upon the great spirit God/Goddess that is All to be here in conscious loving support. And I ask that all parts of you be present and open and relaxed. I also call upon the guides of Sarah to help me in giving the most truthful, empowering, and accurate reading possible."

When she opened her eyes, I could've sworn their blue had become more intense, more penetrating. I admit it, I was a bit scared.

"What would you like to ask?"

All the important questions in life scrolled through my mind. Have I chosen the right career? Will I be happy acting the rest of my life? Will I have children? Will I find true love? There was so much to ask! What did I want to know? I wanted to know everything!

I took a deep breath. I'd just start with what was most important. "Will That Dickhead Actor suffer and regret the day he ditched me?"

Again she smiled rather knowingly, winked at me, and said, "Tell you what, let's start with a life spread. We'll see if he plays into it, but we'll begin with you."

After having me shuffle the cards, she laid them out one by one in the shape of a Celtic cross. With each card my breath lodged in my throat; every card had meaning, yet all I could gather was a vague sense or impression of the pictures, and not all the pictures were pleasant. Apparently just because the deck was round and painted in happy soft colors didn't mean there wouldn't be bad cards. Right off the bat I got the Death card, a lovely pastel-colored grim reaper.

The Death card, it turned out, was a rebirth—and evidently it was my acting career that was being reborn.

"Don't worry. There's nothing to fear from the Death card. People have such limited views of what death means, and they tend to put those feelings onto this card. Really what it is, is a symbol of what you're going through now, essentially a rebirth process. Now this," she said, pointing to a picture of three people holding their cups high, either delirious with happiness or sloppily drunk, "this is you in the immediate future."

Great, I thought. I get wasted to mask the pain.

"You and the other two leads," she said softly. "You're celebrating the success of the film."

Celebrating the success of the film. I tried to act nonchalant while images of me strolling down a red carpet streaked through my mind. Flashbulbs, screams, "Sarah! Sarah, this way; smile for me, Sarah!"

"Really? Yeah, that'd be nice."

And it got better. By the time we got to the end of the reading, I'd completely forgotten about That Dickhead Actor and I wanted more than anything to spring from my seat and leap into my future. Then came the last card, and that card might as well have been a rope that pulled me from the earth and plopped me on a cloud. It was, as she called it, "the overall outcome card." And it was the Star.

I was going to be a star.

Bless Aurelia's soul, she had no idea what she was doing when she introduced me to those cards. The reading not only lifted me from the pit That Dickhead Actor had so callously thrown me into, but it gave me a hope and confidence I'd never really known. Whereas I'd always had faith in my abilities, I had never had much faith in others' abilities to recognize my abilities. But now I knew the future! Someone *would* recognize me for the star

I'd always known I should be! By the end of the year, life would be amazing.

I had to have my own deck. I wanted access to the cards at all times. I needed to be able to experience such happiness and reassurance whenever my pained little heart desired. So I called Aurelia and told her I wanted cards, and within the hour she'd whisked me off to a new-age store with dangling crystals and a haze of Nag Champa incense. It turns out, purchasing your own deck of cards is bad luck. So once I'd selected the happy round pastel deck, Aurelia took my money and paid a man with so many piercings that I pictured him taking a sip of water and turning into a human sprinkler. I'd had no idea they made people like that in Detroit.

The cards were mine. From that point on during the film's shooting, I'd spend my free days either with Aurelia or alone on the floor of my huge suite, surrounded by cards and the instruction booklet, furiously studying spreads and meanings. Never, not even in college, had I been so determined to learn.

Once my evenings had involved long phone conversations with Gina, but all that changed with the arrival of my cards. Not only could they tell me the future, but they could also tell me what someone was thinking. The cards were a portal into people's minds. Sure, Gina made attempts at that as well ("What's he thinking? He's thinking he must be a pretty brilliant fucking actor to have gotten you to fall for all that your-eyes-are-golden bullshit"), but I liked the cards' version much better. Besides, if I wanted them to say something, to send me a certain message, I'd just keep pulling and pulling until they did. Gina, on the other hand, would've snapped long ago. ("I'm on to you, missy. You want me to tell you to give him another chance, but I won't. He sucks, and you know it.") Of course, my repeatedly pulling cards until they said what I wanted was a little like someone dropping her diamond ring into a Cracker Jack box and then exclaiming with joy when she finds it seconds later, but that didn't seem to bother me.

I returned to Los Angeles equipped with my trusty cards and the knowledge that the film, and I, would be a success. As the town car pulled up my street, the Hollywood sign appeared to stand a little taller, the palm trees looked a bit more majestic, and even the smoggy sky seemed not quite as choking. Yes, I was certain. My life was about to begin, and it would be amazing.

2

Tarot Bliss and Live Psychics

HOW WRONG I WAS.

Only a few months after returning to Los Angeles, I'd already run out of money, the only men I met were those who delivered bags of Chinese food to my door, and it looked as though a movie I'd been relying on to launch my career was taking a quick and tragic journey to video. Where was my amazing life?

Still, I believed in Aurelia's words. It takes time, I figured, for a life to do an about-face, to upswing from the pits of despair. All the readings we continued to do—just about daily, much to the delight of my long-distance phone company—stubbornly insisted my world was on the verge of becoming magnificent, but soon I began to wonder whether seeking a second opinion might be a good idea.

Just a few blocks from where I lived was a house, a seemingly normal and dignified white Craftsman, save for the gigantic neon hand looming in the middle of the yard.

Blinding pink, the sign slapped passersby with its message: FIVE-DOLLAR PALM READINGS! I'd glance at the sign as I drove by, somewhat scared yet slightly captured by its command, until one day the pull was just too great. With a small bag of groceries in my car and dinner with Gina planned for an hour later, I threw all obligations and logic out the window and jerked my car to the curb. I had a hand. I had five dollars. I was gonna get a reading.

Walking up the steps, I again had the same vision of a gypsy psychic that I'd had upon meeting Aurelia, all the ridiculous stereotypes one would collect from watching too much TV—the scarves, the jewelry, the crafty smile. I shook my head, picturing Aurelia in her Gap sweatshirt. I knocked on the door.

Apparently I wasn't the only one who watched too much TV. There before me was a psychic straight from Central Casting. Long flowing dress, bright scarves, sequins, ornate gold jewelry. She even came complete with a Russian accent. Was this really how she was? Or was this an act? I couldn't help but wonder if at the end of the day she'd stretch her arms, sigh, and then head off to her bedrooom, where she'd wash away the garish makeup and slip on a pair of jeans to watch *When Harry Met Sally . . .* with her girlfriends.

As the gypsy lead me inside, I knew I should run. Instinct told me to grasp at whatever logic and rationale I had remaining, say "Oh, hi, just wanted to compliment you on your tasteful sign," and bolt. But of course I didn't do that. Instead I followed her to the living room and sat before a crystal ball.

Once the business transaction—four singles, three quarters, a nickel, and two dimes—was out of the way, she got down to business. She studied my palm, her eyes narrowed, her gypsy breath on my skin. After about a minute she sat back and shook her head. Her jewelry clanged.

"You have a curse."

Simple. As if announcing I had brown hair.

In silent horror I listened to the details: An older woman in my life wished me ill and had cast a curse, and till it was gone, my life would be tainted.

"*Tainted*," she said again, "viz bad luck."

I sat back, fleetingly noticing that the red paint she'd picked for the room was the same charming shade as blood from a fresh-cut artery, and thought, "Why, yes, this makes perfect sense." It explained everything. Of course I had a curse! I was supposed to be happy with a career and love, but this darn curse kept blocking those things. It was like some evil force field that no goodness could penetrate. In a way I was relieved, relieved it was that simple. We'd remove the curse and I'd be gifted with the life I was supposed to have. On the way home I'd even buy a lottery ticket, as I figured the universe might tweak some numbers to help make up for lost time.

"Two hundred dollars," the gyspy said.

I'd win two hundred dollars? Had she read my mind?

"To remove zee curse. Is bargain, special for you." She smiled. "Cash only."

Now I lost it. Having the curse was one thing, but not being able to afford to remove it was another. Somehow I panicked my way to the front door, made the gypsy *swear* that she'd get rid of the curse as soon as I found the money, swear that this wasn't a one-time-only offer, and then flew out the door, past the gargantuan hand, and into my car. I could practically feel the curse on me, scratching me like an itchy sweater.

Right as I dumped my last shoe box of bills onto my bed—determined to find at least one credit card pin number—the phone rang. Thank God it was Aurelia; the second she said hello I began frantically spewing words—"scarves, curse, hand in yard, pin number, Russian"—until somehow she was able to locate the pertinent ones, string them together, and then tell me to stop.

"It's a scam," she said. "Are you breathing? I need to hear you take a deep breath."

I took a deep, wobbly breath.

"It's a scam. A very common scam. You don't have a curse."

I stared at my credit card statements. The entire bed was filled with them, every inch. "But—but then why isn't my life as good as it should be?"

Aurelia laughed, softly, sweetly. "It'll get better. And I have something you can do, if you're still worried. Get some sage. It's purifying. Burn it around your house, visualize the negative energy leaving, feel the air being cleansed. If there is any kind of negative energy around you, the sage will help."

I didn't need to hear another word. Within seconds I was in my car and about to pull away from the curb, when there was Gina, standing on the sidewalk, ready for the dinner I'd neglected to cook, and looking rather confused.

"Get in," I yelled.

Obediantly she climbed in, bottle of wine in hand, and buckled her seat belt. She glanced at me as I threw the car in drive and punched the accelerator.

"I don't know what's going on," she said, "but I like it."

. . .

An hour later we had sage. The man at the new-age store said we'd only need a bit, but to be safe I bought bundles. I wasn't messing around with this cleansing business. I was serious, and now I was holding a match.

"Ready?" I asked Gina.

She, too, held a bundle in her hand. She nodded solemnly. We lit the sage.

At first it was fun, traipsing around the apartment from corner to corner, waving the sage as we cleansed my aura and purified my energy. But then the smoke got thick. Really thick. Apparently there was a reason you only needed a little bit. I opened the windows, but the smoke was everywhere. We started to cough. I doused the sage in water, we fanned at the smoke, but it was no use. The room was a dense haze.

And then the fire alarm went off. We both stood there, fixated by the blaring contraption at the top of the wall, until finally Gina was spurred into action and grabbed a broom. Furiously she beat the thing, yelling at it to shut up, while in the background I heard my neighbors stirring. People were smelling the smoke. There were sounds in the hallway. Knocks on doors. I could only imagine that the fire department was already howling up the street.

Sage extinguished, every window open, we eventually had no choice but to join my neighbors on the sidewalk. As my unit faced the street and had windows through which smoke was still drifting, it was pretty obvious who had some explaining to do.

. . .

A couple months later I had no proof the sage had done anything. The only change in my life seemed to be the addition of a new cat—which was then accompanied by the fear that I was on my way to becoming Crazy Cat Lady. Though, really, to be a Crazy Cat Lady you must live in an old wood house with chipped gray paint and an unkempt yard. Crazy Cat Ladies mutter strange things from their porches, and kids dare each other to approach on Halloween, spooked by creepy feline silhouettes in the windows. I had no house, and thus no porch, no yard, nothing—so, in truth, being a Crazy Cat Lady would've been a step *up*.

The bottom line was, China wasn't living up to her catly duties. Everyone else had cats that cuddled and nestled and purred, while mine did nothing but judge me and piss in the tub. Actually, that's a lie. She'd started doing more than just piss in the tub; she'd started doing another little number that seriously challenged the pledges of Clorox. So, with hopes of having a normal cat, I adopted Onyx, a tattered little black kitten from the pound. As we pulled out of the parking lot, Onyx wailing in a box beside me, I knew soon she'd be the cat I'd always wanted. Happy, curled next to me at night, and greeting me with meows of love when I returned home. Versus China, who howled from the window when she saw me approach, a cry I'd long ago learned could be translated as "Are you trying to kill me? It's been almost two hours since I've eaten!"

So yes, I had high hopes for Onyx. Yet this sweet little kitten must have read some instruction booklet on how my luck tends to go, and in accordance immediately took up residence inside my closet and refused to leave. My only Onyx sightings involved glimpses of her sprints to the food bowl or her stealthy endeavors to the bathroom, where she'd gnaw on the toilet paper's plastic wrapper, her eye on the door.

I hoped this wasn't an indication of my future as a mother to human children. Who was to say it wouldn't be the same? One daughter rebelling against toilet training altogether, the other sneaking food at the crack of dawn and then hiding out in darkness, nestling in shoes.

Not that I needed to worry about kids, as I was still in my midtwenties, and the children bridge wasn't one I'd be crossing for quite some time. No, at that point I was even afraid of dating, in part due to the dreadful luck I'd been having in that department. The last time I'd gone out was with a man who'd told me I reminded him of his mother, and that his father had proposed after having known her for only one day. Red flags began to wave, bells and whistles began to chorus, and the sky practically lit up with stars that spelled "Run!" But I saw the date through to the end, even resisting the urge to leap from the car when he turned to me with a syrupy gaze and pronounced that my skin was "like a song." In case I hadn't heard him, he then proceeded to demonstrate how my skin was like a song—by bellowing in full operatic grandeur "Your skin is like a song . . . *ahhh-ahhhh-AHHHH!*" My knuckles were white as my grip on the door handle became deadly. Finally I was able to sneak back inside my building, hoping my neighbors wouldn't identify me as the one who'd elicited such an aurally offensive compliment. After that, I vowed to take a break from the dating world, just a temporary one, but a break nonetheless.

• • •

China, The Bathtub Destroyer, was not pleased with the friend I'd gotten her, and she began to unleash her skills on other parts of my apartment, depositing little presents by windows or tucking them into corners. With each discovery I'd recoil in horror, as she lay innocently in her leopard-print bed, quietly plotting, a well-fed cat who clearly had issues.

"Go to a pet psychic," Gina said as she watched me frantically scrub the carpet.

I glanced back at her, trying to ascertain her expression. Face turned openly toward me. Smiling. Eyes clear and wide. But then one eyebrow twitched slightly, and I was on to her.

"No, seriously," she continued. "I bet she has issues from her childhood. Neglect and abandonment. Sibling rivalry."

"I hate you. I'm traumatized, and you're making jokes."

"I'm not kidding; I really think Miss Shitsalot needs therapy."

Pet psychics were far too expensive, and sadly I knew this because I'd already looked into the option. My reliance on Aurelia and her readings had grown and grown, and I was beginning to see that psychics were a great place to turn for just about any problem. Need to know how that audition went? Ask for a reading! Curious if you'll be able to pay your rent next month? Bust out the cards! Want to find out if that freak will stop singing "Your Skin Is Like a Song" into your answering machine? Do a spread!

"Don't worry," Aurelia said one night on the phone, after she'd told me that no, she could not read my cat's energy. "Things are going to really improve for you. I've been feeling a shift in energy coming on, a massive swing for the better."

I needed a swing for the better. Though just a year ago life had seemed so promising, with my face in publications and a hail of praise from critics, nothing much had materialized. The only result was that I now had a box full of cutout articles under my bed, with the magazine that featured twelve actors to watch hidden at the bottom. I'd kept the magazine whole as a way to torture myself, as every girl *other than me* had apparently been worth watching. Right across from my page was a girl who'd soared into stardom almost immediately, while the girl on my flipside was currently in at least two movies. Meanwhile, there I was with my guitar, painfully wedged between them, evidently nothing more than an upset musician with no hope of an acting career. Surrounded by success, I couldn't help but wonder what the hell I was doing wrong.

Just to be certain of this swing for the better, I demanded a reading. I heard the shuffling begin, such a wonderful, comforting sound, and curled up against the pillows on my bed.

"In five days," she said, "you're going to lose something."

I sat up.

"You'll lose something or have to sacrifice something on the material level. You'll be upset about it."

"What? Where'd my swing for the better go?"

"I'm still sensing that, but this does appear to come first. Sorry."

And that was that.

Five days after the reading I was running late for an audition for a guest spot on a lame-ass show, a job I hoped I'd get as much as I hoped I wouldn't, and couldn't find my keys anywhere. For about ten minutes I'd been kicking mounds of clothing around on the floor, shoving things off my bed, and generally redistributing the mess to try to unearth the keys, an activity that obviously got in the way of China's people-watching at the window, because she turned and glared at me in a way I didn't know was possible for a cat.

At last the keys came out of what I can only imagine was invisible mode, appearing in plain sight on the table by the door, and I was outta there, hurling myself down the stairs and flinging open the door to my building. I'd taken two steps on the sidewalk when I spotted a cat that looked strangely like China hightailing it up to my building, its belly swinging. What the hell? I looked up to my window on the second story, where I knew China would be. What I saw was an open window with no screen. The screen, I noticed, was now decorating the side-walk. Amazingly, China was fine, something that made sense when, back in my apartment, I noticed the awning below the window, completely covered in dust but for a big skid mark from a certain feline's mammoth ass.

Screen secured, I ran to my car, distractedly rehearsing my lame lines in my head. I reached out, about to open my door, but stopped. My car, which had been parked in that exact spot the night before, had turned into an oil stain. Other than a few pieces of broken glass, that was all that was there. The spot was empty. I lowered my arm. Was I mistaken? I looked up and down the street for my little white Honda Civic. Wait. *Broken glass.* Crap.

Whereas *I* was under the impression that my car being stolen was a monumental event, the police seemed to be under the impression that this type of thing happened every day. Robotically they jotted down notes, annoyingly insisting they needed "Just the facts, please" and none of my theories, and then suddenly they got another call about something somewhere else and were gone. Though I was slightly and secretly relieved at not being able to get to the audition I'd been dreading, the whole day's experience had left me feeling rather unsatisfied. Thus I was forced to call everyone I knew to recount the saga of the crime, inserting the appropriate and corresponding emotions, and felt better once I'd been afforded some sympathy. After all, this was Los Angeles, and my being without a car was no joking matter.

When it came time to call Aurelia, it hit me. She'd been right. I'd lost something material *five days after the reading*, exactly as she'd predicted. Forgetting all about my car, I quickly asked her about my future husband, hoping she'd still be on a psychic roll.

Immediately she got the Knight of Swords, a card that represents a man less than thirty-five years of age, with dark hair and dark eyes. Since Aurelia was not just a card reader but also a full-fledged clairvoyant, she supplemented her readings with her visions—and, indeed, the man she was seeing had dark hair, was of average height . . . and, she said warily, he might be an actor. Flashbacks to Gina's drunken prediction over a year ago streaked through my mind. Could it be the same man? Was That Dickhead Actor not who she'd seen after all? Were they both talking about the same amazing not-too-tall actor who would one day propose and give me two beautiful children with whom we could take disgustingly cute Christmas card pictures? Okay, the Christmas card pictures had never been in any of the predictions, but still, I wanted them.

But thoughts of any future holiday pictures or portraits were crushed beneath the weight of Aurelia's next words.

"He's someone you've already met. He's already entered your life."

"What? If he's the love of my life, why wouldn't I have grabbed him then and there? What's wrong with him?"

"It wasn't the right time then."

"Okay, fine, how did I feel about him when I *did* meet him?"

"You were intrigued. Is that the right word? Yes, intrigued."

"By what? Intrigued by what?"

"That's all I'm allowed to say right now."

I hated it when she pulled that, because there was just no room for arguing. It was like a parent telling a child "Because I said so," and each time I wanted to stick out my chin and sulk. But Aurelia stuck to her guns, as she'd long ago learned that if she didn't cut me off at the pass, I'd ask the same question in twenty different ways, stealthily trying to stumble upon another tidbit of information.

That night I worried about my future husband. There must have been a reason I'd met him and never considered him, so I figured he must not have been very good-looking. Obviously, when I do go out with him later, I'll be settling and desperate, willing to date anyone. And "intrigued"? What does that mean? Was he shrouded in mystery? What, was he wearing a cape?

As I drifted to sleep, I told myself to dream of him—*I will dream of my future husband, I will dream of my future husband*—but the only dream I remembered was about Batman, who, contrary to his stellar reputation, had taken me hostage. There I was, being held by the caped crusader, forced to sit at the edge of a skyscraper so tall that fear was what finally woke me.

• • •

A few weeks later Gina knocked on my door. It was a Friday night and, strangely, neither of us had anything to do.

"I had a vision of your future husband," she said the second I let her in. "I got really pissed off the other night that I had no career and no man and no space for this mission-style bedroom set I totally want—not that I could afford it even if I did have space, but whatever—and I may have polished off a bottle and a half of wine by myself. You know that horrible feeling when you wake up the next morning and you see an empty bottle on the coffee table and you're like 'Oh, good, it was just that one.' But then you go to throw it away, and lo and behold, in the trash can is—"

"Are you going to tell me what the vision was?"

"You're not gonna like it."

"Just tell me. The fact that I *have* a future man has already made me pretty damn happy."

"Yeah, but this guy . . . he's on a show."

"An actor?"

"Yes."

"I can accept that. I will *have* to accept that."

"You haven't heard which show." She smiled, started unwrapping the aluminum around the cork of the wine she'd brought, and strolled into the kitchen.

I chased after her—which, in my tiny single, meant I took three very quick steps. "Which show? Which one?"

She told me, and my heart stopped. My future man, it turned out, was on a phenomenally popular yet particularly cheesy TV show. We're talking the kind of show that encourages friends to gather together with tubs of popcorn and boxes of pizza so they can view the supposed drama and have a hearty laugh. I've seen people jokingly reenact the scenes for fun, and act better than the actors themselves.

I was devastated, and it got worse when she told me which actor it was.

"Charles Darnette."

"No. *No.* He looks like a frog."

"What? You're insane."

I was pacing. I couldn't stop. I pivoted furiously, almost spilling my wine. "He looks like a frog! With those froggy lips? And froggy eyes? *Frog.*"

"You're crazy. I think he's cute. I'd totally go out with him. Women love him; he's an established heartthrob. I thought this would make you happy."

"Happy to be married to a frog? Wait, how did you know he was my husband? How exactly did you know that?"

"Because you were standing together—"

"Standing together! People stand!"

"Because," Gina tried again, "you were standing together *at the altar.*"

I sat on the bed. Hmm. "And it was definitely us getting married? I wasn't maybe a bridesmaid?"

"Nope. Sorry. Big white dress." She lit her cigarette and exhaled dreamily, as if she'd just come off a twelve-hour flight with no nicotine, a look I knew meant yet another attempt she'd made at quitting had just now failed. "You guys looked really happy together, though. And isn't it the frog who becomes the prince?"

"Don't pull that fairy tale—" I stopped. He was an actor.

Average height. With dark hair and dark eyes . . . and I'd met him before. "No. No. *No!*"

Gina stared at me, one eyebrow raised as she brought the cigarette again to her lips, apparently too happy to inquire what I was no-ing about.

"I've met him before. Aurelia? Her prediction? Actor with dark eyes and dark hair? Average height? That's him! I met him a few years back with my manager in an elevator. He got in and she introduced us and it was real quick. You know, hello, how are you, nice to meet you. Aurelia said I was intrigued when I met him, and I was! Because he was famous! And I remember thinking, 'Why is he famous? He looks like a frog.'"

I was completely unnerved. Even Gina admitted it was strange and that, yes, it did indeed sound like he'd be my husband. Heartthrob or not, I found him to be disgustingly unattractive and a horrifyingly bad actor, one I didn't even want to watch, much less marry. I mean, this was the man I was supposed to have children with? He'd pollute my gene pool with his frogginess!

From that point on it was as if Cupid were both sadistic and on speed. Charles was planted everywhere. I'd innocently turn on the TV, only to find his froggy face grinning from the screen; or as an irresponsible treat I'd get my nails done, only to be handed a tabloid with Charles's froggy mug on the cover. I couldn't escape. Even getting a bagel proved dangerous, since the second I placed my order, the girl behind the counter mentioned him to her coworker.

Finally, after months of this, I gave in. I was resigned. I was going to marry Charles Darnette, and there wasn't a damn thing I could do about it.

As he was my future husband, I figured I might as well find something about him I liked. I learned he spoke French, which was good. I grew up in a French-speaking household and have always wanted to pass the language along to my children. So okay, he got one point for that. But there had to be more. His disembodied French-speaking voice would be fine, but the way the world is set up requires *him* to be present as well, which means I'd have to look at him now and then. I began to watch his show carefully. Religiously I observed him from every angle, trying to find one from which our morning breakfasts together wouldn't make me weep.

After a while he began to grow on me. He really wasn't that bad-looking, I guessed. Most women did love him. And though I never wanted to marry an actor, I knew Charles Darnette was such a bad actor that it was only a matter of time before people suddenly realized what had been happening and stopped hiring him. Who knew, he could still become a lawyer. A nice frog-looking French-speaking lawyer.

I'm embarrassed to admit it, but a year passed and I was still convinced I was doomed to be Mrs. Sarah Darnette. I knew I would be. Gina had seen it, Aurelia had seen it back when she was on the you'll-lose-something-material roll, and the world seemed determined to shove us together. Seriously, for him to keep appearing as he did defied all odds. It was fate, and I told myself I'd learn to love him. All would be fine. In my mind I saw the Christmas cards: me and our two beautiful children prominently situated in red and green velvet, perhaps by a white marble fireplace, while Charles stood in the corner, slightly shadowed, the picture taken from his least froggy angle.

• • •

Christmas, without Charles, came and went with a few Santa sightings on street corners, a wreath on my neighbor's door, and one boring holiday party where a drunken meathead of a man tried to ambush me every time I passed through a door frame, actually once losing his balance as he tilted his head back to point out the mistletoe. Yes, nothing says "Kiss me" like a whiskey-scented man falling backward.

A few trees lost their leaves, and people's light cotton T-shirts now had long sleeves, but that was the only change in Los Angeles. As usual I missed my days back in New York. Not only did I long for the snow and the true change of seasons, but I also missed the accessories that came with actual dips in temperature. You just can't get away with scarves or hats in Southern California's low of 50 degrees. Instead of looking chic or sophisticated, you look wimpy or, worse, like you're *trying*—and much of L.A. is about perfecting the look of groomed and trained neglect.

But this you can count on: Once a year Los Angelenos abandon ship and, to what I imagine is the chagrin of a pretty much idyllic town, take up residence in Park City, Utah. It never fails. When Sundance rolls around, every tanned producer for miles, and every actor, from starving to star, braces himself or herself for the cold, and then, en masse, they invade.

When I got the call that a movie I'd done was going to Sundance, and hence I'd be part of the invasion, I went straight to my closet (accidentally stepping on Onyx) and shook off the dust from my leopard-print coat, otherwise known as my Sundance coat. Within the hour I was packed and ready to go, one entire carry-on designated for accessories.

In general, film festivals are the shining, gleaming moments of an independent film actor's life, and I pretty much lived for them. Since most of my films never actually made it to theaters, festivals gave me a once–in–a–lifetime opportunity to see myself on the big screen, to listen to an audience react, and then— hopefully—to be accosted by congratulatory praise afterward. "Thank you," I'd say later in the lobby, "that's so kind; I appreciate it. I know. I'm really not dead. See? Yep. Here I am. Wasn't murdered after all."

Amazingly, the director of my film had arranged for the entire ensemble cast—all beautiful people almost too hip for their own good—to stay in a condo he'd rented. It was beyond picturesque and perfect. There was snow; there was a fireplace. I searched for a bearskin rug but thankfully didn't find one, as everyone knows what those make you want to do.

During this time I got to know Jonas, the lead in the film. Jonas, the product of a French–Vietnamese mother and an Irish– with–a–touch–of–American–Indian father, had an interesting and exotic masculine beauty, with longish brown hair, and cocoa brown eyes. He was completely indefinable, something I related to. Because although I'm entirely French, I was born in Canada (though, to make things a touch more complicated, I am *not* French Canadian), spent my childhood in Australia, my adolescence in New York, and my adulthood in Los Angeles, and I have somehow always felt I come from nowhere and everywhere all at once. How I felt was essentially how Jonas looked. "Where are you from?" people would ask him, in response to which he'd smile and say "Here."

After much glamorous partying in the snow—highlighted by

my dancing the "Stand" dance with Michael Stipe—I returned home to the dark pavement and crisp hillsides of Los Angeles. Jonas, it turned out, lived just half a block away from me. Since Los Angeles's traffic can turn just about anyone into a seething blabbering monster, the fact that we were neighbors was like an endorsement straight from heaven. "Look," God was shouting through his celestial bullhorn, "I put him within walking distance! Befriend him, you lazy girl!"

So friends we became. Everything was perfect, until the thought twisted through my paranoid little mind that he might be interested in something more than a friendship. In a tizzy, I called Aurelia. "No," she assured me, "he sees you as just a friend. Don't worry about it." So, with the guarantee of my trusty psychic, I didn't think about it again . . . until, that is, Jonas threw me for a curve by blurting out, "Will you be my valentine?"

This actually did make sense, because the next day was Valentine's Day, yet I was still confused. I stared at him. "You mean like a real *valentine* valentine?"

"Yes," he said. "A valentine valentine."

I didn't know what to say. This hadn't been in the cards. Jonas had completely abandoned the universe's script and was *improvising*. Confused, I stumbled out "Yeah, okay," and went home to fret. *Just go with it*, I told myself. Jonas was actually a really good-looking guy, but I valued him to the point that my only concern was keeping the seal on our friendship. You break that seal, things can go bad in a hurry.

Poor Jonas. If he'd harbored any expectations of a romantic Valentine's Day, he'd been sorely mistaken.

During the last years of college, and the couple of years right after, Gina lived with her father, an artist with a great house in a hip community called Silver Lake, not far from where I lived. Though she adored him, and he was actually friends with just about all her friends and threw parties people talked about for years, she realized it was perhaps time to leave, to stumble from the nest and find a place of her own. And though I'm sure much of her decision had to do with independence and growth, I also suspected much had to do with her insane urge to decorate, an urge that had been rather stifled, since she'd been confined to a ten-by-ten-foot bedroom.

The answer was for us to find a new place and be room-mates. After all, two cats (three if you went by mass alone, since China should surely count as more than one) had turned my studio apartment from charming to suffocating, and the idea of actual living room furniture had an irresistible appeal. Almost immediately we stumbled upon a great two-bedroom apart-ment not far from her father's house, an older building with a fantastic view of the city and a rather drastically sloping living room floor. Since we'd figured we'd be dateless, we'd thus opted to move on the devil's holiday, aka Valentine's Day.

Amid grunts of "Be careful" and "Shit, this is heavy," I began to look at Jonas in a different way. He actually had some very nice muscles, and because it was a hot February, I was getting a full display. "Would you grab that?" I'd ask, then pause dis-creetly to watch him stoop to pick something up. Hmm. "And that, too?"

The day skidded into night, and soon we had everything stacked and shoved into our new place. Jonas offered to hang a few paintings in my room, an offer I jumped at not only because of my strange inability to hang anything straight (I could be equipped with a level and a tape measure and still hang things as if I'd been on crack) but also because I got to lie on the bed and watch as he reached and stretched, hammered and hung.

Just as he finished with the last nail, we caught it . . . very soft, barely audible. The sound of Gina in her room, crying. Jonas turned to me. First, I'm sure he was shocked that Gina cries, as picturing her in a vulnerable moment was a little bit like imagining a blizzard blanketing the Sahara. Second, I think we both were a bit horrified at how thin the walls were. That, we both knew in a way that made me blush, could be problematic.

"I need to spend some time with her," I told him. "She's a bit freaked out. You know, first time on her own and all."

Of course Jonas understood. I walked him downstairs, but at the door he hesitated, lingering as if trying to remember if he'd left something behind.

"Did you forget something?"

"Yeah, I did."

Already I was picturing the mess in my room. Anything he'd forgotten wouldn't be unearthed till May. I hoped it wasn't important, because it was as good as gone. "What?"

"This," he said, and leaned in . . . and kissed me.

3

Finding My Sparkle

BEING IN LOVE IS LIKE WEARING AN IMPENETRABLE cloak of happiness, like sleeping on clouds, like discovering unused gift certificates in your wallet. My joy was out of control. Every ex I'd ever had and every actress who'd ever gotten the parts I'd wanted could all have moved in next door, yet still I'd be smiling. Not even the fact that China was *more* disgruntled in our new apartment, and hence more focused in her "gift giving," could upset me. Jonas loved me, and that was all that mattered.

One of the first things I did was call Aurelia, who revealed she'd had a feeling he liked me. Why, I wanted to know, had she deceived me by saying he saw me as just a friend?

"Because you weren't meant to know. You were meant to relax and just go with it."

Of course, that made perfect sense. Relaxing for me is a near impossibility. I'm a control freak. If I could, I'd own the world and hand out daily memos on exactly what everyone was to do that day, exactly what they were to say, and exactly what they were to feel. Should anyone stray from the plan, I'd fire them. Simple. *Fired.* And Jonas's liking me wasn't something I'd been ready for at the time. On the contrary, I was so focused on keeping his friendship that if I had known that he was interested in me, I would've freaked and embarked on a sabotage mission, thwarting any and all chances for romance and developing a strange claustrophobia that would have demanded that he stay at least two feet away. So what Aurelia said made sense. Perfect sense.

But now she was free to sing his praises, to claim she saw us together *forever.* I just smiled as she said this, though inside I was doing cartwheels. I'd found him!

Overall our relationship was going well, and in most ways we were scarily compatible. Of course there are always exceptions, and ours came in the form of *Star Wars.* Jonas, it turned out, was a *Star Wars* freak and often bolted out of bed at five a.m. on a Saturday to be the first to get the newest action figure. Being the supportive girlfriend I was, I even endeavored to help him in this, a one time and one time only attempt on my part. There by his side at the crack of dawn, I accidentally dropped what I considered to be a "doll," a grave misnomer on my part, I soon learned.

Before I knew what was happening, he'd swooped down to retrieve it, gently touching the corner of the box, and narrowing his eyes into slits. When he looked back up at me, it was as if he'd just caught the kid who'd been egging his house and smashing his mailbox.

"This," he said, "is the super-rare variant of Slave Leia from *Jedi*, with the *brown* chain instead of the *gray* chain." Then his eyes went back to the box, as if having seen me, the perpetrator, had been too much. "You have to be careful," he cried. "The corner of the box is dented. Do you know how much this is worth?"

My eyes went to the price tag by his thumb, and I suggested $4.99, as that seemed to be what the store was asking for the action figure. The look of dismay on his face was like that of a modern art professor who'd just overheard Picasso described as "That dude who painted the f'd-up people," and in that moment I realized that Jonas and I were on very different wavelengths regarding all things *Star Wars*. After that I stayed home and slept in, knowing somewhere out there was my boyfriend, carefully carrying boxes to a register, speaking a language I was incapable of understanding.

One day Jonas and I were sitting in his Jeep, waiting for a light to turn green, when beside us grew the furious revving of a motorcycle, the ridiculous sound of a man desperate to look cool.

Jonas laughed and pointed out the window. "Hey. It's Charles Darnette. What a dork."

Sure enough, though his froggy face was slightly obscured by his helmet, it was *him*. My future— That's when it hit me. Jonas was an actor, with dark hair and dark eyes, he wasn't too tall, and, in fact, we'd met years ago when I'd auditioned to play his girlfriend in a movie. I remembered that at the time I *had been* intrigued by him, enraptured by his curious beauty.

All the predictions were coming true, and I knew this was it.

Jonas and I would be together forever. I smiled, and thanked God for his kindness that my future husband wasn't the black leather-clad frog on the motorcycle that had just stalled.

Other people hear of the hottest movie, the hippest bar, or the best mixed martini, and they can't resist. They must see it, they must go there, they must down it. Me? Someone tells me of a good psychic and I've made an appointment before the story's even finished.

One of the first times I discovered this about myself was when a friend told me about Drew. "He was so right on I was terrified! I couldn't sleep for days!" With glowing reviews like that, how could I stay away? Next thing I knew I was parked in front of a smog-gray apartment building in the midst of Culver City, certainly not a mecca of spirituality but close enough to Sony Entertainment Studios that I'd known how to get there without a map, an accomplishment that always gave me a slight thrill.

I stared at the bars on the lower windows and began to doubt myself. Was this wise? But I'd heard such good things about him, how could I walk away? Whatever. As long as there wasn't a gigantic fluorescent hand in the front yard, I figured I was doing okay. In I went.

Drew was about seven feet tall, super thin, and had a voice like a drag queen on helium. Part of me instantly loved him and wanted him to be my new best friend, while the other part was already checking for escape routes.

"Your grandmother's spirit is here," he said immediately.

I scooted my chair in closer to the kitchen table, relieved. See? Everything's fine.

He made a little tsk–tsking sound. "And boy is she *pissed*."

I looked up and caught him rolling his eyes, like he and my grandmother went way back and this was just so typical of her.

"She's really upset you're here, getting this reading. Don't worry, though. I'm gonna send my grandma's spirit to talk to yours. She'll settle down."

Okay then, I thought, envisioning some spiritual conference with ghostly shrieking little old ladies.

I can't say it got much better. When I pulled out a photo of Jonas, excited for confirmation that he was indeed the love of my life, Drew was silent. He chewed his lip, studying the photo as if he'd have to do a police sketch later. Finally he spoke. "Is this your brother?"

To say I was horrified would be an understatement. No one wants to think of their boyfriend as their brother—but even more upsetting, I don't have a brother, nor do I have a sister, so what did this say about Drew's psychic ability? I'd just paid this man a hundred dollars to fully creep me out. "No, that's my *boyfriend*."

Drew shook his head and tossed the photo on the table. "Oh, no, honey. He's not the one for you."

I was shattered, completely devastated, and trying not to lose it in Drew's kitchen. All my emotions were careening, and I felt the need to upheave the table, cry like a fiend, and pelt Drew with the salt and pepper shakers. Perhaps he saw the look of trauma on my face, or realized I hadn't taken a breath since he'd last spoken, but he picked up the picture once more. "You guys aren't done, though."

Gee, thanks.

"You still have more growing to do. The guy you're with after him? *He's* the one you'll marry."

The devastation hit me in bits and pieces. I didn't know what to think anymore. Jonas and I did have problems, problems that developed after our peaceful honeymoon period, problems I'd overlooked due to Aurelia's insistence that we were meant to be. I'd started to wonder, for instance, how two people could be meant to spend a lifetime together if they couldn't even decide on dinner without breaking into a brawl. Or, for that matter, how enjoyable that love would be if *progress* was considered backing out of the driveway without already having commenced in the screaming match. Gina, who was now dating an Irish musician and suffering for such a perilous choice, tried to comfort me. "Listen to *yourself*," she said. So I turned to my tarot cards, asking over and over again how I truly felt.

The splinters in our relationship burrowed deeper each day, and our fights began to escalate to sensational proportions. Putting two actors together could be risky, but when those actors were Jonas and I—both stubborn and prone to drama— the combination was positively volatile. Soon our evenings together began to resemble scenes from *The War of the Roses*, and still Aurelia persisted that ours was a destined love. *Destined for what?* I began to wonder. Romeo and Juliet's had been a destined love, but that hadn't worked out so well, now, had it?

Somehow, through tears and determination, I stayed with Jonas, though I continually felt twitches of instinct, nudges of insight. *Leave. This isn't right. You shouldn't be fighting like this.* But was that just because of Drew? Each psychic sat on my shoulders like a devil or an angel, barking commands into my poor befuddled brain.

During a rare peaceful time with Jonas, I decided that Aurelia was right and Jonas was *the one*, and, this being the case, clearly we should move in together. After I approached him with a sweetly worded ultimatum, he agreed, and Gina began the hunt for a new apartment. Well, really it was I who was hunting for her, as she'd recently started working at a literary agency for a man who called her Servant Girl, and time was not a luxury she had. Every day I'd scan the papers for new listings and then plan my life with Jonas, envisioning romantic dinners at home, copper pots, and a lifetime of free foot massages.

When we found Gina a place she liked, she packed up to leave, informed me she was taking Onyx (who, upon our moving in together, had slighted me by choosing her closet over mine), and then, before I knew it, was gone. I filled the resulting void with the beginnings of my life with Jonas. She took her TV, and I convinced Jonas to buy a new one. She took her couch, so Jonas and I went shopping—eventually and mistakenly buying one that was too big to fit through the door and that had to be hoisted through the balcony, and may be permanently stuck there. Still, everything was so encouraging, so wonderful . . . except for the fact that he wouldn't move in. He'd been furnishing and paying rent at our apartment, but the *our* part was a bit misleading, because at the end of the day he was nowhere to be found. He kept going home, "home" being the place where I wasn't.

It seemed there was always an excuse, and three months later the only thing that had made it from his apartment to mine was a life-size Princess Leia cutout. I sequestered Leia in the empty room, sat on my gi-normous couch, and told myself all was fine.

Facing facts isn't easy for me. If I want something, I have a very, very hard time giving up. My brain is like a Venus fly-trap—even *I* can't make it let go of certain things—and when it does finally release, it does so at a disturbingly slow pace. So, after four months of having a Princess Leia cutout as a room-mate—during which time Jonas actually got a new roommate himself at *his* apartment—I had to face that perhaps he wasn't ready to move in.

After countless tarot readings, we broke up. There I was, in my great apartment with a view of the city and all the makings of a wonderful life, completely alone and frantically pulling tarot cards to see if I'd done the right thing.

With time I did feel I'd made the right choice, but the frantic card pulling never stopped. Two very celibate years passed, and I tried to ignore that not only was I about to turn thirty, but I also had no real source of income and had been reduced to buying groceries and anti-aging creams with the checks MCI and AT&T sent me (a blessed benefit of my long-distance friendship with Aurelia). Thank God for those checks because, although eating tends to be important, I'd have done just about anything to anti-age. Thirty, as far as Hollywood is concerned, is one shaky step away from cutting out coupons for PoliGrip and comparing walkers on a large community porch. You age in actress years, each birthday hurtling you forward with such speed, such vicious force, that when someone at a liquor store asks to see your ID, you're so overjoyed that you could throw a party and send out a newsletter. And, if truth be told, that clerk will forever be one of the few who knows your true age. So trained is an actress at keeping her age a deep dark secret, that some of my friends genuinely have no idea how old they are and must call upon rusty math skills to come up with a number they will never ever speak aloud.

And it wasn't just my career that was telling me I was old. Even my mother got in on the fun, informing me one day that it was okay, she was coming to terms with the fact that she'd never have grandchildren. It seemed that the hill I'd thought I'd been approaching was actually a cliff, and it was only a matter of time until my unemployed and single self was falling through the air, about to land in a place called Too Late.

Gina too was enduring single life, vowing never again to date a man who referred to Guinness as Vitamin G, and together we shared our fantasies about fleeing the city and moving to a place to which beauty queens, models, and the female prize of every small town didn't migrate each year. (There's no shortage of pretty girls out here, a fact of which the men in L.A. are damn well aware.) One day, we decided, we'd move to a place where a man would open a restaurant's door for you because he was polite, not because he was using those seconds to scope the room and determine who was who and which table would be the most advantageous. In this new land we'd find not only love but also a one-bedroom house that didn't cost a million dollars simply because it was in an area where the sounds of gunshots were a bit more distant.

But there would be no moving. All predictions pointed to my

taking on this town and beating it at its own game, so the love I decided to concentrate on was that of acting. I didn't need a man to act. I didn't need a man to be successful. I'd simply get a part on the next hit show and buy myself a cute little silver Bug, a Spanish-style house, and a Chihuahua that would bounce around and periodically go for dips in my infinity pool. From there would come the guy, because men are drawn to confidence and a girl who's got her shit together. And, my God, if I had the Bug and the job and the house, then I'd have my shit together and I'd be happy and who *wouldn't* want to be with me? I'd radiate all that good stuff that draws men in like moths. Yep, my new plan was to trick love into finding me.

Unfortunately, it wasn't that easy. Hollywood is where dreams go to shrivel up and die—the town itself being the ultimate unrequited love. Though I focused on my career, my career refused to focus on me. Audition after audition yielded nothing but more and more miles on my car (a death trap Del Sol I'd bought with the insurance money) and an increasing confusion on my part as to why people were stubbornly refusing to see me as the starlet I should be. And, to add to my delight, I was fired from my agency. It was devastating, but I still don't think they ever really knew who I was. All I had left was my manager, Holly, who continued to stick by me through thick and thin . . . or thin and thinner and thinnest. God bless her.

Upon discovering the small, insubstantial role of a French girl in a movie called *Until the Night*, Holly immediately called the director and tried to sell me for the role.

"Actually," I was told he said, "we were thinking of Sarah for one of the leads."

I can only imagine Holly fell out of her very expensive ergonomically correct chair. At the very least her jaw dropped. This shift in conversation would be much like if Holly had asked someone to do her a favor by hiring a friend as an errand boy, only to hear the words "Actually, we were thinking of making him vice president." It turned out the director was a fan of Abel Ferrara's *The Blackout*, a film I'd done that hadn't been a financial or critical success but that had garnered a fan base of young edgy directors, who, with any luck, will all hire me.

When I heard the description of Karina, the character I was meeting for, I was shocked: a high-priced call girl/L.A. party girl/model. Not that I have any qualms about playing a hooker, but in my mind I pictured her as absolutely soaring in height and with cleavage that cost more than my car. To cast this they could seriously go to any Starbucks in Los Angeles and find ten of those girls. Why me? Not that I considered myself unattractive, but I liked to think of myself as more sophisticated, more chic. Apparently, though, I was wrong. And thus commenced my Play a Whore phase.

Now, nudity is not something I shy away from—as long as there's a reason for it, and that reason isn't to jack up ticket sales or give the crew a reward for working long hours. Of course, it also has to be my choice, and not just because they "accidentally" got a shot of my right breast—something that happened early on in my career. How one *accidentally* includes a breast in a shot, and then goes on to edit that scene over and over and simply never notices the renegade breast, is beyond me. But after reading the script for *Until the Night*, I decided this was one of those cases in which a touch of nudity was fine. Actually, the way I saw it, Karina being topless in one scene was important, as it established her as a free spirit. See? I'm seriously a director's dream.

And, apparently, I was this director's dream. "Great," he said when I told him I was okay being topless. "You're the only actress we're considering for the role."

I was momentarily stunned, and then completely exhilarated. Right as I was about to say something like "Finally!" he continued with, "No one else will do the nudity."

He realized his mistake when I gasped sharply. After listening to him stumble about, trying to get out of what he'd just said, I laughed it off. Really, who cares? I needed a job.

I left feeling pretty good. For the first time in years I felt certain I would land the role, or at least be seriously considered. This sentiment was quickly trampled to death when Holly informed me of the director's concerns. It appeared that now that he'd met me in person, he had concerns about my stature. I'm petite. Short. Whatever. I'm no midget, but I'm five-two, which doesn't exactly put me in the Amazon category. In the script there's one line that refers to Karina as being tall. *One line.* This, to my horror, was cause for some serious consideration on the director's part, and my response was to immediately call Aurelia.

"Will I be offered the role of Karina in the film *Until the Night*?" Over the years I'd learned to be very specific about such questions. Saying you want to know if you'll get a job soon could easily be misconstrued by the very busy and often very ironic universe as meaning any job, and "soon" could be viewed as relative to your entire life . . . so, best to include as many details as possible.

Aurelia sighed, never a good sign from a psychic. "I don't think so. No. You'll be disappointed. There's something blocking him from giving you that role, but I feel like he'll offer you something else. Is there a smaller role he could give you?"

Of course, I should've known I'd be playing the insubstantial French girl after all. To be sure Aurelia wasn't just in a bad mood when pulling my cards, I busted out my own deck, but no matter how many different ways I asked the same question, there was no swaying the message: I was not getting this job.

A few days later I was about to get in my afternoon bath when Holly called. *"You got it,"* she said, her voice as excited as it could possibly get. Holly, by nature, never gets very excited. Next to her my calmest state sounds absolutely hysterical. *"They're offering you the role of Karina."*

"Yeah?" Obviously she was mistaken; this could get embarrassing. I shook my newest gardenia bath salt into the tub, breathing in to see how badly I'd overpaid. This salt was seriously expensive and supposedly from the Dead Sea. Why had I bought it? Something, I realized, was undeniably wrong with me. I'd drive past a grocery store with longing, wishing I could afford to stop and eat, but then spot a beauty supply store across the street and practically leap from my car as it was still screeching to a halt. Why didn't this smell like gardenia?

"Hello?" Holly said. "They're offering you the part of Karina?"

"I thought I was too short."

"I guess he changed his mind."

I waved my hand in the water, trying to bring the damn bath

salts to life. Somewhere, hidden deep within the air, was a small trace of gardenia. I furiously shook the bottle, practically emptying the entire thing into the now very pricey bath. "Are you sure?" I said. I was trying to give her an out, one more chance to realize her mistake.

"I just got off the phone with him. Are you okay?"

"Yeah, I'm fine." Holly was going to feel awful later, when it dawned on her that the part he'd wanted to give me was that of the flippin' French girl. "I'm about to take a bath, that's all."

"Well, you got the part," she said, sounding slightly puzzled as to why I wasn't more excited.

"Okay." I tried to muster a little enthusiasm for her benefit. "Well, that's great, I guess."

We hung up the phone and I got into my bath, reclining so far, sinking so deep, that my nose skimmed the water. *There*, I thought. There was the gardenia.

Two hours later it hit me. There was a chance, though slim, a miniscule flimsy little chance, that perhaps the cards weren't right. Did I have the job? The cards weren't always right, were they? A call to my manager (who was growing increasingly concerned) seemed to confirm it: I'd gotten the job! And though it seemed pretty obvious to everyone else that I'd definitely been cast as one of the leads, it wasn't till I was finally on-set and about to take off my shirt that I truly believed the job was mine.

As is the case with independent films, the work was rewarding but the paychecks were like drops of water on a sizzling day. What little money I'd been paid, disappeared. I began to panic.

What was I doing wrong? I examined my life, and then—to me this made perfect sense—I focused my anger on Aurelia. For years she'd been giving me false hope, setting me up for disappointment, essentially lying to me. Where was the success she'd been promising? Where was my wonderful life? Just the other day I'd agreed to take home leftovers from a dinner party simply so I could eat later. That was not supposed to happen. I was supposed to be *hosting* lavish dinner parties, all scraps going to my rhinestone-adorned sweater-wearing Chihuahua!

I called Aurelia in a fury and let loose a string of complaints, a barrage of failed predictions. Aurelia, as if she'd known this was coming, took it in stride.

"The problem is that the negative energy you're projecting is blocking you from getting the roles you would otherwise get. It's your negative attitude that's preventing you from being successful."

I attempted to breathe, and then calmly explained that I wouldn't *have* a negative attitude if I *were* successful, which she'd always said I would be. Was this really going to morph into a chicken and egg debate? I was supposed to be a star! It was that simple! But no, Aurelia continued to insist I had something to do with my own failure.

"The casting people don't know why they're not casting you; they just feel this underlying negative energy. What you need to do is find your sparkle."

"*Sparkle?*"

"Yes, sparkle. Imagine all the blackness moving up from your toes, up your body and through the top of your head. Let it out. Imagine it turning into white light. As it turns whiter and brighter, imagine it exploding and turning into golden glitter that falls back down onto you."

I wanted to chuck the phone out the window. Of course I was being bitter and resistant, but *please*. No one who's trapped in an abyss of despair wants to talk about glitter exploding over her head. To make myself feel better, I asked about my future man. Maybe if I had a wonderful love life I wouldn't care that I was in danger of turning into one of those tragic older actresses with perilously sculpted hair and heaps of fake jewelry—that aching, overly painted woman who still tells stories of a job she had fifty years ago. And honestly, my heading in that direction was a distinct possibility, since I had a ton of worthless jewelry.

"No, Sarah."

I blinked. "No what?"

"I'm not doing any more readings for you. You're getting too dependent on them, and it's not healthy."

Not *healthy*? Not healthy was feeling as though you had nothing to live for, that nothing good was ever going to happen to you, that you'd be alone forever! I needed these readings to feel better, that was all. How could she say that was unhealthy? Unhealthy was *not* getting the readings!

I informed her that I'd do my own damn readings, and that's exactly what I did. Nonstop. For weeks on end I shuffled the cards, actually relieved to no longer have to rely on someone else, relieved to not be accused of asking the same question over and over. If I so desired, I could ask about my future man until my fingers ached and the room went light with the rising sun, and not once would I hear "Please, Sarah, no more. I need to go; I have to sleep." Instant gratification was another plus. Before, I'd been at the mercy of Aurelia's schedule. Now I could have readings whenever I wanted. Ten seconds after walking in the door from an audition I could get answers to my questions: *How did the director feel about me? What did the producer think? Will I get the part? Will it lead to more work?* The immediacy was a nice change from all the times I'd returned home and been forced to wait and stare at the phone until Aurelia returned my call.

The only downside was that after countless readings, my mind would grow wild with confusion. *This reading said I wouldn't get it, but that one an hour ago, didn't that one say I'd get it? Better try once more. . . .*

One thing there was no doubt about was that the Knight of Wands was determined to be noticed. No matter how many times I shuffled, that one card persistently showed up in my readings, its resolve like that of an annoying neighbor who constantly pops up when you least expect it, determined to be noticed and not caring that you've got ice cream melting in your grocery bag. The universe, I realized, was telling me something, so I found my tarot card book and looked up the meaning.

"The Knight of Wands is physically attractive and focuses on style and look. Blond or light hair and light blue or green eyes. Someone who sparkles and glows with the fiery element of the wands."

Sparkles? Why was this word haunting me? Wait, could it be a *man* who was my sparkle? Did finding my sparkle mean finding my man? My Knight of Wands? Had I cracked the code? Intuition kicked in and I knew this was a man. This was my man they were alluding to. Soon he'd be in my life. I could feel him approaching.

Locked in my room, I began chatting with the cards. "What do you think of him?" I'd ask. "You like him? Oh, good. And he's polite? Okay, well on a scale of one to ten, how is he in bed? *Really?* Well, that's certainly something to look forward to, now, isn't it?"

Meanwhile, the messages Gina left on my answering machine were becoming increasingly fevered. "Where are you? Are you pulling cards? Put them down and pick up the phone! What's going on?!" I was all right, I thought, still functioning in the world, still going about my daily activities and fulfilling all my obligations. The only differences were that now I had a few more readings a day—fine, *many* more readings a day—and that I didn't feel like talking to Gina about my love affair with the cards or the future they predicted. What business was it of hers? What business was it of anyone's? I was fine, and I certainly didn't need a lecture. In a stroke of what I considered brilliance, I found the knob on the side of the answering machine and turned the volume down, thus solving the problem of her disruptive wailings. *There,* I thought, *now let's find out if my knight speaks a foreign language.*

One day there was a loud, insistent knock on the door. Figuring it was a script, perhaps even the one that would lead to the job the cards had just predicted, I ran downstairs, and found Gina standing at the door. Without saying hello or why she was there, she pushed past me.

I followed her up the stairs and watched as she turned in the direction of my bedroom. "Where are they?" she asked.

Panic sped my steps. "Where are what?" I said innocently. "What are you doing here? You want some wine?"

Nothing could distract her, and of course she didn't have to look hard, since the cards were spread out on my bed, in exactly the spot I'd left them just seconds before. With one swoop she gathered them all up, stuffed them in their worn and tattered box, and demanded to see the others.

"I know you've got more. Tell me where you're hiding them. I'm not leaving till you tell me."

"But what will you do with them?" The thought of the cards, my friends, discarded in a trash can, forced to nestle Gina's empty box of American Spirits for warmth, or turn to a crumpled Diet Coke can for companionship, filled my heart with anxious sadness. "You won't hurt them, will you?"

"No. They're coming to live with me until you get your sanity back. I'll return them when I think you're ready."

"So it's not good-bye?"

Gina rolled her eyes. "It's a temporary good-bye. It's a little break, that's all. Now, I know you've got an Aleister Crowley deck too." She watched as I shuffled to my nightstand. "And the Rider Waite deck. And the Arthurian Legend. And the Tarot of the Cat People." She nodded. "That's it. Keep 'em coming."

One by one I gathered the decks together and agreed to be good. One month, I was told; if I went one month without tarot, she'd release whichever hostage I chose. I eyed my Aleister Crowley deck. I agreed. I promised. I wanted her to leave.

She was halfway down the stairs when suddenly she stopped. Head tilted, a smirk on her face, she turned to me. "And the Goddess deck."

With that, with the removal of that last deck (which I kept beneath my pillow in preparation for late-night readings), it was official: I'd just been heaved onto the wagon.

In a way it was a relief. Amid uncertainty, worry, and panic, I felt a certain amount of freedom being cardless. To celebrate my liberation, and to give myself something to do so I didn't sit around all day missing my cards, I convinced my parents to buy me a plane ticket to visit my cousin in Paris. Before I knew it, I was in the sky, flying above clouds so thick it seemed impossible to think they wouldn't catch us if we fell. My visit would only be for a few weeks, but these weeks were monumental in their importance, as they were the last chance I'd get to recharge my battery and prepare myself for the impending hard whack of reality. Upon my return I was going to have to get a job. It was that simple. A real job—one that could interfere with auditions, one that could make me sit in more traffic, one that could make me . . . work. I was so not happy about that.

Still, I had weeks to enjoy denial and live up the last remnants of my unshackled life. Once settled into my cousin's apartment, I informed her of several things I wanted to do: visit the Louvre, go for strolls in the park, see the new exhibit at the Musée d'Orsay, climb the Eiffel Tower (I figured I'd try that "exercise" thing), and, naturally, drink wine and eat blocks and blocks of Brie.

"All this is fine," she said cheerfully. "Oh, did you bring your cards? Can you do a reading for me?"

I shook my head. "No, I left them at—"

Before I'd finished my sentence, she was gone, bounding into her room and then racing back out. The world now had a horrible slow-motion quality to it, like when a glass slips from your hand and the seconds spread out in a way that only happens when something terrible is about to occur, when a horrible shattering mess is inevitable.

I took a deep breath. There before me stood my well-intentioned cousin, and, of course, in her hand was a deck of French tarot cards.

4

The eBay of Psychics

THERE ARE FEW EVENTS IN AN ACTOR'S LIFE MORE traumatizing than the Hunt for a Job. Working nine to five in an office is pretty much out of the question, since an employee suddenly emerging from the bathroom in, let's say, full disco regalia, can be quite a workplace disturbance ... but when that employee then bounds out the door with the promise that she'll try to maybe return in a few hours, the reception isn't usually all that welcoming. Disappearing for auditions is frowned upon, to say the least, and without auditions or meetings or some kind of activity that involves acting, you don't feel so great about calling yourself an actor. To a lesser degree, obviously, at that point you could almost equate yourself to a high school dropout who one day declares he's a neurosurgeon. To be an actor you must act, and, after a while, perfecting random accents while doing the dishes just doesn't cut it.

Hence, actors turn to waiting tables or bartending, jobs with flexibility or vampire hours. Unfortunately, in a pressured situation like a loud and crowded bar with desperate and drunken cries for drinks, I knew I'd end up hiding beneath a table, eating maraschino cherries, and pretending that I, too, had no idea where that damn bartender had gone. Waiting tables was also out of the question; long ago I'd discovered I possessed a strange inability to carry a tray. Seriously. The manager who actually really wanted to hire me for the position was shocked and ended up studying the angle of my wrist and the bend in my fingers, in an effort to discover the root of the difficulty . . . yet to no avail. That damn tray simply wanted nothing to do with my hand.

I anticipated that the Hunt for a Job was going to be traumatic. But then, in an odd stroke of luck, a friend of mine (another actor) got a job at an Internet start-up that was not only hiring but was understanding of actors' "special needs." Word spread, and with barely a clue of what the job entailed, several actor friends and I enlisted. Soon we learned the company specialized in something called "buzz marketing," also enticingly known as "viral marketing," and that our job was to go undercover to online forums and chat rooms and pose as fans of upcoming movies, to create a "buzz" around the film's release. If we did our job right, people everywhere would end up at theaters, buying tickets for movies they had no desire to see.

Though I'd started with only a very fundamental understanding of computers, within a matter of time that drastically changed. In addition to the more standard ins and outs of a PC,

I also learned how to deviously cover my tracks online and hone the art of creating phony identities and fake e-mail accounts. It was my job to learn the tricks of the trade, and it was a very sneaky trade with very, very wily tricks.

Unfortunately, the most popular forums, and those with the most traffic, were porn sites, and hence that's where we spent the majority of our time. I can safely say there were some images I wish I'd never seen. Yet the other, almost less appealing option was to spend my days at movie-gossip sites and film-fan forums, gushing about actresses I'd once been in direct competition with, actresses whose careers had taken off while mine remained curiously snagged on the starting gate. But that was my job. It was up to me to learn everything about all the up-and-coming movies I was in no way a part of, to study up on all the actors whose careers were golden and gleaming. Essentially, it was my job to torture myself in long, drawn out twelve-hour shifts.

The fact that I'd gone from a supposedly rising star to an earthbound Internet marketer who helped other actors' careers soar was an irony that was not lost on me, and within a matter of time I sank into a depression like someone starved for sleep would fall into a feather bed. I couldn't get out. I didn't want to get out. The rest of the world was simply not one I wanted to be a part of, as, among other things, it often lacked the sensitivity a struggling artist requires. For instance, though the phrase "What have you been up to?" is a seemingly innocent inquiry, it is actually Hollywood's way of determining if you're someone who's just completed work on the next blockbuster and are hence essential to talk to—to be *seen* talking to—or if you're a loser who's not had a job in a while and thus, in terms of strategy, now rank one step below that of the valet. "What have you been up to?" can be directly translated as "What was your last film, and when's it coming out?" And in response to such a question, I could only shrug and eye the door.

All this was reiterated to me like a smack to the head the night I mistakenly lifted myself from my downy nest of nothingness and headed off to a party at the Chateau Marmont. The Chateau Marmont combines a mixture of horrors, the first being its location on Sunset Boulevard, which involves fifteen-dollar parking and streets plugged with poor misguided souls who enjoy "cruising"—the art of creating traffic jams so thick that traversing the length of one block can take twenty minutes. Another aspect of the Chateau's horror is that it can be hard to get into, so once inside, you're generally surrounded by people who tend to remind you of why you should've stayed home.

After using a considerable portion of my paycheck to park, I showed my ID to the doorman and beelined my way toward the models, I mean "bartenders," who were haughtily pouring drinks. If I bought a drink now, that would mean I'd have to use the latest AT&T check for food and not skin care. So I was trying to figure out who might want to have me over for dinner for the rest of the week, when I heard my name. As the voice was male, and coming from the vicinity of the bar, I turned with hopes of at least a free Coke or just something to sip, and saw, a few dark wood stools over, the editor from the magazine who'd once deemed me one of the twelve actors to watch. His smile was big, he was motioning me over, he certainly could afford to buy me a drink.... Yet the one thought that had grabbed my brain and wouldn't let go was *He remembers my name! Yay!*

"Sarah," he said again, "it's so funny I'd run into you. We were just talking about you in the office the other day."

My heart started pounding—was there some publicity in my future? I had no idea what the publicity would be for; I had no movie coming out, no upcoming projects. Could it be just because they liked me? I was likeable! I deserved good things! See? There was a reason I'd gotten out of my pajamas on a Saturday night! "You were?" I asked coyly.

"It's coming up again, the Twelve Actors to Watch issue, and we were going over a few back issues, looking at the girls we'd picked. There you were."

There was a long, painful pause, during which I wouldn't have been surprised had one of the model bartenders gazelled her way over the bar and finished his sentence with, "... *the only one who wasn't worth watching.*"

The editor continued, oblivious to the knife he was wedging into my heart. "Whatever happened to that movie you did?"

His clone friend, whom I'd not noticed till now (perhaps because he wore almost the exact same outfit as the editor, had the exact same haircut, and effectively appeared to be nothing more than a slightly skewed and miniature reflection), chipped in. "Which one? Which movie?"

"*The Blackout,*" the editor said. "Abel Ferrara."

The clone paused, his face tilted toward the impossibly high ceilings—a necessity in such a bar, in order to allow for the egos. Clearly the clone was trying to place the movie, and I prayed for a swift and dramatic subject change. Had the clone suddenly said, "Gosh, I'd love to have a lengthy conversation about football," I would've done a dance of joy. Unfortunately, I had no such luck.

"*The Blackout*," the clone said. "I'm just not placing it. Who else was in it? When was it released?"

"It wasn't," I said. Then I smiled brightly, proudly said the dreaded words "Straight to video," and excused myself. With a speed I never knew I had, I raced out the door, flew across the traffic on Sunset, and was back in my room, where for hours I tortured myself with variations of the conversation that took place earlier in the week between the editor and a coworker. "Check it out, it's our past issue." "Who's this one?" "Who?" "This girl, I've only ever seen her here, on this page." "Oh, yeah. That's Sarah Lassez . . . right. I don't know. Obviously she wasn't one to watch. But five outta six ain't bad. You feel like a Mojito? I feel like a Mojito." "Nah, I'm much more in the mood for a sidecar." "A *sidecar*? We just time warp back to the thirties?" "Last week a guy I know told me Drew Barrymore was drinking one." "Drew? Really? Okay. Sidecars it is. Put that magazine away." "Yeah, but I gotta say, it's a great shot. This Sarah chick with a guitar, posing as a depressed musician. You don't get better than that. Great work, man. Sidecar's on me."

To make myself feel better I pulled out my French tarot cards. *Will I get an acting job soon? Will it lead to more acting jobs? Will I be able to support myself as an actor?* For hours I asked questions, and each time I shuffled, there it was, insistent on being seen: the Knight of Wands.

"Who are you?" I wanted to scream. "And why aren't you here yet?"

• • •

Misery loves company. I admit that the saying is true, but if I could, I'd add "and a couple bottles of wine and a block of Brie." I had the wine, and Gina stopped at Whole Foods for the Brie, a mission that involved her calling—completely overwhelmed—from the cheese section, whereupon she told me how pretty all the cheeses were and that she just knew I'd like Jarlsberg if only I gave it a chance. I agreed to try it simply to get her out of the store, and then found a platter I hoped would fit her final selection. Mercifully she showed up with only a handful of choices: Edam, Jarlsberg, Gouda, Brie, and a farmer's cheese she swore was "refreshing." After a little rant about how Panela should be sold at more stores and accepted as the amazing cheese that it is, she sat back and announced that she hated her job.

"So, you work at a literary agency," I said. I was still trying to figure out exactly why she'd taken the job. "But you don't want to be an agent."

"Nope."

"And they rep screenwriters, but you don't want to write screenplays; you want to write books. That's what you went to school for, why you have all that student loan debt."

"Right. Thank you. But just being around writers makes me feel better."

"You're around the writers?"

"No. They don't write *at* the agency. We get what they write. All the scripts. And writers are very close to their agents, you know. You learn a lot about their lives."

"And your agent, the one you work for, he reps some good writers?"

"Well, no. My agent actually just reps directors. Mostly TV. No writers."

"But you don't want to be a TV director?"

"God, no."

"So you want to write books, and you're working for a man who gets television directors jobs."

"Give me the wine."

"I'm just saying it makes perfect sense."

"I know what you're saying, Miss Internet Marketer, now give me the wine."

We spent the next bottle comparing notes on our miserable states of employment. Gina eventually won the You'll Never Believe What Happened Award with her tale of an agent who'd witnessed a car accident while driving, and then called his assistant to have her *conference* him with 911.

"I mean, had he forgotten what number you dial to reach 911? Or does he really think he's so important that he needs to be announced when he comes on the line? 'Yes, Officer, please hold for Ken Steinberg. He represents several Emmy-nominated writers and has just seen an accident.' Seriously, who *are* these people?" Gina laughed.

"I'd say they're the successful ones."

"Oh my God, that reminds me. I forgot to tell you. I was looking for Gouda earlier and started thinking about you and totally had a vision of you and your husband. You were standing with him in front of a really gorgeous two-story brick house, with a black SUV in the driveway. A *new* SUV."

"So, we're married? We have a house? And why does Gouda make you think of me?"

"I don't know. I can't answer any of that. I guess it could've been my future house, but I'm totally out of my wanting-a-brick-house stage. It's Craftsman or nothing. The woodwork is amazing. Some of the built-ins will literally give you palpitations, and the—"

"*Gina.*"

"Yeah, okay. I don't know if you were married, but you were definitely *with* him, and I think it was your house, and he was cute, too. Very preppy-looking. Blond hair and green eyes."

A couple things struck me about this latest claim. First, preppy-looking with blond hair and green eyes is pretty much the polar opposite of the type of man I'm drawn to. Just that description brings to my mind a guy who's got a semblance of a life, someone with a job, someone who plays golf and showers regularly. That is not who I date. Blindfold me and stick me in a party full of men, and I'll sniff out the empty wallet and pained soul of the one actor/musician in the building. Dark and messy is how you'd describe the men I date. *Not* preppy with blond hair and green eyes.

The other, more alarming aspect of this claim was that the description perfectly matched that of the Knight of Wands. It was then that I knew, without a shadow of a doubt, that he was coming.

My knight was on his way.

A few weeks later I was at work, enjoying one of my self-imposed "breaks," when I discovered Angel, a phone psychic with lofty promises. I scrolled through her site, temptation twitching in my fingers as I learned that she had a special rate for first-time callers and, even more tempting, that she didn't use tarot cards.

Lately the tarot cards had been annoying the crap out of me. In addition to the unrelenting Knight of Wands, I'd also become—less pleasingly so—haunted by the Disappointment and Strife cards. If I saw either card one more time, I swore I'd launch myself off the Hollywood sign, which stood as a painful reminder outside my window at work. Even a sidelong glimpse of those letters made me sad, because I remembered with aching clarity the first time I'd seen them in person. I remembered feeling that those letters cast a promise to all who viewed them, a promise that anything was possible. Yet here, years later, stuck in an office with a clear view of the taunting sign, those letters only brought to mind Peg Entwistle, the out-of-work actress back in the thirties who couldn't bear it any longer and hurled herself to her death from atop the *H*. As if that in and of itself weren't tragic enough, two days after she killed herself, her uncle received news that Peg had just been offered the leading role in a play at the Beverly Hills Playhouse. The way I view that final twist has always been dependent upon my mood, as it's either a reminder to find a way to last another day (or two), since things will get better, or it's a harsh statement about the universe's sick sense of humor.

At any rate, I needed answers. I looked around and determined that the other employees were also on breaks: I caught glimpses of poker Web sites and eBay on flickering computer screens. What the hell, I decided, and slipped out of the room and into an empty office.

As I dialed the number, I felt guilt the way one does when

cheating on one's hairdresser. I was about to betray Aurelia; I was about to have a dalliance with another psychic. But Aurelia wouldn't read me anymore, so what choice did I have? Essentially she'd driven me to this. This was, basically, her fault.

I was scared to ask Angel about my career, but forced the question. Without pause she told me there would be success in my future, but what I needed to overcome was fear and a karmic block. "You used to be a very famous actress in a past life," she said. "That's where your strong ego comes from, but your karma in this life is to be humbled and rejoin the masses."

I was conflicted. Part of me was thrilled at having been a famous actress, while the other part heard the phrase "rejoin the masses" and wanted to stomp on the phone. I mean, *rejoin the masses?*

What came out was, "Sarah Bernhardt? Was I Sarah Bernhardt?"

"I can't say. But the sooner you learn the lesson and are humbled, the sooner you'll be freed from your karma and go on to great success."

My eyes flickered to the Hollywood sign. I was stuck in an office with computer nerds high on café lattes. Wait. I *was* a computer nerd high on café lattes. Hadn't I already been humbled?

Then, with words that certainly wouldn't lend to my humility, she announced that I'd go on to win a Golden Globe.

My smile could've blinded passing airplanes with its brilliance, and my eyes stung with tears of joy.

• • •

Needless to say, I began calling Angel all the time. With Aurelia's refusal to read me I'd been left with a huge void in my life, one that Angel with her uplifting readings lovingly filled. Of course Angel wasn't free, but for some things you just have to find money any way you can—and hearing that I had a future as an actress and wouldn't be stuck forever in the fishbowl computer room as an Internet marketer certainly qualified as one of those things. Before I knew it, the credit cards I'd once wisely left at home were in my wallet at all times. And lucky for me, and for Angel, I had a huge credit line.

And then it happened: I had only two weeks left before turning *thirty*.

Granted, I'd contemplated this event every single day since my twenty-sixth birthday, but I was still in no way prepared for the actual experience. The actual experience involved me actually *being* thirty, as in, no longer in my twenties. In a stroke of what some people may have considered regression but I considered genius, I decided to throw myself a party: a good old-fashioned child's *The Wizard of Oz*–themed party, complete with my parents in the other room sipping spiked drinks. I utterly rebelled against aging, and did so with the Wicked Witch of the West stuck beneath my couch, a yellow brick road twisting through my apartment, and a slightly hazardous game of Pin the Heart on the Tin Man.

And I survived. I awoke the next day with such a feeling of relief. I'd tackled turning thirty and lived to tell about it! But then it hit me. I'd now have to turn thirty-one.

In fact, turning thirty had never been the problem. It was all the years *after* that I should've been afraid of. But no matter, I clung to the idea that turning thirty-one or even thirty-two wouldn't sting nearly as much if I had the love and fame that had been predicted.

One day Angel, my lifeline to my Golden Globe future, told me she was joining up with a psychic Internet site, a place called Psychicdom. I was horrified. I'd just gotten used to our little routine, to my relationship with her, and now all that could change. I'd have to go through the site to reach her, and what if someone else was talking to her? She was *my* psychic, and I was not happy about sharing. Sharing, as a concept, has never been one I've embraced. I mean, why share when I can have my own? Why settle for half when I could have the whole? No. Angel, like Aurelia, was betraying me, and I vowed never to forgive her . . . but decided to check out the site first.

What struck me was that Angel, in whom I'd put my utmost confidence, wasn't the sharpest tool in the shed. Essentially she'd just led me to a smorgasbord of psychics. I could barely breathe, I was so overwhelmed. *Look at them all. And they're all here for me!* I tried to remain calm as I did a little searching on the site, contemplating the psychics' names. Would Desire to Love lead me to my knight? Or would Astro Linda point me in his direction? And then there were the photos, sedate Sears portraits and disturbing Glamour Shots, a whole range of psychics from what appeared to be councilmen to cowboys, housewives to waitresses, and of course a few stereotypical gypsies thrown in for the more traditional callers.

Beside their names were stars, five being the highest, so one could feel assured they'd get their money's worth, money being the obscene amount per minute written in a much smaller font and nestled somewhat off to the side of the alluring stars. And, like eBay, there was feedback, so I was sure that irate callers would expose anyone who failed to live up to their price tag. The system itself was like a security blanket that smothered any doubts I had, and before I knew what was happening, a Visa card with my name on it had jumped from my purse and settled by the phone.

I leaned in toward my computer, studying up on a man named Erlin, who was rated as one of the top three on the site. He looked remarkably like Valentino, his smooth smile, slicked-back hair, and black tux lending the impression that should you request a reading, he'd be forced to set his champagne glass on an ivory-topped table and exit the ballroom, much to the chagrin of a line of women either coyly fanning themselves or discreetly hoisting their cleavage. Surely this Erlin understood romance and love, unlike Ask Ursula, who looked as though the only thing she understood for certain was the location of the best buffet in town.

When I looked up, away from my computer, I realized how late it had gotten. My room was dark but for the eyestrain-inducing glow of my laptop, and I could see from my bedroom window that most of the houses on the street were now only lit by porch lights. The world was going to sleep, but I refused to follow its cue. I needed a reading, and nothing could stop me.

Erlin cost a bit more than Angel, but what the hell. I'd always been taught to appreciate quality not quantity, and I figured if

I started straight off with one of the top three psychics on the site, I'd have no need for the hacks. In truth, I was saving myself money by spending so much.

"Hello," a soft airy voice said, "and welcome to Psychicdom. Please hold while we connect you with your adviser. You will be charged the rate of $4.99 a minute. Please don't forget to leave feedback at the end of your call."

I barely had time to panic before a calming, almost hypnotic voice came on the line. "Hello, this is Erlin. I sense you're calling about love ... about a love relationship."

"Well, sort of. I mean, yes. Will I ever have one again?"

I could almost hear him smile through the phone, and the sweetness of what I felt was like sugar after a lifetime of salt. It washed over me. I will have love again, of course I will! Then my mother's voice, informing me she was okay never having grandchildren, hit me with a thwack, and I tightened my grip on the receiver.

"I see him," he finally said. "He's your heart's desire, everything you've ever wanted and everything you never knew you needed. He will absolutely sweep you off your feet."

"When?" At some point I'd leapt from the bed and begun pacing frantically. I pivoted right as I reached my nightstand, then again as I reached my bookcase. I needed sweeping. I desperately needed sweeping.

"It's soon, actually. I see him so clearly. He has blondish hair and blue or green eyes. Light eyes."

I froze. Could he be talking about my Knight of Wands? My Knight of Wands who'd been teasingly announcing his arrival for the last year? "When? *When* do I meet him?"

Though I expected Erlin to ponder the question, to look into his crystal ball or summon the spirits, he instead immediately spit out, "Two weeks." And that was that. There was no guessing, no big window of time, no room for error—simply "two weeks." His confidence had completely sold me, and my belief in my knight's arrival was so firm it was as if God had just faxed me an itinerary.

For kicks I decided to ask about my career, which, despite Angel's encouragement, I'd pretty much given up on. Erlin again seemed very confident, very assured. "I see a lot of success in your future. Money will not be a problem."

After a few seconds of joy it occurred to me that the success he was seeing could be from a career as an Internet marketer. I began pacing again. "Can you make sure you're looking at my career as an actress? Because I'm doing another job on the side."

"The side"—the side of what? I hadn't been on an audition in so long that I was an Internet marketer through and through. There was no side. I worried that I was lying to the psychic, something that's always terrified me. Even getting annoyed with psychics freaks me out, because what if they can read your thoughts? Shouldn't they be *able* to read your thoughts? What if the words "You crazy bitch, where's my Golden Globe!" randomly course through their brains as they're mopping the floor, and they know it's you? What if they feel your bad thoughts and put a curse on you? What if you never win a Golden Globe *because* of your bad thoughts?

But Erlin gave me no reason to think anything negative, as immediately he responded with, "Yes, your talent will be recognized. You're very creative."

"As an actress, right?" I knew I was being picky, but I had to be sure. I'd become pretty damn creative as an Internet marketer, too.

"Yes, as an actress. I see success and recognition."

"When? When's that happen?"

"This year there's a little success, but I see a lot coming in the next few years. I see a role that fits you well."

A role that fits me well . . . like on a TV series? A long-running TV series that would mean I'd get my Spanish-style house and my infinity pool? "So, I'll be famous? I'll be rich?"

"Yes, you will be famous—and money will never be an issue."

Beep! The soft airy voice interrupted. *"You have one minute remaining."*

"Do you see anything else? What else do you see?"

"You'll be presented with an opportunity. You'll be on a roll. You'll feel strong and successful and fulfilled. You need to suspend doubt. Clear your head and make it your intention."

Beep! "To continue your call at the rate of . . ."

I yelled a good-bye over the soft airy voice and hung up.

Wow. Love, career, fame, money, being swept off my feet—that was the best call ever. Of course, that call cost me about seventy-five dollars, practically a whole day's work at my job from hell. . . . But a glimpse into the future was worth it! Erlin was like a gatekeeper who'd just swung open a door for me, his tux-clad arm indicating a path paved in dazzling gold. And it must be true, he must be right, because he was so highly rated. With Angel or Aurelia I'd always felt a slight tickle of doubt, since I had no proof they were accurate; they had no feedback. But Erlin, Erlin came with an accuracy report!

I ran myself a bath and knew it was just a matter of time. Now *three* psychics had predicted I'd be famous, so obviously I'd be famous. And love ... the great love of my life was just around the corner, just about to appear!

I thanked my lucky stars I'd been led to Erlin and to Psychicdom, and dumped half a bottle of valerian and hops into the bath to promote sleep. It was close to midnight, yet I was so awake I could've painted the entire apartment.

As I slipped into the blue overpoweringly fragrant water, I was so excited about my future it almost hurt.

5

Wilhelm the Metrosexual

NOTHING TAKES OVER AN ANSWERING MACHINE LIKE one of Gina's phone calls. It never matters that she's essentially talking to herself; once she has yelled "Pick up the phone" a dozen times and is thus satisfied you're not home, she will then have an entire conversation, asking questions, answering them, elaborating and debating. If you weren't sitting idly by when she called, screening the message, then you'd get home later, press play, and stand there, legs aching, tempted to delete her rambling halfway through. But you can't, because she tends to leave the important bits right at the very end. The tricky, sadistic girl.

So, almost two weeks after my introduction to Psychicdom, when I was searching for the right psychic for a little pick-me-up reading and I heard Gina's voice careening into the room, I prayed for a full message box. However, that wish sometimes backfires, because the message would then be left on my cell phone's voice mail, along with a supplemental speech on the importance of clearing your messages. I lay down, resigned to a long sprawling message. I just couldn't handle a conversation with anyone right then, much less someone who might insist I leave my house. Just days prior the company I worked for had floated belly-up in its algae-filled Internet start-up pond, and I'd lost my job as an Internet marketer. This actually had made me very, very happy; with my layoff came severance and unemployment, and if there's one thing I'm good at, it's being unemployed. Still, I was a bit miffed that *not one* psychic had managed to predict this. I mean, to other people the loss of a job would be monumental, something to predict. How had they missed it?

I was trying to zone out Gina's ramblings and was about to put the pillow over my head, when suddenly my mind latched on to something she said. I sprang from the bed and yanked the phone from its cradle. "Who? Who's my future boyfriend?"

It seemed she'd just met a friend of a friend, a sous-chef at a fancy hotel, whom she claimed was perfect for me. "He's not an actor. Sarah, are you getting this? He's got a normal job."

"Yeah, I heard you. But *what* are you calling him?"

"*Villll*-helm."

"What the hell is that?"

"You know. Wilhelm. German for William, I guess."

"Wilhelm? He's German? Great. His ancestors probably gassed mine, and we'll have some fucked up karma."

All right. Even I knew how ridiculous I sounded. The truth was that for all my talk about wanting a boyfriend, I was terrified of getting involved again. So far it seemed that the universe tended to intervene in any way it could to mess with my love life, so it seemed a distinct possibility that this Wilhelm and I would be settled on the couch on some rainy day, flipping through old family photos, only to make the gruesome discovery. "This is my great-grandmother," I'd say, right as he said, "Holy crap. That's my great-grandfather with the gun. How funny!"

"Sarah, you're being a freak. Listen. I have a feeling this is important, like this *needs* to happen. And he's totally your type. He looks just like Elvis. A blond Elvis with green eyes."

I paused for a moment, wondering where on earth Gina had gotten the idea that Elvis was my type. "Young Elvis or old Elvis?"

"Young Elvis. Jesus, like I'd set you up with old Elvis."

After she insisted he was a pretty, clean, young Elvis, I agreed to meet him. Then my insides started doing somersaults when I realized his description matched all the predictions. Was this my knight? Was my knight a young blond Elvis look-alike German sous-chef?

On Saturday night Gina arrived at my house, took one look at me, and asked me why I was dressed as Superman.

"The *S*," I informed her, pointing to my baby doll Superman T-shirt, "stands for Sarah."

"Uh-huh. Okay."

I realized then that in my mission to not be vulnerable and to keep my guard up, dressing as a superhero might have been overkill, but we were already late at that point, and Gina wouldn't let me change.

"We're supposed to be on the west side in ten minutes," she said, pointing to the door. "Get in the car, Clark."

With that she turned and clomped down the steps, stopping at the door and then looking back at me with an encouraging grin, as if to say, "Ready? Ready to meet your future husband?" I nodded, and finally followed her, because as a matter of fact yes, yes I was ready to meet my future husband.

It turned out there were three stages to this particular evening. The first was to meet her friend Dustin, an enormously tall German, at his place. The second was to head to the hotel where Wilhelm worked, so he could join us. And the third was to go to another bar, where, almost two hours after we'd left the house, we'd then officially start the evening. Such genius planning was only one of many reasons why going out seemed like work, but I didn't complain as we pulled up in front of Dustin's apartment building. Ever so casually, Gina turned off the car and dropped a bombshell.

Seat belt still on, I twisted toward her as much as I could, staring in disbelief. "He's *how old?*"

Gina smiled. "Dustin's age."

"And that's *twenty-five?* I thought Dustin was older!"

"He just seems older because he's so tall. People often make that mistake. But no. Twenty-five. Come on, let's go." She grabbed her purse and got out of the car.

Not budging, I yelled after her, "I cannot believe you're just telling me this now!"

I saw her heading to my side of the car, and I locked the door. I wasn't getting out. No way. Not for a twenty-five-year-old. No. Twenty-five-year-old guys are still submerged in their frat boy lives; are still stuck in bouts of womanizing, bachelor pad black leather couches, and cinderblock end tables. They think a date means picking up the tab at McDonald's and romance means not having a football game on in the background. You date a twenty-five-year-old guy when you're eighteen, not when you're thirty. In fact, if we got a move on, this thirty-year-old could be resting her ancient bones beneath a blanket and watching *Grease* within the hour.

Gina attempted to unlock my door with her key, but I planted my hand on the lock and foiled her plan. "No. I'm not getting out. You tricked me. You ambushed me with a child."

"Sarah," she said, trying to unlock the door and at the same time pull on the handle, a combination that was decidedly ungraceful and yet highly entertaining. "Open up. Come on, unlock it! You will not be sorry; I promise you. He's mature for his age! He's German; they're *born* mature!"

"No."

Then, suddenly, she stopped pulling. She knelt by my window. In the glimmer of her eyes I could practically *see* her brain switching gears.

"Look," she said in a very calm and scarily soothing voice. "At the very least you'll just want to mess around with him. That I can definitely promise you. When you see him, you won't be able to resist. Okay? Just look at it that way, that this is a really cute, nice guy who will buy you drinks and maybe a dinner or two. He'll get you out of the house and make you smile. He's someone to think about. Who cares if he doesn't turn out to be *the one*? What else do you have right now? This is a cute boy to kiss! Isn't that a good thing?"

Damnit. She was right. I glared at her as I took my hand off the lock. This whole time I'd been thinking I was about to meet my knight, my future husband, and had been on a cloud nine of anticipation like a girl told there was fine-jewelry shopping or drunken disco dancing in her future. Now I'd have to completely realign my thoughts. I opened the door and stepped out, my heels immediately sinking in and aerating someone's lawn. *Cute boy to kiss*, I repeated in my mind as Gina quickly locked the car behind me.

I admit, I took one look at the hotel, a glamorous and historic building with opulent décor and views of the ocean, and thought maybe this Wilhelm guy wasn't that bad. Certainly they wouldn't have a Senor Frog's T-shirt wearing, beer-bong-partaking frat boy working here. Maybe he was mature for his age. Maybe there was hope after all.

Gina and I waited at the hotel's glossy bar while Dustin disappeared to find his friend. The plan was to wait just a few more minutes till Wilhelm was off work, join him for a bottle of wine courtesy of his incredible employee discount, and finally all head over to a different bar, where he could knock back a few more drinks without being scrutinized by his employees. It was actually a shame, because his hotel was gorgeous and equipped with some great people-watching. Glancing around the room, I noticed that someone had meticulously planted a celebrity at every table, as well as in the entryway, for that matter. On our way in, Dustin had almost stepped on a little sitcom actor.

Just for kicks I imagined dating this Wilhelm creature. I'd

meet him at work and sit demurely at the bar with my leopard–print handbag and a black fifties–style coat, my lips glossy red, my dark hair shining. The bartender would rush to make me an apple martini as people looked on with awe. "Who is she?" they'd ask, discreetly trying to catch my reflection in the bar's mirror. "She looks familiar. She's got to be important for that bartender to move like that."

Gina nudged me. "That's him."

I looked up. With mounting excitement I scanned the room for a clean, pretty, young Elvis, but saw no one who matched the description. What I did see, however, was Dustin heading toward us with someone who looked like a skinny human version of Mr. Burns, the boss from *The Simpsons*. I was about to ask Gina whom she was talking about, when I realized that this human Mr. Burns did kind of look like Elvis . . . if I squinted. Panic looped through me and I felt the need to fling Gina into their path and make a break for the door. *She set me up with Mr. Burns?*

Then he was before me. He took my hand as he said hello, and I had to admit I liked his voice. He had a debonair quality to him, like he'd own pocket watches and go to the opera, def–initely not a frat boy. Yet now I couldn't stop thinking of him as Mr. Burns. *Stop it*, I told myself. *Give poor Mr. Burns a chance.*

We took a seat at a table with a view of the dark and endless ocean. Along with the wine, Wilhelm had a tray of desserts sent over, and I saw Gina, across from me, eyeing the chocolate tortes with alarm. Gina was always on a diet and lacked the ability to have just one of anything, so I knew she'd either skip them altogether or within minutes have the tray on her lap and crumbs on her chin.

Wilhelm turned toward me. "Is this your first time here?"

There was a pause while everyone waited for me to answer the question, but I couldn't; I was too busy studying his head.

"Yes," Gina finally said, furiously waving the dessert tray away when Dustin tried passing it to her, "we don't come to this side of town too often."

As she explained that there was nothing wrong with this side of town, that it was quite lovely but she'd become allergic to traffic, I figured it out. *It's his widow's peak.* I flashed back to just minutes ago, when he'd been heading toward us. *It was the gigantic widow's peak,* the skin around it reflecting the overhead lights and shining like a mirror—that was what made him look like Mr. Burns. I squinted and this time saw Elvis. The sideburns! That's why he also looked like Elvis. Sideburns. I'd never dated anyone with sideburns, and I wondered if they were his attempt at hair. Clearly he wasn't having much luck with the strands on his head, so possibly the sideburns made him feel better. Wow, balding at twenty-five. Good God, he's *twenty-five.* . . . *What am I doing here?*

It took me a second to realize everyone was staring at me. Apparently I'd just been asked another question. Drat.

"Right?" Gina said, kicking me under the table. "Silver Lake is where you live?"

"Uh-huh," I said. "Silver Lake." Wilhelm had really nice lips. Nice full, luscious lips. I'm a sucker for lips, their lure so powerful they could tempt me to overlook the rest of a person, though I was realizing that Wilhelm needed no overlooking. Once I'd torn my eyes from the very present sideburns and the glaring widow's peak, I saw his actual face and was pleasantly surprised. He was very cute.

In the background of my mind's appraisal I heard laughter at something he'd said, so of course I joined in, relieved to learn he appeared to have a sense of humor. Nice lips and a good personality. This was promising! And, I reminded myself, there were drugs for the whole balding thing. If he had insurance, we'd promptly order some prescriptions, and if he didn't, we'd get some drugs in Mexico, maybe take a weekend trip and stay at a hotel perched on a cliff above the ocean, where we could eat gigantic bowls of cherry pit clams and buy lots of silver jewelry. Then, while the hair drugs took effect, I'd present him with baseball caps. He'd look cute in baseball caps. I was trying to decide what kind—not a sports team cap, since instinct told me he was too much of a pretty boy to be a sports fan, but maybe an Abercrombie & Fitch hat—when Gina whacked me in the arm. "We're going to the next bar," she whispered. "You can stare at him there."

And that I did. We journeyed off to a dimly lit, crowded, humid bar, one of those charming places that reeks of decades of spilled beer. On any other occasion I would've caught wind of said beer vapors from the sidewalk, turned, and fled back to the car, but I'd somehow become glued to Wilhelm's side, so that wasn't an option. I couldn't stop looking at him. He was a charmer, a gentleman. I'd heard of guys like this. They existed in past generations. They were stories our grandparents told. They opened doors for you, brought flowers, and helped you with your coat. Never would they be caught on a ragged couch from the seventies, unshaven, and taking a deep toke off a Coke can that had been scientifically transformed into a pipe, as tended to be the case with most of the men I'd dated. This, I thought as Wilhelm ordered me a drink with such refinement I immediately asked for another, was a new experience.

It didn't take long for me to be completely smitten—and completely drunk. I wanted to touch his lips, and literally had to hold my hand down so it wouldn't reach up and feel them. At one point the boys excused themselves, and I decided now was the perfect chance to write down my number so that at the end of the evening I could sexily and suavely hand it to him, impressing him with my moves and sophistication. I asked the waitress for a pen, and Gina, perched beside me, elatedly handed me a napkin.

I leaned in close to the napkin, maybe two inches from its surface, and painstakingly wrote the number. I tried to make it as legible as possible, but ultimately was just too drunk to trust my handwriting, or my vision for that matter. Strangely, no matter at what angle I held the napkin, what I'd written just didn't look right.

"Gina? What's wrong with this?"

She glanced at the napkin. "For starters it's not your number."

I tried again and displayed it for approval.

She shook her head. "Uh, no. Try again."

I crossed it out and made another attempt.

Gina watched with anticipation. "Nope."

One more attempt and she began laughing so hard she had to cover her mouth not to spit out her wine. I told her I could do this and got back to work. But I just couldn't. Even when I did remember my number, I'd start to write the digits, and they'd morph on their way out, becoming different numbers entirely. I had no idea why this was happening, but soon we were both laughing hysterically at my drunken state and all the napkins on the bar with messy fake numbers. Perhaps that was it, we decided. I was so used to giving out fake numbers to men that when pressed for my real number, my very being simply rebelled. "No!" my well-trained hand was trying to tell me. "You give him this number and you'll be screening your calls for weeks! We've been through this before! Think back to the 'Your Skin Is Like a Song' guy! Don't do it!"

By the time Wilhelm and Dustin returned, I'd written out something Gina promised was my phone number. Though at that point I didn't even trust her, as I'd noticed she had a bad case of Wine Lip, the telltale stain that indicates more than a couple glasses of red have been consumed. I watched Wilhelm take his seat, and that was when it hit me: He looked exactly like the Knight of Wands. It was as if the knight had sprung to life, climbed from the cards, and perched himself on a barstool.

It was too much. It was freaking me out. He was twenty-five; I was thirty. This couldn't be my knight! There was no way this was going anywhere! I knew there was no way he wanted to settle down and have kids. My clock was furiously ticking away while he didn't even have a clock.

Though he did seem much older. The problem, I realized, was that I was used to actors, who are basically perpetual children. Wilhelm only seemed beyond his years because he had an actual career and direction in life, a quality I'd never experienced in anyone I'd dated. Essentially he was a mirage of an older person, and I worried it was only a matter of time before his sophistication crumbled to a pile at his feet, leaving behind a true twenty-five-year-old boy pounding his fists on the bar and shouting, "Drink, drink, drink!" No, I couldn't let myself be fooled here. *Remember your Superman shirt*, I thought, *and be strong. Embrace your superpowers.*

I leaned in to Gina. "He's *twenty-five*," I slurred into her ear. "And he will be my play toy."

She smiled. "Famous last words."

I laughed, turned to Wilhelm, and, without an ounce of sexy, stuffed what I hoped was my number into his hand.

Gina had indeed helped me write down my real number, because the next day I heard Wilhelm's voice streaming through my machine. I was shocked. The cards I'd been pulling all morning, well, ever since my hangover had subsided enough that I could see, had indicated fast communication, but this was unheard of. Had he not been told, upon entering the United States, that men were required to wait at least three days before calling a girl? That it was practically a mandate to call only once the girl had panicked, cursed the guy's name endlessly, and then given up, figuring she'd never hear from him? Who was this guy? And how had he passed, undetected, into the U.S.?

Spurred into action, I picked up the phone. I noticed—now that I didn't have his pretty face as a distraction—that his accent was a lot stronger than I'd remembered. It was cute. *He* was cute. As he spoke, I pictured his full lips forming the words. *Stop it, Sarah. Pay attention.* Evidently he wanted to do something that night, and as soon as we'd made plans for him to come over at eight, I tornadoed my way through my room, on a mission to embody the perfect combination of "sexy" and "refined class." Essentially I needed to be a Gucci-clad librarian with an impeccable French manicure and come–fuck–me heels. It wasn't easy, and I definitely didn't have time to do my nails. Finally I settled on a pink cashmere sweater, distressed jeans that had cost a fortune, faux diamond stud earrings, and elegant red lace underthings (such preparation thus ensuring nothing would happen). There. Outfit secured, room a wreck, I looked at the time: four o'clock. I had just enough time to clean up (shove everything into the closet or under the bed), soak in the tub for three hours, search the house for any presents China may have stashed, and then carefully apply a bunch of makeup that would make me look natural.

It wasn't till I was in the tub that I realized it had been exactly two weeks since Erlin had made his prediction. I craned my neck toward the bathroom door and debated about getting out, grabbing the phone, getting back in, and having a nice long conversation with Erlin as I relaxed in my detoxifying rosemary fango mud bath. He could tell me what the evening had in store, and thus I'd be prepared. *No,* I told myself, *I can do this. I can charge forth into the unknown.* And though I'd like to say it was sheer strength and willpower that kept me from getting out of the tub and calling for a reading, it may have also had something to do with the fact that a couple days prior I'd heeded some advice I'd read in a magazine and frozen my credit cards in a big bowl of water, and I knew my bath would be cold by the time I got those suckers thawed. That, I must say, was some great advice, and I made a mental note to nuke the bowl in the microwave the second the date was over.

At exactly eight o'clock the doorbell rang. I waited a bit, so it didn't look as though perhaps I'd been staring out the window for the last twenty minutes and had just now seen his car pull up. Then I took a deep breath and answered the door.

There he was. Smiling and looking very . . . clean. I don't think I'd ever seen anyone look so clean, so shiny. I also don't think I'd ever been on a date with a man wearing a pink button–down shirt. But there he was in pale pink, a selection he'd paired with black dress pants, a shiny black leather belt, and black shoes so polished I could've used them as a mirror. I suddenly became very conscious of my chipped nail polish and distressed jeans, and decided I should find a way to slip into the conversation that these jeans had cost a fortune and were *meant* to look like this, were in fact coveted by many *because* they looked like this. As I led him upstairs, I worried he was looking at my purposefully frayed back pockets, pockets that to the untrained eye could simply look used, as if I had spent the majority of my life sitting on rough surfaces. It hit me that for the first time ever I was with a man who made *me* look like a slob, and the realization was both impressive and profoundly disturbing.

Once he settled on the couch, it became clear he had no intention of taking me out. Apparently the date was to happen here, and it seemed this had been established in our earlier phone conversation, perhaps right around the time I'd been picturing his lips moving and had zoned out his actual words. Crap. Staying at my place was a twist to the evening I was not prepared for, since I'm in no way the consummate hostess. I knew I should've called Erlin. Erlin could've told me to buy food, wine, plates, and wineglasses that weren't from Mexico with the thick blue rims that only margarita glasses should have. Erlin could've told me the night would involve my standing in the kitchen, panicking, as a sous-chef in a pink shirt waited patiently on the couch for something that wasn't a half-eaten carton of chow mein.

Thankfully I managed to find a bottle of Two Buck Chuck that Gina had ignored, because she claimed even the fumes gave her a headache. *Whatever,* I figured. *If I can drink it, so can he.* I grabbed two glasses, making sure to pick the ones without chips that, the way my luck goes, could easily have led to an emergency room visit. Now, looking back on the night and knowing what a wine aficionado he was, I cringe to think that on top of my seemingly slovenly appearance I then proceeded to present him with a bottle of $1.99 merlot in a glass that looked as though it should be dipped in salt. Despite my best intentions, I was not off to a rip-roaring start, and in truth might as well have been in sweatpants and about to pour him a mug of Night Train.

To my relief he took a sip of the wine and was kind with his response. Soon we were seated on my gigantic couch, talking about his job and his move from Germany a few years back. This lead to a discussion of all the places I'd been, and then, as is typical of any conversation of which I am a part, the talk migrated to my acting career. Clearly he'd never dated an actress before, because he actually listened. Not only did he listen, without fear, to my talk of my acting career, but he was impressed with what I'd done, with what I'd accomplished. He was especially impressed when I mentioned I'd been in not one but *two* films with Claudia Schiffer, Claudia being one of Germany's national treasures. Yes, to Wilhelm I was a star.

Then, somehow, the conversation turned to tarot cards.

Whereas normally on a date I'd learned to, to quote a friend, "hide the crazy," this was different. Wilhelm revealed he tended to see ghosts, and once that was said, I dashed into my room for my cards, returning with the offer of a reading. I was thrilled. I mean, what better way to learn about a person than to read their cards? As he shuffled, I felt as if the universe were handing me a Wilhelm cheat sheet. It was great.

Immediately two cards jumped out: the Empress, which usually signifies an older woman, and the Devil, which tends to signify sex. Without thinking, I said, "You're going to be involved with an older woman and have lots of sex."

Silence fell over the room.

It was as though a bubble had appeared above my head, with an arrow pointing down at me and the words "Older woman! Older woman!" in flashing piercing-pink neon. And what if I weren't the older woman? What if I was predicting the impassioned love affair he'd have with someone else? The whole thing was just too weird for me, and it was confirmed it was weird for him as well when I saw his face: a slight, embarrassed smile, mixed in with something I'd later learn was a mad conservatism, a German restraint one could almost classify as self-punishment. Clearly sex was not something he wished to speak of on a first date, which was fine, because I really didn't want to think of myself as an older woman, either.

"I can't read your cards right now," I said. "It's not the right time."

He smiled, most likely relieved. "Okay."

After chatting for a while longer, the one pathetic bottle of wine completely drained, it naturally seemed like the end of the evening. He got up to leave.

I was shocked. Not once had he made a move, and now he was *leaving*? Why hadn't he made a move? It wasn't like we were at a fancy restaurant with a table of fine china and considerations of public etiquette in our way. We were at my apartment, just the two of us, on the same couch . . . for hours. And we'd been getting along, laughing and having fun. What the hell?

I walked him to the door. This was not happening. I wouldn't let this happen. If there's one thing I am, it's direct, so I cut to the chase. I smiled sweetly. "You'd better not leave without kissing me."

And to my relief, he kissed me.

Within weeks we were seriously dating. Wilhelm was sweet, kind, entertaining, and, of course, an incredible cook. Despite the fact that I was now better fed than I had been in years, I felt lighter than ever. My every step was lifted with happiness, a happiness that, by the way, somehow commanded me to call psychics. I was pretty sure I knew Wilhelm liked me, as all signs and statements seemed to indicate the sentiment, yet confirmation from the psychics made me feel free to enjoy the feeling, to relish in his affection. "He's afraid of the intensity of his own feelings," I was told, to which I could relate, as I too was becoming afraid of the intensity of my feelings. "He finds himself daydreaming about you when he's at work." Again, something he and I had in common. Even though I was technically living on unemployment and wasn't working, I daydreamed about him to the point where, if I'd had a job, I certainly would have been unable to get any work done. And then the best: "He's in love with you," in response to which I thought, *Yes, Wilhelm. I think I'm in love with you, too.*

Still, I tried to keep my wits about me. Erlin had certainly been right that I'd be swept off my feet, but what he hadn't seen was that I'd fight tooth and nail against that broom. I'd been hurt too many times to let myself go, and while I privately cherished the positive words of the psychics, I struggled to be rational and grounded. Sure, all evidence seemed to point to that I now had a serious boyfriend, but I couldn't help being worried. I was suspicious of my own happiness and was determined to avoid injury. *Go ahead and tell me how much I mean to you,* I'd think, *but you are still only my play toy. You may be a play toy whom I need to see and talk to constantly, but you are nonetheless a play toy.*

And then tragedy struck, and my fears were confirmed. One day, ever so casually, he informed me that, "All American girls are desperate to marry and are out to shackle men any chance they get."

I was silent when he said this, as it was certainly not what I'd wanted to hear. But what could I do? It was just proof that my instincts had been right and that this relationship had no future. *Play toy,* I repeated in my mind, though now a bit less firmly, and with a bit of sadness. After all, if Wilhelm was my play toy, I'd essentially been living at Toys "R" Us for the past few weeks and had been quite happy there.

But then, just a week later, things really got complicated, because he started to pepper our conversation with talk of marriage . . . of *our* marriage. *What the hell? He's testing me,* I thought, and I knew that if I admitted I would one day like to marry, he'd claim his theory had been right and he'd run for the hills. *Be strong! He means nothing to you! Play toy!*

One afternoon, while we were on the phone, he threw in yet another mention of marriage, and I became irate. He was so obviously trying to trick me into revealing my true intentions that I did what any normal girl would do and lied my ass off.

"I never want to get married," I said. "And I never will."

There was silence. At last, I figured, I'd put an end to this hurtful topic and we could move on, as would any normal couple with no future. But then he spoke again.

"You're breaking my heart."

"*What?*" I was angry and confused and now burning a hole in my living room floor with my furious pacing.

"Because," he whispered, "my intention is to marry you."

I froze. My heart literally stopped beating. And then it started beating very fast. Too fast. What was going on? Had the man I supposed was indeed my boyfriend just told me he wanted to marry me? I think he had! And to this, to this sweet utterance, my reaction was to scream, "Fuck you! How *dare* you say that to a thirty-year-old woman!"

"But I mean it."

"No, you don't!"

"Yes, I do," he insisted, and went on to promise to prove it.

Sure, it all sounded good, but I wasn't buying. As soon as we hung up the phone, I called Erlin. "Is Wilhelm being honest?" I asked, still furious. I mean, really, no one should mess with a thirty-year-old about marriage. It's just cruel. There should be a jail for that kind of thing, for leading on someone's skeptical and aging heart.

Psychic Junkie

"Yes," Erlin said. "Trust him. There's an engagement soon, in August. I see marriage in a year to a year and a half."

Huh. Erlin seemed pretty sure, so I hung up the phone and started shopping for a ring.

Yes, I was still a touch doubtful, but Erlin's psychic seal of approval allowed me to let go of my fears and apprehensions enough to enjoy the idea . . . and it was an idea I loved, as Wilhelm was quite possibly everything I'd ever wanted. He spoke foreign languages; was well traveled, an amazing cook, gorgeous, polite, intelligent; and had fabulously full lips. Could I see us getting married? Absolutely! And, I realized with an almost frightened thrill, Drew, the drag–queen–on–helium psychic, had said the man *after* Jonas was the one I'd be with forever. *That's Wilhelm!* With both Drew and Erlin having seen it, I suddenly felt free to relish in the warm sunny thoughts of our everlasting love, and thus spent hours at diamond Web sites, building and constructing my ring. Did I want radiant or princess, round or oval? There were so many cuts and shapes. Where to begin?

It didn't stop there. Wilhelm continued to toss about little hints of marriage like colorful sparkling confetti. "I need to have a conversation with your father," he'd say, or "Have you found your dress yet?" To that last question I laughed and shook my head, because no, of course I hadn't found my dress yet! Geez. Who did he think I was? I was utterly confused about my dress! Completely torn over ivory silk charmeuse, or white satin organza; a ball gown or an A–line silhouette. Had I found my dress yet? *Please.*

To keep myself assured that all was true and I should be as

happy as I was, I periodically checked in with psychics. Since I'd first called Erlin, I'd also ventured out and called others, and began keeping a log of their names and readings in an effort to find one who was cheaper than Erlin and yet just as accurate. As much as I loved Erlin, each call escalated the balance on my credit cards in a rather alarming manner, and the way I saw it, if one psychic insisted we'd be engaged in August, I was tempted to believe, but if a dozen all agreed, it must be true. And amazingly, most did agree. Of course there were a few psychics who insisted on a different outcome, who'd say horrible things such as "I see a breakup, and it's going to be a bad one." Upon hearing those bitter and cruel words, I'd simply hang up the phone and make a note in my log to never ever call that "psychic" again. And then I'd leave really negative, scathing feedback. There. Problem solved. Bad psychic. Bad.

Each day, we fell deeper for each other, though he—with the innocence of one who'd never before had a broken heart—tended to express his feelings, while I stubbornly fought to reign mine in. With tears in his eyes he'd profess he'd never been this happy before, and I'd smile and nod and make a note of the exact words so I could later mentally replay them over and over, savoring a private elation that would keep me awake and planning our honeymoon or naming our future children till the sun sliced through the curtains.

Everything was just about ideal. He talked of us moving in together, we walked hand in hand, he called me "darling." And, being the true metrosexual he was, fashion was a prime concern and hobby of his. Now *this* was an interest I could share. Proving to be the supportive girlfriend by accompanying my boyfriend in his lengthy shopping excursions was definitely something I could handle, and my role was one I took on with vigor.

What I quickly learned, however, was that though he shopped for hours, he never actually bought anything. Instead, on just about each and every one of his precious days off, he went *window-shopping* ... at discount stores. For an entire afternoon he'd wander through the crowded and chaotic aisles of Ross and Big Lots, then cap off the day with a tour of T.J. Maxx. Loehmann's, a discount store in Beverly Hills, was reserved for special occasions. Loehmann's was his treat.

This never ceased to confuse me. I mean, if you're going to window-shop, why not meander through the clean and tasteful floors of Barneys, Saks, or Neiman's? Window-shopping at Ross was simply some strange form of self-deprivation, not an act of fantasy. Still, who was I to judge? I was Miss Live Beyond My Means, an unemployed actress with tens of thousands of dollars of debt (a number that was growing exponentially), and still I could justify charging a very pricey pair of pink Chanel sunglasses. But you know, I had to have those sunglasses. It's L.A. It's sunny.

So in truth I respected his thrifty approach. I figured we'd balance each other as a married couple. He'd keep us from dangling into the jaws of bankruptcy while I'd bestow upon him the joy of throwing caution to the wind, and the unbridled bliss of designer accessories.

• • •

Soon our custom was to end a long day of discount-store window-shopping by unwinding in Wilhelm's apartment building's hot tub. This involved Wilhelm in his spot—across from me, on the top step, water only halfway up his calves, an ashtray by his side, a cigarette perched in his lips, and a beer in his hand—and me practically lost in bubbles as I stared at him in frustration. At first his little routine, his position from which he would not budge, amused me. He'd take his spot and I'd laugh at how predictable he was, how settled into his habit. But then ... then I'd start to look at other couples with longing, couples who sat in the hot tub side by side as, you know, a couple. I'd try to comfort myself by making up excuses, like he must not like hot water (though, him being the one to suggest we go to the hot tub, a place pretty much known for hot water, tended to challenge that theory), or that maybe he just didn't like getting wet. Maybe he was worried about his hair?

Ultimately, the excuses proved little comfort. With jealousy I'd watch other couples, like the flighty big-chested redhead and her sexy surfer boyfriend who lived in the corner unit, both constantly in the hot tub and practically sitting on top of each other—until, that is, with almost ritualistic certainty he'd start tickling her, and she'd squeal and pretend to get away, and they'd grab their towels and run off, giggling. My heart would clench and I'd look away, consoling myself with the knowledge that *she* wasn't about to go upstairs and be served a homemade gourmet three-course meal with the appropriate accompanying wine. No, that was me! I was getting the three-course meal! I was about to go upstairs and start the evening with a sweet chenin wine and foie gras!

Of course what I didn't like to dwell on was that while Wilhelm arranged garnishes on a plate or decanted a bottle of wine, that redhead and her hot surfer boyfriend were most likely getting it on. They weren't consumed with food, or the meticulous presentation of food; they were consumed with each other. This was something that had begun to concern me about Wilhelm. I was coming to terms with the idea that perhaps it wasn't just the long hours and stress he was under that rendered him too tired. . . . It was that he had very little interest in sex.

I'd *never* encountered this problem before. After some lengthy debates with Gina—who herself had gone through a bout of dating gay men—we decided he wasn't gay; he simply had a low sex drive. I did hours of research on the Internet and learned that many men had low sex drives, though the discovery was little comfort. Being with someone who has a low sex drive is like continually heating an empty teakettle, as no matter what you do, you ain't gettin' tea, and after a while you get tired of standing at the stove.

Naturally the psychological fun and games kicked in. As I was essentially being told he was off limits, I thought about him constantly, always trying to conjure new ways to seduce him or at least get his attention. The one time he actually truly noticed me, and initiated things, was when I decided to cook *him* a three-course meal . . . topless. Of course, I'd interpreted "three-course" in a slightly different way, and what I prepared was actually one main dish and two sides, but I figured that equaled three, and I was quite impressed with myself. Though even then, standing at the counter, his lips light on my neck, I had a sneaking suspicion it wasn't so much a sexual drive that had brought him to me, but rather a commanding need to get a close-up view of my culinary effort. If I had to wager, I'd say that as we kissed, his eyes were open and he was studying, with alarm, my overzealous attempt at mincing mint—practically a green puree—on the chopping board.

And then, one evening in the hot tub, I was studying him for any signs of amorous intent, when he said something that killed any and all of my ardent thoughts: One of their partner hotels in Johannesburg was looking for a chef.

"As in *South Africa?*" I sputtered, then recovered. I had to be cool. No panicking. I sat up straight so my ears were above water. I had to pay attention.

"Yes, that Johannesburg."

"You're not thinking of moving, are you?"

And to this, to my masked plea of, "Don't go! I'll die if you go!" he simply shrugged. As casually as I possibly could, I asked what would happen to us if he took that job, and to my horror he looked surprised, as if he'd just now been told I was his girl-friend and not merely an accessory that came with the hot tub.

"If I took the job?" he said, still looking confused. "Well, you'd come with me, of course."

Of course. I would go with him.

Despite everything, despite Erlin and all the psychics' prom-ises, and despite anything Wilhelm had said in the past, *that moment* was the cannonball to the walls I'd built around me. Whereas before I'd indulged in happy optimistic thoughts and designed rings and shopped for dresses, it was all different now.

Suddenly the knowledge I had came from deep within; it was a feeling of conviction, of certainty, of confidence. Just like that, I believed. And just like that, I let myself go.

Our future life together. Fiery sunsets in South Africa; hills of fig and almond trees in Portugal; the crisp, whitewashed, mythic beauty of Greece. We would go everywhere. Sand in our shoes, the sun on our shoulders, our passports filled and worn. And of course we'd stay in all the luxury hotels, places with mini sewing kits and fluffy white robes. Granted, Wilhelm would be *working* in these hotels, but whatever. I wasn't about to let his employment mar my fantasies.

Then arose the issue of what *I* would do. I never wanted to give up acting, but without knowing, let's say, *Thai*, I wasn't so sure I'd be able to strike up a career as a starlet in Phuket. And although I don't know where the idea came from, I started picturing myself as a lounge singer . . . and I dug it. I'd be a dark-haired version of Michelle Pfeiffer in *The Fabulous Baker Boys*, wearing a sexy red dress and slithering about on a piano, my sultry voice stopping busboys in their tracks, my glamour making wives eye their husbands. And then later, after my show, once he was off work, Wilhelm and I would meet in our dark room atop an impossibly high building, below us a light-streaked ruby-and-sapphire city.

The best part of my new plan was that as a lounge singer I'd still be an entertainer, yet I'd be mercifully removed from the twisted pressures of the A-, B-, C-, or F-list life. It was simple. I didn't need Hollywood; I just needed a bar, a piano, and a killer dress. That was it. It was the answer. I had a new identity: I'd be

Wilhelm's wife and the best damn luxury-hotel lobby/lounge singer ever.

A few days later I remembered a reading Aurelia had done for me, back when I was still with Jonas. She'd said she'd seen me with my own business—and she'd said it had something to do with hotels and entertainment. At the time I'd had the fleeting worry I'd end up an independent call girl, but now it all made sense! Wilhelm works in hotels, and I'm a lounge singer!

Everything was wonderful. My gleaming future was about to unfold, and August was the month when it would happen. As I went off to the bank to cash my unemployment check, I was in absolute heaven.

6

The End of Round One

THE PROGRESSION FROM GIRLFRIEND TO FIANCÉE to wife can be documented in the magazines found on a woman's coffee table. As a girlfriend, I poured through the pages of *Marie Claire* and *Glamour* and *Vogue*. As a fiancée, I should have been compiling stacks of *Modern Bride* and *Elegant Bride* and *The Knot*, but since I couldn't let Wilhelm know I was on to him and his plans to propose, the only logical thing to do was to prepare for the role of Sarah the Wife. So as August approached, I started up subscriptions to *Martha Stewart Living*, *O*, and *Real Simple*. I even considered making a doctor's appointment so I could hijack a few issues of *Redbook* or *Better Homes and Gardens*, though ultimately I decided that those magazines were really for mothers, or at least wives in a later stage.

I hurled myself into my new role as Sarah the Wife, and at the end of each day had practically memorized entire articles on making curtains or the best ways to organize a closet. In the evenings Sarah the Wife cut out recipes from magazines with surgical precision, carefully adding them to a cookbook she was making, one tailored to the tastes of Wilhelm the Husband, a very discriminating creature who couldn't be satisfied with basic dishes such as macaroni and cheese. And though difficult, Sarah the Wife completely ignored her Neiman Marcus catalog to instead focus on the Williams-Sonoma catalog, coveting with a scary passion the Le Creuset pots shaped like hearts and the KitchenAid Tilt-Head Stand Mixer in the exclusive pink satin pearl finish. Eventually, I decided, Sarah the Wife would even take up knitting (just as soon as she'd managed to give up buying bath products rather than buying yarn) and would be perfect in every way, like an ad for how the job should be done: young (fine, "not old") and sexy, combining with flair the worlds of pot roasts and stilettos, teddies and All-Clad copper pots.

The one thing I, as Sarah the Wife, had issues with was décor. Perhaps as a result of his metrosexuality, Wilhelm had a very clear sense of style and a very firm choice in interior design—and that was stark and modern, clean lines and no frills, Lucite and Le Corbusier. In contrast, I favored antiques and toile fabrics, messy bouquets of flowers, and velvet curtains. My room had ornately carved French walnut nightstands, a floral bedspread, oriental rugs, and a sense that someone had been living there for approximately two hundred years.

I quickly came to terms with the fact that everything I owned would have to go. It was okay, I told myself, I loved him enough that his tastes would become my tastes, his interests my interests. Though I'd always considered myself something of a feminist, touting women's rights and the importance of independence, it was becoming evident that perhaps that wasn't really the case. I guess deep down I was a 1950s housewife, a 1950s housewife who doubled as a lounge singer.

After brimming with shame over my unevolved state, I got over it. I saw things logically: After ten years of struggles and pain and rejection, would being taken care of be so bad? No. What was so wrong about being a housewife, anyway? Nothing. I mean, sure I'd have to get rid of all those pesky hopes and dreams I'd always had, but it's not like my efforts had been panning out. Might as well focus on Wilhelm, the one thing in my life that was on the right track.

Still, I needed to maintain *some* of my identity and not completely fold myself into him. Thus I decided to absolutely put my foot down and insist on being allotted at least one little room in our future house, where I could sequester all my belongings. There. Identity secured.

Yes, Sarah the Wife was the answer. In the face of stark unemployment, dwindling funds, and a life with no career, I simply counted the days till August, and debated over china patterns.

Suddenly August was two weeks away, just fourteen days off, which meant Wilhelm had only about 336 hours to come up with a romantic and wonderful proposal. Not that I really thought he was going to propose *on* August first—I'm not *that* crazy. But I figured I should be prepared and looking memorable starting on the first of August. No more figuring my hair was fine unwashed as long as it was in a ponytail, no more deciding my chipped nail polish would go unnoticed if I wore big distracting rings. No. When he told the story of the proposal to our future children, Max and Madeleine, he'd tell them their mother's hair was shining, her nails were gleaming, and her eyes were sparkling between perfectly applied eyeliner. "She looked radiant," he'd say, and beside him I'd smile from my lounge chair, the reflection of our infinity pool wavering in my tearing eyes.

Strangely, I was so caught in the momentum of our approaching proposal that I barely had time for readings. It was, in a sense, time to sit back and let the predictions I'd been waiting for happen, to enjoy the life I was about to have. Besides, one of my last calls had been to a psychic named Evangeline, a woman who'd cheerfully said in a Southern drawl, "M'dear, your relationship is an impendin' train wreck." Immediately I recognized her as the evil person she was and decided her accent was brash and disagreeable, and then I noted that her ratings weren't nearly as stellar as Erlin's. I had nothing to worry about, but I decided to take a break from readings just so I didn't upset myself with people who undoubtedly had miserable existences and enjoyed hurting younger women whose entire amazing lives were about to unfold. They were bitter, I knew, and nothing's worse than a bitter psychic.

July thirty-first arrived, and something horrible occurred to me. He didn't know my ring size. How could he buy a ring? Obviously I couldn't just tell him, so I went to my jewelry box and lifted from its depths all the rings I'd ever owned. Carefully

I cleaned each one so they'd catch as much light as possible, then slyly planted them around the house, leaving a couple on the coffee table, a few on the end tables, one on the bathroom sink, and a dozen on the kitchen counter. I knew it was just a matter of time till Wilhelm seized his chance, pocketed one, and took it to a jeweler. Then again, I reassured myself, there was the chance he'd somehow already figured it out, and I realized that as a metrosexual he might possess the ability to determine ring size *visually*. Of course! I was almost certain that was it, and tried to remember all the times I'd seen him looking at my hands, my heart racing as I realized he looked at my hands *a lot*.

Content that he'd already found a way to ascertain my ring size, I watched him like a hawk for any signs of debating about my ring, ordering my ring, or receiving news that my ring had arrived. Then one evening, a few days into August, I saw such a sign. We'd just returned from a long, strenuous day of discount shopping at an outlet mall and were relaxing at my house, when he requested to use my computer to check his e-mails. Of course I let him, and pretended to watch TV in the next room as I pictured him grinning at an e-mail that, oh, I don't know, maybe said something like, "Your 1920s platinum 1.79 carat Old European–cut diamond ring is ready for pickup, and we've made sure that all six French–cut sapphires on the sides are secured and certified."

After a while I got hungry and wandered to the kitchen, a trek that involved passing through the dining room, the location of the computer. Sensing my presence, he quickly minimized something, something that looked like an e-mail, and pretended to study an eBay listing for a Giorgio Armani shirt. Hmmm. My ring suspicions pretty much confirmed, I continued into the kitchen, found a bag of potato chips, and was about to pop a chip into my mouth, when an absolutely horrible, wretched thought swept over me: *I might not like the ring.* What with our vastly different tastes in décor, there was a huge chance we wouldn't agree on jewelry. I liked antique rings that people consider heirlooms, and he'd like contemporary rings people consider art pieces. This, despite my detailed mulling on the subject, had never occurred to me, and with horror I saw him on bended knee, presenting me with a modern ring made of titanium, a stark ring consisting of only one single stone— clean lines and no frills. I lost my appetite. I put the chip back. I *had* to see the ring.

But what could I do, even if I did see the ring? That would be a problem for later, I decided, the key right now was to prepare myself. Not only am I not a fan of surprises, but I detest surprises and don't handle them well at all. I was a child who couldn't be left unattended in the house near Christmas, because I would tear everything apart in a hunt for my presents—and not because I wanted them early, or was even excited about my gifts, but because I simply couldn't bear the suspense any longer. The suspense hurt. And though my parents should've taken note of my quirks and ruled out surprise parties, they did make one unfortunate attempt at such a celebration for my ninth birthday. There I was, convinced that they'd forgotten, when suddenly I was confronted with a room full of people smiling and singing and holding a cake. I was so completely caught off guard that I burst into tears and bawled uncontrollably for hours. From that point on they practically drew up programs for all events.

Thus I knew: I could not be caught off guard with this ring. Very easily Wilhelm would be able to discern that my tears were not tears of joy, and that would pretty much be that. I went back into the dining room and put my hands on his shoulders, massaging like a caring, plotting girlfriend would.

"Almost done?" I asked sweetly. "I've got some e-mails to write."

"Sure." He got up, and I took his spot, and waited until he was in the other room, till I heard him channel surf and land on his new favorite TV show, *elimiDATE*. "It's a marathon," he said with excitement. "An *elimiDATE* marathon!"

I scooted in toward the table. "Mmm–hmm. Good. I'll be there in a bit."

Though the browser was now on Yahoo!, I hit the back button, and *Bingo!* There was his e-mail account, and, of course, being trusting and technologically inept, he'd not logged out. My heart, as if it were just clueing in to what was going on, started pounding furiously. What was I doing? I was being bad, this I knew, yet I couldn't help but also feel exhilarated. Briefly I pictured myself as an undercover agent who'd slipped into a den in the midst of a party to hack into the host's computer, and immediately felt better. Ah, yes, secret agent stealth mode. Very good.

With Wilhelm safely snickering in the other room, I swiftly scanned his e-mails, searching for anything with the word "diamond" or "ring" or "purchase" in the subject line. Though I came across nothing with those words, I did stumble upon an e-mail with the subject *"liebling,"* a word I recognized as German for "darling," as it was one of Wilhelm's pet names for me. Um, *darling?* My eyes darted to the sender's name: Nadja. Who the hell was Nadja? I knew it wasn't his mother or sister, but prayed it was an aunt or someone else able to use the word "darling" in a nonsexual way. As far as I knew, the only person he kept in contact with back home was his best friend, a guy named Rolf— *not* a guy named Nadja.

I opened the e-mail. German. The entire thing was in German. But then my eyes focused on two words, two words that needed no translation: Julia Roberts. I took a deep breath. *I* was Julia Roberts. Not that I was actually Julia Roberts, of course, but Wilhelm liked to say I looked like her, so evidently this e-mail was about me. And if it was about me, I had every right to read it—or so I told myself as I copied the entire thing, closed his e-mail, went to a site that offered free instant translations, selected German to English, and hit paste and enter. There. Heart racing, I leaned in. What sat before me was a passage Shakespeare might have written when completely hammered.

Darling. It has been too long now since for the last time we saw or wrote. How is your treasure? Is truth resembles Julia Roberts? Remember my favorite that the woman you marry and the woman you have a fling with are completely separate pair of shoes. American women are to the shackle quick to the altar. But when the torches are out and the festivities done they resign to the cupboard. Yours, Nadja.

The first thing I did, after reading this highly suspicious note to my boyfriend from a girl whose name conjured images of a six-foot-tall Aryan goddess, was try to envision my last Visa statement, in particular the itty-bitty amount under "Available Credit," an amount that would hopefully serve as a psychic buffer zone before I hit the sharp and unsympathetic "limit." There would be calls about this, of that I was certain. Of course, I couldn't just pick up the phone with Wilhelm in the other room. I had to wait. So I shot off a copy of the e-mail to Gina, figuring she'd been an English major and should hence be familiar with passages that made no sense. Then, just for fun, I read the malevolent little note over and over and over again.

This wasn't symbolism here; this was mistranslation. "The woman you marry and the woman you have a fling with are completely separate pair of shoes." I got that, sort of, though I was curious what in German could mistakenly lead to "pair of shoes." Perhaps it was just some wacky German saying? Next was the part about American women. The word "shackle" was one that Wilhelm had used, and without having to be told, I knew that this girl, this evil Aryan goddess, had been the one to plant such a word in his head, because she wanted him. This was a thinly veiled manipulation, a letter written by a cunning woman posing as a friend, a woman who wished to destroy a relationship so *she* could get the man. I recognized this tactic because this was a letter I myself could've written.

I was trying to figure out what "cupboard" meant when I heard Wilhelm get up.

"Are you getting hungry?" he asked.

"Uh, no, not yet." I quickly saved the translation in a Word document, minimized everything, and stopped breathing as he passed behind my chair and into the kitchen.

Nadja could be a stalker. He might not like her at all. Maybe he hates her but she just won't leave him alone. In fact, she could be dangerous. Maybe she's jealous and hates me, and Wilhelm's kept this all a secret so I won't worry! Or, or, I told myself, the whole thing was perfectly innocent. Nadja could be some overprotective cousin, a well-intentioned relative who just happened to hate American woman and felt the need to offer evil advice. The point was, I couldn't jump to conclusions. I had to be cool. I might have wished to run into the kitchen and rip what was left of Wilhelm's hair out, but I couldn't do that. No. I couldn't ruin our upcoming engagement over something that could be completely insignificant.

I tried to be calm, but my only thoughts were that Wilhelm was cooking, ignoring my shiny rings spread about the kitchen, and having an affair with an Aryan goddess. *Bing!* A reply from Gina hit my in-box:

What the hell is this and why'd you send it to me? Are you a shoe? Who's Nadja? What's up with the cupboard? I have to go out with that guy who's way too old for me and spent most of our last date yelling about his dad. Do you need me to ditch him and come over? Do we need to figure out what kind of shoe you are? Off the top of my head I'd say you're a Charles David gold leather sling-back with dreams of greatness. Call me.

I turned off the computer. I counted to ten. I got up and went into the kitchen.

He was stuffing, oh so tenderly, some sort of cheese and spinach mixture into chicken breasts, so I leaned against the counter and watched him. Casual. Yep, there I was, just watching my boyfriend cook, nice and normal, as if my brain weren't caught in a loop, singing the name Nadja, Nadja, Nadja over and over. Normally his staying the night was a good thing, but I knew I couldn't make it till morning without answers. No. If I didn't address this now, I'd have to wake in the middle of the night, grab my cell phone, and sneak out of the house under cover of darkness for a reading. Thus I'd run the risk of him waking to an empty bed, and quite possibly I'd have to explain my decision to run outside in my nightgown with a cell phone and crouch by the azaleas to make a call.

Obviously, coming right out with "Who the hell is Nadja?" wasn't going to work. I had to be sly. I couldn't scare him off. Subtlety was key.

"Looks good," I said. "So. Is dating American girls very different from dating German girls?"

He tilted his head as if appraising the chicken breasts. And actually, he probably was appraising the chicken breasts. "No, not really."

"When was the last time you went home?"

"To Germany? Last summer."

That was a bit more than a year ago. Okay, we weren't together then. "That must have been fun." I smiled sweetly. "Did you hook up with any old girlfriends?"

He turned, and the look on his face reminded me that my goal was *subtlety*.

"No."

As he focused again on his chicken, I pretended to absent-mindedly pick at the feta he'd left on the counter, trying to look innocent. I had to employ the right tactic here. *The buddy tactic*, I thought. *I must use the "I'm your buddy" tactic and lull him into a false sense of security.*

"Oh, come on," I said teasingly. "I bet you had hoards of fräuleins throwing themselves at you. You, the big man all the way from Hollywood, living by the beach with an impressive job and everything."

Now he smiled in that "Aw, shucks" kind of way, and I knew I had him.

"I guess so."

Good work, Sarah, keep it going. "I bet you left behind quite a few broken hearts that trip."

He shrugged, went to the fridge, and pulled out a bundle of asparagus. Briefly I wondered where the hell all this food came from. Had he gone grocery shopping? Had he brought this food over earlier? I supposed there was a chance he'd arrived at my house with bags and bags of food, yet I'd been so busy eyeing his pockets for the shape of a small ring box that I'd just not noticed. Whatever. I was getting hungry and was now captivated by him browning butter. *Stop it! Concentrate, Sarah! You need to be alert here!* "So," I said offhandedly, "who'd you fool around with?"

I swear his head spun around like in *The Exorcist*. Or maybe it didn't, but he did look at me in a way that told me I had to act quickly. I smiled and jokingly hit him on the shoulder. "Come on, you can tell me. Give me all the gory details. Let's hear it."

"I just kissed a couple girls, no big deal."

Time to go in for the kill. "What were their names? I bet they had funny German names."

He glanced at me, and I saw one thing: It was dawning on him that this could be a trap.

"I can't remember," he said, and quickly looked to the asparagus. He then began precisely, too precisely, chopping off their ends. Usually he'd just snap them off. It occurred to me that ours was a strange relationship, that I could tell my boyfriend was uncomfortable by the way he was cooking.

"You can't remember?" I said this jokingly, yet with a touch of "genuine" shock. "That's terrible! I'm surprised at you. I never thought you'd be the kind of guy who'd fool around with someone and then forget her name." I paused for emphasis. "I always thought you were a gentleman."

I let that last word hover in the air, and watched his brow furrow.

"Well, I guess I just hadn't thought about it. But yes, I do remember."

Manipulation a success. I smiled, feeling a bit like a grinning lion watching a clueless bunny hop into its lair. "So? What were they?"

"Let's see. Hilde and Nadja. Those were their names."

Nadja. He'd said it. With her name finally spoken, I felt as if I'd made some great accomplishment, and then felt the need to sit down, put an icepack on my forehead, and not move or think for the next hour. *Just a few more questions,* I told myself, but then my brain reversed and hitched on Hilde. Who was Hilde? *Who cares, Sarah, get to the point here.*

"Hilde and Nadja. Poor girls. I bet they were brokenhearted

when you left. You didn't lead them on did you? Act like there was a future?" This last part I said in a conspiratorial manner, as if we all led on German girls when we went back to the motherland. Just to be safe, I also lent it a slight "You da man" feel.

"No," he said, his mouth toying with a smile. "It was no big deal. I just kissed them."

Hoping he'd answer without actually digesting the question, I spoke at the speed of light. "Soyou'renotincontactwiththemanymore?"

He shook his head. "Nah."

And that was that. I could do no more. I abandoned him in the kitchen and went to brood on the couch. Why was he lying about being in touch with Nadja? Then again, if he'd only kissed the Aryan Goddess, what was I worried about? They were basically nothing more than friends. Most likely he just didn't want to upset me, and had spun a little white lie to save explaining something completely insignificant. *Or,* I thought, *maybe she is stalking him and the whole subject is just too painful for him to talk about.* The possibilities were endless, but I comforted myself with the fact that Nadja had now been officially identified and discussed. As long as he'd openly said her name, and not kept her as a deep dark suspicious secret, what did the odd e-mail from an ex-fling really matter? Feeling better, I grabbed my *Martha Stewart Living* from the coffee table and tore out a recipe for lemon pound cake.

Though I repeated the mantra "All is fine, all is fine" over and over, my mind still obsessed for psychic verification that Nadja was nothing to worry about and that, indeed, all was fine. Yet still I had to wait. The whole night I waited, and the next morning I continued to wait. And wait. And wait. Finally, when he offered to make me brunch, I told him that sounded lovely but that I had a lot to do that day.

"You," he said slowly, curiously, "have things to *do*?"

Oh, good grief. I'm not *that* bad. Still, I had to be realistic. "Yes, believe it or not. I made an appointment for a milk bath at Burke Williams at two o'clock, but I want to get there early to hit the sauna. You know how it is at a spa. I need time to eat the fruit."

He nodded, apparently assured I was telling the truth. Downstairs I gave him a nice kiss good–bye, paused about ten seconds after shutting the door, then catapulted myself back up the stairs. Attempting to be the spendthrift I knew I should be, I immediately called a cheap psychic, was told there was nothing to worry about, but then had to call Erlin just to make sure.

"She's a friend, Sarah. You don't need to worry. The attraction he felt for her long ago was fleeting, completely transitory. He sees her as only a friend, and doesn't want to take it any further. Trust me on this."

I finally agreed to stop thinking about it, as really, I did trust Erlin.

Upon hanging up I was consumed with a new idea: a Burke Williams milk bath. I vaguely remembered my manager giving me a Burke Williams gift certificate years ago and opting to save it for a special occasion. Since no special occasion ever came, and I never organize my drawers, that fabulous piece of card stock was most likely still buried beneath my socks. In fact, if I made an appointment, I wouldn't have lied to Wilhelm at all.

Sarah Lassez

I'd be right on schedule and not at all deceptive! *Brilliant thinking, Sarah. You are such a good girlfriend; now go treat yourself to a day at the spa.*

August just kept on going. It was unrelenting in the way the days continued, despite the bareness of my ring finger. By mid-August I was fighting to remain patient, but desperately wanted to get the show on the road. If we were to get married next summer, we needed to start planning! We needed to secure a venue! Each day that passed was another caterer hired by someone that wasn't me.

And then there was this: a tenseness that had taken over Wilhelm's demeanor. He seemed distracted, a bit more distant, and rather stressed. I attributed this to his drama at work, as that's what my tarot cards and a few psychics suggested, and the theory was pretty much confirmed when his employees attempted to share their distaste for his German efficiency by keying their sentiments—albeit with a vastly different word choice—across his car's driver's side door.

It all made sense, him being so distracted, but I worried that such troubles would render his mood anything but romantic. There were also the simple logistics of the matter. How could he propose when the body shop had his car? He was far too great a gentleman to make me drive on our big night, of that I was sure. But what else could he do? Keep the taxi idling just around the bend as we enjoyed a picnic? Ride a bike to my house, have me hop on the handlebars, then pedal off to a fancy restaurant?

And then he was struck with depression. Seeing his mood shadow with despair actually slightly pleased me, because depression was my territory and I figured I'd finally be of help. Seriously, I may not have had stellar advice when it came to employees or bosses, but if we were talking about not having reason to get out of bed in the morning, I was your girl.

One night we were at his house, doing absolutely nothing, when I decided to address whatever was bothering him. Well, I guess if you consider my sitting on the couch fretting over him, and his sitting in his hard plastic straight-backed chair, staring blankly at an episode of *The Bachelor*, "doing nothing," then we were doing nothing. To Wilhelm, however, what we were doing was an actual activity: We were "enjoying an evening at home." Of course, as may be evident already, Wilhelm and I possessed vastly different definitions of "enjoyment," a fact that could be illustrated by the chair he was sitting in, a chair that was clearly not meant to be sat in. Calling his hard plastic straight-backed chair "uncomfortable" would be like calling Saddam Hussein "a tad ornery," and as far as I could tell, the chair had been built with no function in mind other than to hold one's purse or show off a stack of books on some obscure architect. It was, basically, a decoration, not a chair. However, this was Wilhelm, a man who window-shopped at Ross, and for reasons I'll never understand he insisted this was how he relaxed: stiff, upright, and unmoving in the hard plastic chair. For hours he'd sit there, which made me theorize that the chair was similar to a bed of nails in that once you got situated, no good could come from squirming.

So what he was doing now, looking pained and uncomfort-able as we "enjoyed an evening at home," was supposedly *relax-ing*, but I could tell something was wrong. I'd been studying him for twenty minutes, and I'd noticed that his eyes weren't tracking movements on the TV, and he hadn't cracked a smile at the ridiculous lengths women went to to get their man.

"What's wrong?" I finally asked. "Something's bothering you."

"I'm fine."

"You don't seem fine. You know you can talk to me. I can help. Tell me what's on your mind."

To my words he showed his comfort, his ease, his relief, by reclining a quarter of an inch. I could tell he was thinking everything over, trying to decide what to tell me, holding up his fears and worries to a mental light before handing them over. *It's okay, Wilhelm*, I thought, *you can tell me anything. I'm here for you.*

"It's work," he finally said. "I'm having problems with Franklin."

I nodded sympathetically, as I'd heard him complain about the head chef many times. Franklin was the cause of much beer consumption, many smoked packs of cigarettes, and countless hours of hard–chair–sitting, and for this reason I had problems with Franklin as well.

"I don't know," he continued. "I feel as though I've gone as far as I can there, that it's time to move on."

Now, as a general rule, unless you're the one talking, the words "move on" are never good. "Move on where?"

"I don't know. There are so many questions I'm trying to answer. It might be time to leave Los Angeles. I don't even like it here."

My heart rate spiked. Shimmery red dress. Piano. Lounge. Would I be ready when he gave me the word? Sure, why not. The plan would be sped up, the move would happen sooner than anticipated. Not a big deal. I'd tell him I was okay with this, which would undoubtedly ease his mind. In fact, maybe now he'd propose, relieved by my support and seizing the moment to ask if I'd be his wife and travel the world! Perhaps this whole time he'd been worried I'd want to stay! Maybe that was it? A fear of losing me!

Now say it like you did before, I thought, coaxing him with my mind. *Tell me I'm going with you. Just give me the confirmation.* I took a deep breath, counted to ten, and asked, "What happens to *us* if you leave?"

But he didn't say it like he had before. He actually didn't say anything. Instead he looked slightly nervous, lit a cigarette, and took a deep drag, holding the smoke in his lungs. "If only I was further on in my journey."

Journey? What are we, in *The Lord of the Rings?* What the hell was he talking about? Where did this "journey" come from?

He exhaled and continued. "I've always dreamt of traveling and working all around the world, but I dreamt of doing it alone. I'm too young to settle down. I couldn't possibly take care of a wife. It's too much . . . responsibility."

Now my heart was racing. What the hell had happened here?

"You don't have to *take care* of me," I said, managing to be completely freaked out and offended at the same time. Okay, yeah, I'd actually been looking forward to being taken care of, but if I had to, I could certainly continue the job myself. It wasn't as if I'd be some weighty wifely appendage who couldn't go out and get herself a job as a lounge singer. In fact, I'd probably end up making more money than he did. "I wouldn't be your responsibility. I'd take care of myself."

He shook his head and sighed in that "This is hurting me more than it's hurting you" way—and that's when I knew.

I wasn't going with.

I closed my eyes. My soothing, sparkling vision of life as a lounge singer started to go awry, and in it I stopped singing. I dropped the microphone. I fell off the piano. There was no piano. There was no me.

"What—," I said, and heard my voice splinter with anger. I stopped. Calm. Calm and rational. Men, Gina has always said, are like dogs. It never matters what you're saying, it matters *how* you're saying it, if you're using your Good Dog Voice or your Bad Dog Voice. The Bad Dog Voice sends them scurrying behind the couch, even if you're professing your love, and that's the end of it. The Good Dog Voice keeps them in the room even if you're detailing your hatred and informing them that the plan is to dunk them in an ice-cold bath and then toss in a toaster just for fun.

I tried again. *Good Dog Voice.* "What about what you said before? That I'd go with you? All that stuff about marriage?"

He stared at his hands. "I meant it, at the time."

It was official, I was panicking—and completely overcome with the need to burst into tears, furiously hurl sharp and pointy objects at him, and at the same time tell him that he didn't have to worry, I would take care of myself as a lounge singer and he could propose as planned and I'd say yes.

I tried to focus. "So . . . what you're saying is . . . you don't mean it now?"

Still unable to meet my eyes, he simply *shrugged.*

Now I was mad. Wilhelm was a *bad dog.*

"So, what, our relationship had an expiration date? You didn't bother pointing it out to me? You totally led me on and now you're just gonna go, leave the country, and it's *over!*"

Although he was still silent, I caught him scoping the room as if trying to determine the fastest way out.

"Just because things don't match up with some vision you created years ago doesn't mean things are *wrong*. So your life doesn't go according to your master plan, so what? Sometimes when you love someone you have to make *sacrifices*."

Now his green eyes took me in, his mouth became a smirk, his face smug. "And what do *you* have to sacrifice, being with me?"

Oh, hell no, I thought. *This motherfucker's going down.* For the first time since I'd met him I felt the air that separated us, everything crisp and clear. "Well," I said calmly. "For one thing, I have to sacrifice a satisfying sex life."

His mouth fell open, and I quickly landed the next blow.

"And it's not like you have much money."

Honestly, that last point didn't really matter to me, as I made it a habit to date men without jobs or any source of income, so in truth Wilhelm was rich in comparison. But I knew that he'd reel from that one because he was a prideful man, and all I wanted to do was give him a taste of the hurt I was choking on. And I think I did. He looked genuinely shocked. Tears, I could've sworn, were welling in his eyes. *Don't feel bad for him, Sarah. He's the Antichrist.*

"Well," he said after a pause. "I'm too young to make sacrifices. I want my freedom. I can't be tied down right now."

"So, let me get this straight. Though you spoke of marriage, of *our* marriage, and led me on, the actual truth is that our relationship will last only as long as you're in Los Angeles, and who knows how long that'll be. There is, essentially, no commitment. So what it boils down to is that I'm nothing more than a story you'll tell your grandchildren, the actress you had an affair with during your stay in Hollywood."

"Sarah, don't say that. You know how much you mean to me."

"Yes, *Wilhelm*, I'm just *now* finding out how much I mean to you. And in addition to *that*, I'm also learning you're not a man of your word. You're a man of 'I meant it at the time.'"

He stared up at the ceiling, as if asking for assistance from God, perhaps requesting an earthquake that would bounce me out of his apartment. "If only I was a little further on my journey."

I sighed. *Again with this journey business.* If this journey was so important, why was I just hearing about it now? Sure, I knew he wanted to travel and work around the world, but he'd never spoken of a *journey*, a journey that evidently involved him by himself. Why hadn't he mentioned this when we first met? "Hi, I'm Wilhelm and I'm on a journey" might have been a bit odd as an introduction, but at least it would've been fair and honest. "So is it over? Are *we* over?"

And to this, he said nothing.

Let me interrupt here to explain that one of my least shining moments in life, in fact my most dulled and marred moment, happened during a breakup. It occurred in my early twenties and involved the abandonment of all dignity and pride while I literally begged a guy not to leave me. Yes. His last image of me was shameful: a crying, crumpled mess on my knees, arms outstretched as I wailed at the top of my lungs *"Please don't leave me, please don't leeeeeave meeee-EEE-eeee!"* And though that was his last *image* of me, that certainly wasn't the last he heard of me. Upon his shutting the door to his apartment, almost crushing my desperate, clinging fingers in the process, I planted myself right there and sobbed uncontrollably, begging to be let in. It wasn't till a neighbor with a gun—a man who must have mistaken being a part of the Neighborhood Watch for being on *Dragnet* and was apparently under the impression that robbers tended to sob uncontrollably at front doors before they broke in—rounded the corner and scared the shit out of me that I finally fled home. Once safe, I enlisted my phone and my ex's answering machine in my mission. Since then I have vowed to always maintain my dignity, to be strong and stand tall even as my heart is breaking.

So, after I waited for Wilhelm to say something, anything, I took a deep breath. Dignity, pride, here I come.

"Fine. I'm not going to be your entertainment for the rest of your stay in L.A. You want your freedom, you got it."

And with that I held my head high, grabbed my purse, and sashayed out of his apartment and to my car—where I then collapsed in silent heaving sobs, my head against the steering wheel. Just in case he was peering out the window, I quickly gathered my composure, started the car, drove a bit, and then, once safely out of earshot, started howling.

Somehow, amid sobs that racked my body and made it difficult to drive straight, I careened down the freeway and made it home. I collapsed on my bed, exhausted and now in a rather shocked state. What had just happened? Had we really just broken up?

I rolled on my back and stared at the overhead light, noting the silhouettes of dozens of flying creatures trapped in the glass fixture—now thankfully dead, but alarmingly once alive and most likely having taken respite on my forehead as I slept. It was August, late August, and instead of getting engaged we'd broken up. What had gone wrong? Had I done something wrong? Maybe we weren't meant to break up and I'd forced it? Maybe this was my fault. *Oh my God, I'm single.*

But it still didn't feel real. Nothing felt real. Was it real? I closed my eyes. I'd paid *a lot* of money for my future, and something had gone amiss. Were all the psychics I'd been talking to just wrong? Unreliable? The brash, disagreeable voice of Evangeline the Evil scratched its way into my mind . . . "M'dear, your relationship is an impendin' train wreck." This, I believed, certainly qualified as a train wreck, and while it occurred to me I should call Evangeline, as clearly she'd been right, I just couldn't handle her. She was the kind of insensitive person who would cheerfully declare "Why, yes, darlin', you will be miserable and in just a matter of time you'll slit your wrists in the most adorable little pattern!" No, I needed comfort; I needed someone who knew me and knew Wilhelm, someone to tell me that this was some horrible mistake that would be fixed in the morning when my love recovered from his bout of insanity. I needed a friend.

Within minutes I was on the Psychicdom Web site, studying which psychics were online and ready to take calls. There was Erlin, my tux-clad hero, gazing at me with an expression that said, "Sarah, I've left the ball and am waiting to give you comfort." *Oh, Erlin,* I thought, *I won't let you down. I'm coming.*

And thank God for Erlin. His voice calmed me; his words stopped my sobbing. He assured me Wilhelm and I were *not* over, and he affirmed his prediction—we would not only be together, but we would still marry. I sniffled, and he continued.

"You should feel confident, Sarah. I see all this so clearly, the two of you together, happy and as one. He loves you, and the intensity of that emotion scares him. You've heard the expression "cold feet"? That's what's happened here. What you need to do is stop thinking about him. Right now he's thinking of himself and you're thinking of him as well—so who's thinking of you? You need to take care of yourself, focus on you, and he'll come back around."

Eventually I hung up, breathed a sigh of relief, and then hid my MasterCard inside a stack of bills, with the hopes that by tomorrow I'd either have forgotten where it was or be so horrified at having to rifle through the multitude of bills that I'd leave it be. Of course, Erlin was right. Wilhelm simply had cold feet; he'd come back around. Nothing was over. We'd just hit a snag *because* of how much he loved me.

The comfort and relief lasted for all of about ten minutes, and then the crippling anxiety returned. What if Erlin was wrong? What if Wilhelm didn't come back? What if it really was over? Like the true psychic junkie I'd become, I needed another reading. Another one would make me feel better. If someone else said the same thing, I'd believe it. Tearing through my stack of bills for my credit card, I reached for the phone again . . . and again . . . and again.

• • •

A little more than a week passed and I'd already lost ten pounds on the Heartbreak Diet, as saltines and ginger ale were the only things I could get down. My upset stomach and inability to chew was a typical Sarah reaction to suffering, but in this case it was confounded by the fact that food itself reminded me of Wilhelm. My kitchen reminded me of Wilhelm. My pots and pans, my refrigerator, my wineglasses. But then, of course, my hallway, my front door, even my loofah, which he used because he said it made his skin so soft—everything reminded me of Wilhelm. I was living in a trap of Wilhelm-ness, each memory a nail on which I couldn't avoid stepping.

On top of the torturous reminders, it was hitting me that it was real. I wasn't about to wake up with relief from some horrible nightmare, Wilhelm beside me in bed asking if maybe I'd had a bad dream, because I'd been crying in my sleep. No, we'd actually broken up. The understanding that I was alone and might never see him again rose before me, growing like a mountain I had to climb, one that just kept getting higher and higher, one with cliffs in every direction.

I couldn't leave my house. I couldn't face friends or family. Gina left messages, many long rambling messages, but since she had no idea we'd broken up, she was under the impression I was in some Wilhelm state of bliss. "Step away from your man, leave the kitchen, pick up the phone, and talk to me!" she'd scream into my answering machine. "I met someone! Don't you want to hear about him? We like each other! He's like a young Jeff Bridges. I love Jeff Bridges. Don't you love Jeff Bridges? Who doesn't love Jeff Bridges? Uh! But thank God he's not an actor! Where are you? Are you at Wilhelm's house? I'll try your cell."

I'd listen to her message, then to the sound of my cell phone ringing from my purse, and do nothing. My entire existence was about doing nothing.

Well, that's not entirely true. The one thing I could do, and did quite well, thank you very much, was take it upon myself to test every single psychic at Psychicdom. When I wasn't curled in the fetal position in a state of shock, I called psychics with such fervency that one would've thought *I* was the one getting paid. Credit cards fanned by my side, I started each day lovesick and on a mission to find the perfect psychic. Erlin was great, but I couldn't keep calling him, he was just too expensive and had to be saved for special occasions. I needed someone I could consult with daily, maybe twice a day, without going bankrupt by the end of the week, and until I found that person, I knew I had to call as many psychics as I could. It was my mission, my goal, my duty.

Let me tell you, psychic duds abounded. Not that Andre was a psychic dud, but after the fabulous reading he'd given me, he promptly disappeared from the site. What good was he if he could no longer be located? Then, in addition to the woman who compared our relationship to celery, and Glenda the sultry bonbon–eating psychic, there was a slew of others who seemed determined to confuse or enrage me, or just piss me off by telling me I needed a room filled with crystals.

"In particular, rose quartz," Miss Aura said. "Tons of it."

Rose quartz? It was some random day of the week, I had no idea which one, and I'd awoken in a fit of panic and reached for the phone. Now I was being told I needed to live in a geode.

"You need to recharge the crystals during the next full moon," she continued. "Put some under your pillow when you go to sleep. Yes, I feel you need this. Rose quartz inspires feelings of love and friendship and removes repressed anger. I sense repressed anger. And the rose quartz, it aids the spleen—has anyone told you about your spleen? It's often overlooked as an important organ. May I tell you about your spleen?"

"No," I wanted to scream at her. "I can safely say I'm in *no* mood to learn about the wonders of the spleen. And as a psychic you should've known that, so clearly you suck!" Of course I didn't say this, as there was always the possibility that she could put a curse on me, so instead I simply hung up and decided to call someone else.

Unfortunately, freaky crystal/spleen lady had exhausted the money I'd had in my account, so it was time for another deposit. I emptied my mind of any thoughts that would point out the insanity of my actions, gathered my credit cards together, closed my eyes, and shuffled them as best I could. Without looking, I spread them on the bed and ran my fingers over their numbers. My hand stopped on one particular card. I opened my eyes. *Well, hello, little MasterCard, how would you like to lead me to my future?*

The day went on, overwhelming me with varying scenarios of my upcoming life, as if the universe were fitting me for my fate the way a confused girl tries on an entire closet full of clothes before making a selection. Each minute that passed presented another option, another alternative, and though I'd called for comfort, I soon found myself staring at a long line of future heartbreaks and pain.

Psychic Junkie

151

10:13 a.m.—Madam Clara announced we'd get back together, which, though it sounded positive, proved to be not such a good thing. "He'll convince you to come back with him," she said, "but in June *he* makes the break, and that's it. You're over."

10:18 a.m.—Psychic Jane revealed a more optimistic course, saying we'd get back together and have three children, all healthy and blond. "I feel a set of twins. Yes, definitely. I see you pregnant and very large."

12:39 p.m.—Love by Paulette also made a stab at being comforting. "You'll hear from him soon. He's definitely *willing* to change, but, well, unfortunately the cards are resistant to tell me if he actually does change."

3:42 p.m.—Royal Star alleged, in a staunch English accent, that we'd never reunite, and I'd instead meet an artist who'd propose during a full moon, though evidently that was where the fun would end. "I see struggle. Creatively you two are dynamic, but financially your relationship is marked with issues."

3:57 p.m.—Tarot by Sophie decided we'd get back together, in a "romantic and surprising way." But two years later I'd also be surprised to learn he'd been having an affair with a coworker. "But I see you really benefit from the fresh start. Sure, it'll be devastating, I won't deny that, but there's a silver lining."

4:28 p.m.—Fairy Whispers said, in a deep smoker's voice, there'd be a long stretch of silence and it wouldn't be till next year that I'd hear from him, at which point he'd return "from a place of a high elevation," sorry for everything, and wanting me back. "You reunite, and though I'm not seeing much beyond that, I *feel* marriage."

Sarah Lassez

I should've just stopped at the feeling of marriage, but at 6:11 p.m. Ask Ruth proclaimed we'd get back together in four months and he'd seem absolutely wonderful, but then one day I'd catch him in bed with a male neighbor.

Clearly there was no ending the day on that disturbing note, so at 6:17 p.m. Erlin told me to be patient. "You will be together again, don't worry. And yes, I still see the proposal very clearly."

Thank you.

Another week of psychic binging passed, and I realized I had to try to be healthier and fill my time with things that didn't make the folks at Mastercard and Visa jump for joy. I found three such free activities, and attempted to intersperse them for the longest durations possible between calls. The first was reading each and every psychic's feedback on the Web site. For hours I would read commentaries written by troubled people, noting which psychics they deemed reliable, studying up as if doing a thesis on fortune-telling. The second activity involved online tarot readings, because Gina had captured my French deck when she'd learned of its existence. And the third was to obsessively cut my split ends, something that tended to have a calming effect on me, much like yoga for a normal person. After the intensive split-end-cutting sessions I'd return to the computer—eyes crossed and hair becoming more and more lopsided—cry for ten minutes or so, and then figure out which psychic was next on my list.

For three weeks I did this. I also finally admitted to Gina what had happened, but insisted I was fine and just needed some time to be alone. I then changed the subject to that of her new man, and she briefly, and with as much toned-down enthusiasm as she could manage, told me all about him. "And," she said, trying to be helpful, "he's got a bunch of guy friends you've never met! It's like an entire untapped vein of boys! Forget about Wilhelm—he wore *pink shirts.*"

And though in theory meeting new people sounded nice, the reality was that I was still trying to find the will to take showers and feed myself, and hence leaving the house and dating was a far off and lofty goal. For now the only relationship I could handle was with my local Thai restaurant's delivery person, a kind-looking man who'd begun appraising me with growing concern each time he arrived at my house. Part of me wanted to take him inside, sit him down in my living room, give him a plate of Pad Thai noodles, and tell him everything. I knew he didn't speak English, so it would be perfect. I could talk and talk and talk, and he'd chew and nod, and that would be it. I'd feel better and he'd be full. But I couldn't let him in, because then he'd actually see the state of my apartment and really grow alarmed, so I instead simply gave him hefty tips, courtesy of Visa or Mastercard, and he'd smile and head back to his car, tossing back one last glance in my direction, perhaps to check if I'd collapsed at the door. I'd wait for him to do this, meet his eye, then wave like a healthy person and head upstairs, where I'd force a couple noodles into my mouth, concentrate on chewing, then close the carton and set it in the fridge with the rest of the white Styrofoam collection.

One day, after the best shaft of light for identifying and obliterating split ends disappeared, I decided to put my scissors away and call Misty Mystical. Her photo made her appear kind and soothing, understanding and gentle. She was a large woman perched in a rocking chair with an expression that said "Come here, little one." And so I did.

"What's your question, my dear?" she asked with a sweet Southern drawl that was very un-Evangeline-like.

I wanted to curl up in her massive lap and let her rock me to sleep. *Sarah, time is money. Spit it out.* "How's Wilhelm feeling about me?"

"Give me just a sec while I shuffle the cards." There was the recognizable flapping of cards and Misty's mothering coos of "Just a sec more; we're almost there." "Alrighty, then," she finally said. "Now you pick a pile. Left, middle, or right."

"Left, please."

There was a pause, and then, "He loves you, honey. He misses you."

"Really?" My heart was aching.

"Oh, yes. He knows he's been a fool. You'll hear from him in three to ten days."

"Thank you, Misty!" I cried, and then hung up before she could tell me what would happen after those three to ten days.

Three to ten days. As much as I wanted to believe her, there was absolutely nothing to give credence to her prediction. Erlin as well maintained that Wilhelm was suffering and that I should be patient, and even I couldn't shake the feeling that things weren't over. We all seemed to be under the ridiculous impression that Wilhelm and I would reunite, but what if we were all just flat-out wrong? What if Wilhelm had moved on? What if he were dating? Writing love letters to his Aryan goddess? I had no proof of his supposed suffering or that we'd get back together. In five weeks I hadn't heard a peep out of him, and the only time there'd been a hang up on my machine, I'd raced to the phone and pressed star sixty-nine, only to end up talking to Gina and having to tell her no, I did not feel like bowling with her and her boyfriend, and no, I really didn't think imagining Wilhelm as the pins would help.

That night I lulled myself to sleep by reading notes from all the readings that foretold Wilhelm's return. I did that the next night as well, and the next, the notes becoming bedtime stories that fed my dreams with happiness and made waking in the morning painful. On the seventh night of doing this, I was almost asleep, the pages spread beside me, when the phone rang. I glanced at the time, saw it was one a.m., and figured it was Gina, tipsy and trying to entice me to meet one of her new beau's friends. I was about to pick up the phone and yell at her when the machine clicked on . . . and the voice that spoke stopped me cold.

"Sarah . . . it's me."

I stared at the machine, my heart pounding against my chest in a way that only happens when you know someone's words are about to change your life.

"You don't have to pick up the phone," Wilhelm continued. "I just can't take it anymore. I can't take one more night wondering about you. I've been a fool."

My breath caught—"I've been a fool"—Misty Mystical's exact words!

"I've been praying to God that if only he'd give me one more chance with you, I'd do better, I'd be different. I swear I'd be really committed this time."

As he paused, I noted with excitement that though his voice sounded sad and small, it did not sound drunk. As any girl will tell you, this is key.

I couldn't take it anymore. I felt as though the world had grown bright and my room had filled with rainbows and dancing kittens. I leapt for the phone.

"Hi, Wilhelm," I said as calmly and as casually as I could, as if I hadn't been a raving, wailing, psychic-calling lunatic for the past forty-two days.

I listened to him profess how sorry he was, how badly he wanted me back. I tried to remain composed, my face frozen in a smile as I found my star stickers and my "Psychics I Like and Why" document, the three pages of names I'd stapled together, buried beneath the notes on Wilhelm's return.

It was happening.

I told him I'd give him a chance, and just like that all became right again. Wilhelm and I were back together, and Misty Mystical got a gold star by her name.

7

Ding-Ding! Round Two

THERE IS, SOMEWHERE OUT THERE, A BOYFRIEND boot camp. You may not find it in the yellow pages, you may not be able to point it out on a map, you may not actually find any proof of its existence at all—but I'll tell you this: It's out there, and it's the place where bad boyfriends go to become good.

Wilhelm's six-week enrollment in the camp completely changed him. Suddenly he was attentive, romantic, and loving, and didn't even mind my repeated requests to "Say again what you did on my answering machine." I was in heaven, and out of sheer happiness I was eating everything in sight.

"I don't know about this," Gina said one evening.

We were at her place, on one of the few nights her boyfriend, Mark, wasn't over, though his existence was still seen in a pair of large tennis shoes in the hall, a coat slung over a chair, and a cell phone he'd left behind on her coffee table.

"What don't you know about?" I took a sip of wine and stuffed a large wedge of Brie into my mouth.

"About you taking him back just like that. What about all that moving-to-another-country stuff?"

I chewed and chewed and chewed and finally swallowed. "I don't know. I asked him about it, and he said he hasn't thought about it lately. All he could think about was getting me back."

"It just worries me. What he said about not liking L.A. But maybe it's no big deal."

I shrugged. "I'm telling you, he's completely changed. He's totally committed, which means if *he* leaves L.A., *I* go with him." I leaned over to saw off another chunk of Brie. "I can't believe Mark just left his cell phone here. Did you go through it? Look at missed calls?"

"No," Gina laughed. "Hey! Look who's here!"

I turned and saw Onyx, my former cat . . . at the same moment that Onyx saw me. Though I was happy to see her, the feeling, apparently, was not mutual. Like an animal in the wild who spots an enemy and wishes not to draw attention with movement of any kind, Onyx completely froze, midstride, in the dining room. We stared at each other. I opened my mouth to say hi, and that was it; she did a 180 and flew back down the hall.

"I saved you, you know!" I shouted after her. "Geez. I'll try not to be offended."

"She's a freak; she does that with everyone. She *loves* Mark, though. It's so cute. When he gets ready for work, she just circles around him, practically begging him not to leave."

I nodded, familiar with the act.

"And he loves her, too, I can tell. Of course he won't admit it. He keeps saying, "She's a cat," but I catch him talking to her now and then." She sighed. "He's so cute."

Now that Wilhelm and I were back together, Gina was free to express her feelings for her new man. He was *the one*, she went on to proclaim, and I kept silent, resisting the urge to warn her about the dangers of premature ring shopping.

Of course *I* was shopping for rings. Wilhelm was a different person, committed and without fear, exactly the kind of person who'd propose. Erlin told me it was just a matter of time, that this whole fiasco we'd gone through had happened to prepare him for marriage and reinforce his love. To this I laughed with glee and said, "So do you see a round diamond? Or a square?"

"The ring I see," Erlin said, "will surprise you."

I was silent. It better not be a marquise. To me marquise cuts are the Hyundais of the diamond world; no matter what, they just seem cheap. Never should a marquise diamond be a center stone. I tried asking how the ring would surprise me (we all know how I feel about surprises), but to this, Erlin only said, "It will be revealed to you when it's revealed to you." Great, Erlin. Glad you clarified.

Still, for the first time in a long time everything seemed right. Wilhelm was taking enormous leaps to change, even promising that the next time he went to Germany he'd take me with him. "I want you to meet my family," he said, and I felt woozy with happiness. Then, when at last we got into the hot tub, *he sat next to me*. I was amazed, bursting with pleasure, and again a bit woozy. We had become the couple that some other girl would watch with envy and longing—and perhaps a bit of concern, since, finally submerged in the water, Wilhelm bore an uncanny resemblance to a lobster in a pot. Still, as a testament of his love for me, he smiled bravely through the pain, wiped the sweat off his reddened brow, and wrapped his arm around my shoulders. I was in a bubbly, luxurious heaven.

That heaven, it turned out, paled in comparison to what awaited me: a trip to Hawaii. We deserved it, he said. A vacation, a pure vacation of relaxation and rest and *no work*. Not one to argue with a vacation to Hawaii, or to anywhere, for that matter, I simply smiled and agreed and neglected to point out that I didn't work at all, I pretty much laid about the house and did nothing. But whatever. Maybe I could use a break from that.

After Wilhelm's finagling and securing a discount package deal, and my busting out my already exhausted credit cards, we arrived in Maui to air that was strange.

"What's that smell?" I asked him.

Wilhelm breathed in. "Fresh air."

I touched my arms. "My God, it's like lotion. Do people age here?"

We had to move there. It was that simple; I had to live in that air. Wilhelm could work at some hotel, and me, I'd be the host of a Hawaiian TV show, maybe something called *Good Morning, Maui!* or *Wake up, Waikiki!* Every morning my bright smile would tell Hawaiians "Yes, you are about to have a great day, we all are!" And I'd be beloved and drive a convertible and have an endless supply of pink hibiscuses to wear in my hair.

And then, if the whole fresh balmy air thing wasn't already a shock to our systems, we arrived at our four-and-a-half-star hotel, a sprawling and magnificent place built on black rocks that jutted into an ocean so soothingly turquoise that my instinct was to stick a pineapple wedge and a little umbrella in it and take a gulp. It had been years since I'd seen water that color. By comparison, the ocean in L.A. is a sort of grayish menacing navy blue, the kind of ocean that makes one think of shipwrecks and dead bodies and sewage spills. Really, the beaches in L.A. are beaches simply because they're where the ocean meets the land—they're beaches by default. But this, this beach before me, this was a beach that was rated, a beach that was in competition with other beaches to be the best beach in the world, a beach that made me want to bypass my hotel room, go straight to the water's edge with my suitcase, whip out my cell phone, and order a piña colada.

Everything kept getting better and better. Upon checking in we were immediately upgraded to a deluxe beachfront room. Wilhelm smiled and whispered in my ear, "See? Working in a hotel has its perks. Everything's falling into place."

Into place for what? Let me just say here that since coming up with the idea of this vacation, Wilhelm had been beyond suspicious. Even as we packed, he'd been secretive and not allowed me into the same room, had in fact forced me into the living room, where I'd sat and silently stared at the television—which was off—fidgety with hope. As if the packing episode hadn't been suspect enough, when airport security in its post-9/11 invasive and yet welcome way asked him to open up his suitcase for display, Wilhelm ordered me to not only close my eyes but also *turn around.* So "falling into place" for what? I certainly had my sparkly theories.

Our room was like a brochure on luxury. Even Wilhelm, notoriously critical of hotels and known to fly off the handle at the discovery of a white instead of ivory tablecloth, seemed to be impressed, and was particularly thrilled upon finding the hard straight-backed chairs on the balcony. Before we'd even unpacked, he'd moved one of the chairs indoors, I assumed so he'd be prepared should he accidentally find himself comfortable.

Dinner involved scallop and lobster pot stickers in a guava plum sauce, one of the most divine dishes I'd ever had. I tallied up how many days we'd be staying and determined I could order the dish at least twice a day and thus be ensured of eight more heavenly experiences. "We need to buy an ice chest," I told Wilhelm. "And take pounds of this home."

At this he laughed and smiled, but then suddenly became somber. All traces of fun and enjoyment were gone and he leaned in so close to his plate, he could've opened his mouth and snatched a pot sticker with his teeth. It seemed my words had just flipped a switch, and now he was all business, no longer eating or enjoying, but picking apart his dish with a meticulousness that would put a surgeon to shame.

Though I would've been thrilled to have the dish re-created for me at home, for about ten minutes there, I was pretty much dining alone while he examined each fleck of spice, each shade of color, closing his eyes for long periods of time to taste and ascertain the ingredients, essentially shutting me out as I downed a daiquiri and waited patiently for conversation to resume. I wondered if I had enough cash to just bribe the chef for the recipe and get it over with, but knew that would never make Wilhelm happy, Wilhelm whose motto could be "I don't want it if I don't have to suffer for it." All around us other couples were laughing and eating and talking and actually looking at each other. But me? Me, I was with the guy who'd just scraped a green speck off his tongue and was now studying it by candlelight. I smiled. You had to love him.

We took the beach route back to our hotel room, shoes in our hands, our feet caressed by the softest, most cloudlike sand I'd ever experienced. I eyed a little cove not far off and thought with longing how nice it would be to have our own little *From Here to Eternity* moment: lying in the soft sand, the surf slipping around us, our eyes filled with yearning. I smiled and turned to Wilhelm, about to suggest a late-night sandy excursion, when he patted his pocket, announced he'd left his smokes in the room, and quickened his pace. *Alas,* I thought as I hurried to catch up with him, *some things never change.* My amorous contemplations were so far off his radar that I might as well have been pondering a jaunt into outer space, a little tour of Pluto and a spin around Mars.

Once back in the room, I freshened up with a shower while Wilhelm relaxed on the balcony, smoking and rigid in one of the hard straight-backed chairs. Though I'd already taken inventory of all the little hotel freebies I'd walk away with, the second I undid the cap of the plumeria-scented shampoo (a heady feminine floral that made me want to rinse and lather the whole night long), I knew I'd have to take serious action. I'd have to tuck all bottles in my bag, religiously, so the maid would be forced to replenish the supply, and then I'd have to stalk the maid and her cart. And Wilhelm, Wilhelm with his barely-there hair, was not allowed to use any. It was *mine.*

Walking back into the living room, I was about to inform my

balding boyfriend of the plan, when I saw him on the balcony. He watched my approach with a smile, his hand on a silk pink tote bag. *Well, hello there, little present,* I thought with nervous excitement. *How are you doing?*

"It's for you," he said, a point I obviously didn't need stated, since by the time he'd completed the word "It's," I'd already flown onto the balcony, torn into the tote, and extracted a multitude of gifts.

Everything was pink. I squealed with joy. Being a quintessential girly girl who is hopelessly drawn to glitter and gloss and sparkle and shine, pink is my color. There was a pink beach towel to luxuriate on, a pink notebook to record my memories, a pink sundress to look relaxed yet chic in, and a pink body lotion I recognized from Wilhelm's favorite discount store since it was a brand that had recently been discontinued.

Then he revealed pink champagne, and my heart really started pounding. Oh my God . . . What could be both sparkly *and* pink? A pink diamond! That would certainly be a ring that would surprise me, but one that I would absolutely love. Clearly he'd tapped into my love of pink. I'd never considered a pink diamond before, and wondered if they were cheaper. I bet they were. Hence I could get a bigger one. One people would call a "stunner." Yes, I wanted a ring that stunned people, one that made them stumble backward and blink and then gather their composure and shriek, "Oh my God, let me see that! Holy shit!"

Wilhelm poured me a glass of champagne, and I studied his shirt pocket for the shape of a monster pink ring.

"It's a family custom," he said, waiting for the fizz to settle, then pouring a bit more. "Every time we go on vacation, we give a gift."

I'm included in "family." I've been brought into the fold. I took my champagne and smiled, trying to look radiant and memorable. He looked into my eyes. He held out his drink for a toast, and I did the same, my heart pounding.

In my mind I'd already started telling the story of the proposal. "Well, there we were in our pretty-much-five-star hotel, a resort to end all resorts, sitting on the balcony, listening to the waves crash on the rocks below. The ocean was glittering, the palm trees were rustling, the air was like lotion, my hair smelled like flowers. He handed me a glass of pink champagne— Wilhelm knows how I just love the color pink, he's so thoughtful—and then he raised his glass, and with love in his eyes said—"

"Here's to a great vacation." Our glasses clinked. "And lots of good food."

And with that he took a swig, sat back against his hard straight chair, and lit another cigarette.

The next day was torture. Every step we took landed us in the perfect setting for a proposal, and soon I was exhausted from looking radiant and memorable. The road to Hana was an almost three-hour drive that wound us through rain forests and scenery that made my breath wedge at every turn; it took us to red sand beaches, black sand beaches, waterfalls, pools, and so many romantic settings that I knew in my heart it was going to happen. That morning I'd considered calling Erlin while Wilhelm was in the shower, but decided maybe in this case a surprise *would* be good. After all, Wilhelm had put so much work into this trip that spoiling his plans seemed cruel.

After watching him swing on a vine and do an odd impression of a German Tarzan, I found a perfect spot to just sit and relax. To do nothing. For a while I did nothing, just watched my boyfriend swing through the trees. Eventually I mustered the energy to eat some banana bread, which was so delicious I found the energy to eat all the banana bread and then scrounge for crumbs. Full and absolutely content, I leaned back against a black rock and closed my eyes. I felt the sun through the foliage, the slight mist of the waterfall. In the air was the fragrance of the tulip tree's flaming red blooms, the sweet spice of white ginger, the fresh, clean scent of rainbow eucalyptus. I don't think I'd ever experienced it before then, but it was the feeling of pure bliss.

When I opened my eyes, Wilhelm was before me, on bended knee.

I sat up, my heart pounding. It was happening! I didn't know what to do. I tried to conjure my Proposal Face, but suddenly forgot how to look radiant and memorable and so instead simply grinned like a fool and stared expectantly. He was facing me, on both knees actually, which was perhaps some odd German tradition? I waited. Maybe I'd cry. Would I cry? I felt like I might cry.

And then, with a slightly pained look on his face, he put one hand on the back of his hip and slowly got up. *What the hell?* "What are you doing?"

He raised his right arm above his head in a stretch. "I think I pulled something on that last swing. I was trying to stretch it out. I think it's okay, don't worry."

I stared. "Oh."

"We should go, though. It's getting late and I don't want to drive back in the dark."

On our return we opted for a different route, one that was surreal in its stark contrast to the scenic road we'd taken earlier. Somehow we'd found the dark side of paradise. The land was barren, black, and foreboding, and I knew without having to be told that there would be no proposal now. Soon we'd fallen into complete silence, as if harboring a fear that the sound of our voices could alert evil beings to our presence. Hands folded stiffly in my lap, I concentrated my energies on keeping the car safe, the tires full of air, the gas from running out. I did not want to be stranded there in that spooky place while back in the land of blue water and coconut trees my pink sparkling diamond was waiting and lonely.

After driving for what seemed like forever, we came upon a policeman, who greeted us with the fun news that a flash flood had submerged the road, and therefore we needed to turn back around. We looked at each other, and then peered past the cop to assess the situation ourselves, as at this point nothing short of the Rio Grande was going to keep us from getting back to our hotel as fast as possible. Sure enough, the pavement stopped at one point and then started back up a great distance away. In between there was what looked like a raging churning river, as if some lazy schmuck had been meaning to build a bridge but just hadn't gotten around to it. A few Jeeps with four-wheel drive were braving the rapids, fighting their way to the other side, but all the little cars were doing awkward three-point turns and heading back toward us, the drivers' faces dejected and slightly shamed, like kids embarrassed in gym class.

I thought of my ring. I thought of my pot stickers. I did not want to turn around. Yet there we were in our little rented Kia Rio, a car that appeared barely capable of taking on a slight rain, much less a flash flood. We had no choice but to go back through the creepy dark land.

Or so I thought. I looked back at Wilhelm and saw in his eyes what I can only describe as an insane flicker. He grinned, faced the road, whooped like a cowboy, and hit the gas.

I screamed. I grabbed the armrest, the seat, the ceiling, the window, anything. We met the water, and our car churned, lurched, and struggled. Beside me Wilhelm was still whooping, though now he was whooping rather frantically, like a cowboy on speed. We were going to be swept into the ocean. Such an unromantic and stupid way to go. *So yes, all in all Sarah had a wonderful life, and then she was swept into the ocean in a rental car. That was that. They only ever found her pink beach towel and a pine tree air freshener. So senseless. I mean, a Kia. Who would brave a flash flood in a Kia?*

Half-submerged, we fought against the raging current. I couldn't look. I squeezed my eyes shut, but then couldn't help but envision our car crashing and sinking into the Pacific. *Stop! Traction. Picture traction. See the tires gripping something, anything, propelling us onto dry land.* I tried. I really did. I fought to picture us moving forward, but all I saw was us moving sideways, floating slowly at first and then faster and faster toward a white rumbling ocean.

It took me a bit to realize that not only were we moving forward, but we were moving forward *quickly*. That meant either our car had turned and angled toward the ocean, or we'd hit dry land. Cautiously I opened one eye first and then the other, as if opening both at the same time would have yielded a different result. We'd made it. We were on dry land! At the top of the hill we paused, looked at each other with astonishment, and then looked back at the policeman, who'd turned from us with disgust, most likely calling us crazy *haoles*—"pale-skinned foreigners" in Hawaiian.

Wilhelm was exhilarated, completely breathless from the thrill. I'd never seen him that excited; it was as if he'd just conquered nature at the wheel of a Kia Rio. I *loved* this side of him. So sexy, so brave!

Unfortunately, it was also a side that was rather short-lived. The next day we went snorkeling, and Wilhelm became instantly frightened and fled back to the hotel. I stayed in the water, happy as could be, though now and then I'd glance up toward the balcony, at the little speck that was my boyfriend, a speck that was apparently afraid of fish and masks and snorkels and was now chain-smoking and keeping an eye on the ocean from a safe distance.

A few more days of pot stickers, piña coladas, sunburns, and no ring, and it was time to leave. Saying "Aloha" to Hawaii—a phrase that means both "hello" and "good-bye" and would, I'd imagine, be cause for much confusion—we packed our bags, raided the maid's cart one last time, and then found ourselves standing miserably at LAX, watching our luggage plummet onto a conveyer belt.

Back at home, surrounded once more by smog and traffic and my messy apartment, I called Erlin. Again he said the engagement would happen soon, and that I needed to be patient. Patient?

Patience, clearly, has never been my strong suit. Actually, that's not entirely true. I could be extremely patient when it came to one thing, yet when it came to another, I could snap without warning. If anyone had carefully examined my childhood Rubik's Cube, they would've seen evidence of this, for although I'd lasted only five minutes before determining that the stickers indeed needed to come off, I'd then spent over an hour removing and reapplying them carefully, so as not to be detected. Perhaps, I suppose, it's not a patience issue at all but a focus issue. My brain stubbornly refuses to follow the logical, trodden path. Instead of sliding those cubes around, as the game intends one should do, I'd embarked on sticker extraction. While another child might have seen fifteen minutes as enough time to get all the yellows in order, I saw it as enough time to get the water boiling for the steam bath my Rubik's Cube was about to have.

Annoyed with Erlin, I called Gina.

"Please tell me you got laid," she said right off the bat.

"Yeah, when we landed at the airport. I got a really pretty pink and orange one."

"No. I meant the other kind. Jesus, has it really been that long?"

"Oh, *that*. Yeah, once. It took him swinging on vines like Tarzan and then charging through a flash flood like a cowboy to put him in the mood, though."

"Wilhelm swung on vines?"

"I know. It was hysterical. He was the whitest Tarzan ever, just this white flash through the trees. By the way, why don't people have compatible sex drives?"

"If everything were perfect, we'd have nothing to talk about? A cruel trick of the universe?"

"I'm thirty and my hormones are out of control, and I've got a guy who wants to stay up all night smoking, drinking fancy wine, and chatting."

"Does he call it 'chatting'?"

"No, that's me."

"Well, there's hope, then. And at least you're not screaming at each other in the street, like with Jonas."

"True. We totally get along. I just need to find some vines in L.A."

After Gina convinced me that encouraging Wilhelm to drive across the Los Angeles River during the rainy season wasn't the answer, we hung up and I fixated on my relationship. Everything would be fine. Really, all was good, better than good in fact. Other than the incompatible sex drives—and honestly, I didn't know any couple that was perfectly matched in that department—our relationship was pretty ideal. We weren't screaming at each other in the street, police weren't being called to put an end to our dates, we had fun together, and wanted to spend time with each other. This was, in truth, the best, most easygoing relationship I'd ever had.

And actually, not one psychic had predicted the proposal would take place in Hawaii, so that meant it was still coming. Wilhelm probably figured proposing in Hawaii would be too expected, too typical; I bet hordes of people got engaged on vacations. What was unique about that? For all I knew, his goal was to truly catch me off guard, to sneak in the proposal in a way I'd never see coming or in a way that was much more true to who he was. Perhaps he'd nestle the ring with parsley on a plate or bake it into a chocolate soufflé. After all, platinum and diamonds can withstand high temperatures, right?

8

Pandora's Box and Other No-No's

NATURALLY, AS ANY NEUROTIC GIRL WHO'S JUST come to the realization that her relationship is bordering on perfection would do, I self-destructed.

It couldn't be as good as it seemed. Hidden beneath the surface of our seemingly ideal relationship had to be something horribly, horribly wrong. I'd never had such a good relationship, so that in and of itself was a fluttering bright red flag. Nothing was this good. Somewhere, I knew, was a loose thread that could unravel our relationship, and by God, I had to find it.

The first order of business was to embark on intensive snooping sessions. This involved my staying at his house, waiting till I heard the click of the door that told me he was safely on his way to work, and then ransacking his apartment. I had no idea what I was looking for, but I knew with certainty I'd find it. *Just keep looking*, I told myself as I finished rummaging through his desk and turned to face the closet.

And indeed, the second I hit the closet, I found something. Up at the very top, accessible only by stepladder and buried beneath mounds of sweaters he never wore, was the obligatory shoe box filled with photos of unidentified women. Every guy has this, the shoe box being their version of a photo album, and though they never have the good sense to actually throw these snapshots away, they do have the wisdom to hide them. Though I must say this wisdom is part of a catch-22, since anything that's left in the open is grounds for scrutiny and alarm, but anything that's hidden naturally becomes violently suspect and cause for terror. Perfectly innocent pictures of female friends or relatives thus become immensely threatening as a result of the location in which they're stashed, and hence there is no way a guy can have *any* evidence of a past without running the risk that at some point his girlfriend will go absolutely loony, shove a picture of his great-aunt Edna in his face, and scream, "Who is this? Just who is this!"

I pored through every picture, torturing myself, comparing their attractiveness with mine, picturing Wilhelm gazing into their eyes. Naturally, I determined that the prettiest one was Nadja, the Aryan Goddess. Nadja I'd actually not been overly concerned about for a while, because Gina and I had determined that she wasn't a threat; she was simply a girl with whom he barely kept in touch. Besides, we figured, if he considered her more than a friend, he'd never have told her about me. Reassured after this deduction, I'd tucked the Aryan Goddess into a corner of my mind and only brought her out when in need of another log to toss on a panic session's fire.

But now I held a photograph in my hand. Was this her?

Blond and wearing a tennis skirt? Since when did Wilhelm play tennis? Or was this her, a girl in another picture, gracefully holding a glass of white wine *as she should*, by the stem? I, on the other hand, tended to get my warm little hands all over the bowl and send Wilhelm into a tizzy. In the wine drinker's other hand was a cigarette, and in her eyes was a look that said, "Hello, Sarah, nice to meet you. I'm perfect for Wilhelm and you're not." I flipped to another picture, and then another, trying to determine, based on the intensity of their smiles or the gleams in their eyes, if these girls were in relationships with Wilhelm. I hated them all.

Once every nook and cranny in his closet had been inspected, and I'd recovered from the horror of learning my boyfriend owned more pink shirts than I deemed acceptable, I moved on to the bathroom. Hair products abounded, and bottles of cologne had jurisdiction over an entire medicine cabinet. Good God, my boyfriend was vain. Then I opened the cupboard below the sink and found . . . porn.

Porn. Stacks and stacks of magazines hidden at the very back, all reassuringly heterosexual and not obscurely kinky, but nonetheless all of women who weren't me. I was completely thrown. Wilhelm had no sex drive, what did he need this for? Had the former tenant maybe left these magazines behind? Perhaps, upon finding them, my poor delicate boyfriend had been too afraid to touch them and had left them where they were? *No, Sarah, that's ridiculous. No guy would leave behind his porn.* Along with the TV, porn would be the first thing packed and ready to go.

But why would Wilhelm employ one-dimensional women

and his hand when he had a three-dimensional girlfriend pretty much raring to go at all times? In a frenzy, I ran to my purse, grabbed my cell phone, and returned to the porn. Settled in on the linoleum floor, I flipped through pages and waited for Gina to pick up.

She sounded distracted as she said "Hello," but I charged forth.

"Ask your boyfriend, as he's now a representative of the male species, why my boyfriend, who has no interest in sex, would have a stack of porn magazines in his bathroom."

"Hold, please." I heard her adjust the phone, then yell, "Honey, Sarah's losing her mind. Will you come here for a sec?"

Once she'd explained the situation, Mark offered his opinion, which I heard, followed by Gina's word for word repetition. *Masturbation's different.* "He says masturbation's different." *It's quick and easy, a way to relax.* "He says it's quick and easy, a way to relax." *It doesn't compare to having sex with a real woman.* "He says it doesn't—"

"Put him on the phone."

She handed over the phone, and Mark, sounding a tad nervous, came on the line.

"Okay," I said. "So if it doesn't compare to having sex with a real woman, tell me again why he'd do that and not have sex with me? *I'm a real woman.*"

He took a deep breath, clearly ruing his decision to go over to Gina's house that day. "Well. There could be lots of reasons. I mean, first, it's habit. Ever since he was twelve, he's probably been doing it every day. At this point it's routine. You just do it; I don't know. Then there could be all sorts of psychological reasons, like performance anxiety. Maybe sex with a real woman is stressful? You gotta remember, centerfolds don't bitch—"

Gina snatched the phone back. "That answer your question?"

"Performance anxiety," I said with wonder. "I bet that's it."

"Okay, glad to help, but I'm in the midst of a Virgo moment and have to finish alphabetizing my CDs, DVDs, and books. Gotta run."

We hung up, and I stared at the girl on the cover, a girl whose skin looked plastic and whose boobs looked so filled with helium that it would've made perfect sense if the picture were of her spiraling in the air, passing pigeons and treetops and kites. Of course. Wilhelm was *nervous*. I couldn't believe I'd never thought of that! Early in our dating I'd made the mistake of revealing that I'd had flings with a couple of rather famous actors, and though my objective had been honesty—while also attempting to instill an I-am-so-lucky-to-have-her feeling—the disclosure might have backfired. He could be worried he didn't measure up! Poor Wilhelm!

I vowed not to pressure him anymore. In fact, not only would I not pressure him, but I'd also try to build his ego, compliment him, make him feel like a manly man. Briefly I considered hiding all his pink shirts, but then told myself no, I love him the way he is—my masturbating, sex-hating, pink-shirt-wearing, discount-store-window-shopping, balding, self-punishing, pretty boy chef of a boyfriend.

I also vowed to stop snooping, which, once I'd completed the search of his entire apartment, I did. The only other curious thing I found, besides the pictures and the porn, was a plastic folder from the FBI. How the hell he'd gotten it, I had no idea.

Momentarily I entertained the idea that Wilhelm was *in* the FBI, was perhaps actually here undercover and on assignment, but even that didn't bother me. As long as Nadja wasn't the requisite partner he was in love with, the thought of his deceiving me was not a problem.

I was good. I was trusting. I believed in Wilhelm and knew better than to invade his privacy. I was proud of myself, of how well behaved I'd become—until one day I had a little slipup and put spyware on his computer. Well, actually, it was my computer, the one he used to check his e-mails when at my house, so my reasoning was that it was my property and in truth it was smart to know what was happening on one's own property. If I happened to come across his e-mail password, that wasn't my fault, was it? I know, I know. If there were ever awards for Most Outlandish Justification, I'd certainly take the prize with that one.

So, in a state I dare not describe as sane, I installed the spyware, sat back, and waited for him to check his e-mails. To be perfectly honest, I'd actually been trying to crack his password since I'd learned of the Aryan Goddess's existence, and the effort to do this the old-fashioned way, by educated guesses, was exhausting. I was tired. I just wanted to *know*. Essentially, I wanted to trust him, as one should be able to do when about to get engaged, but in order to do so I needed to search through all his belongings and break into his e-mail account. It made perfect sense.

It was only a matter of time till the plunder of my plot materialized. One bright sunshiny morning, a day when our only plans involved an expedition to Ross and T.J. Maxx, followed by a nice dinner of beef bourguignon and a seductive, velvety pinot noir that Wilhelm wouldn't shut up about, he asked if he could check his e-mail.

"Absolutely," I told him. "Please. Take your time."

Whereas normally I'd agree, let him use my computer, and then somehow manage to hover in the vicinity—dusting the picture frames on the desk, sweeping around the chair he was sitting in, helpfully wiping off the computer monitor—this time I made myself scarce. I went outside to cut roses. Leisurely I selected the fullest blooms, the prettiest shades of pink. I realized that a well-thought-out plan of attack and deception lends a sense of serenity, a feeling of peace and accomplishment. It was a truly beautiful day, and I was happy. Tiny bouquet in hand, I headed back indoors.

Wilhelm was standing in my living room, a look of abject disappointment on his face. "I have to go in to work."

"You do?" I asked, trying to hide my delight.

"Yes. There's a crisis with a private party tonight. They vastly underestimated the amount of—"

"Shoot. That's too bad. Well, you gotta do what you gotta do."

He nodded, no doubt longingly envisioning the cluttered aisles of Ross. "I know. It's true. But I was looking forward to our day together. I hope tonight I can join you, that I can come back. Though, I have a feeling today is going to be bad. Nothing at work goes as it should."

I shrugged and headed to the door. "That sucks. Well, call me later and keep me posted."

Once I'd herded him outside and stood by the window to make sure his car had started and that he was indeed reversing from the driveway, I turned and faced the computer, staring it down as if it were a hostage I was about to interrogate. In truth, all I had to do was press a few buttons. Voilà. I had his password. I must say I was pleased with my detective skills, as Hugo Boss, his favorite designer, had been one of my first guesses. But, being the sneaky Kraut he apparently was, he'd changed it to "HugBoss." "HugBoss" being like a cry for help from a man whose employees had vandalized his car.

I paused. It was rather disconcerting that he knew people would naturally guess that his password was his favorite designer, which, I was learning, wasn't normal. Just recently Gina had asked for advice on what to get Mark for his birthday, and when I'd replied, "Well, who's his favorite designer?" my words had been met with a heavy sigh.

"Oh, my poor Sarah," she'd said. "The way it works with most men is like this: They don't *have* favorite designers. They don't talk about collections or bold new color schemes, and they don't go shopping for fun. When they need something, they get it. The only thing I've been able to tell about Mark is that he often buys his clothes at Banana Republic, and even then— when I asked if it was his favorite store—he said, "I go there because they have one at whatever mall you drag me to." Other than that, I know he likes the color blue. That's it, and that's how it should be."

I recognized this as a good point. Still, I loved my metrosexual. He gave amazing and hip gifts, like the Burberry scarf he'd recently bestowed on me, one he'd *had* to buy me because it was all the rage. Of course, *I'd* known it was a fake, but no one else could tell, because a true metrosexual also possesses the ability to discover and acquire amazing knockoffs. So being with a metrosexual had its perks, and one, I now saw, was the ability to almost correctly guess passwords. Sitting there, about to break into his e-mails, I found his little attempt at being sneaky rather adorable. HugBoss. It made me smile.

And then I got to business.

There before me was Pandora's box, otherwise known as Wilhelm's e-mail account. I felt my hand slowly moving the mouse, watching the cursor inch its way to the word "Inbox." Was this really me? Was I really doing this? Was I really so untrusting, so brimming with trickery, so sneaky? I paused only momentarily. Hell, yeah I was. *Click*.

I was in. I leaned forward and instantly stopped breathing. Nadja. And the date received was today.

There are times in one's life when borders, boundaries, and lines become clear. You know if you take one more step, life will be forever and irrevocably changed, and you can actually iden-tify the moment as you exist in it, feel the weight of its signifi-cance, the sharpness of the edge on which you are perched. This was one of those moments. I stared at her name. If I opened this e-mail, there would be no going back. My life would never be the same. My relationship would never be the same. I felt it. I knew it. People often utter consolations like, "You poor thing, you couldn't have known." Fine, I'm sure that's true in many cases, but not in this one. I was aware. I knew it was bad, and I knew if I crossed the line, there was no going back. Though really there was already no going back, not now that I knew of the e-mail's existence. Short of a lobotomy, there was no way to forget it.

On the other hand, it could be nothing. Most likely, I tried telling myself, it was nothing. She's probably just saying hi again, talking about shoes and cupboards, in which case I'd be needlessly torturing myself with the idea that it was *something*. Whatever. There was no way around it. I had to open the damn thing. So I did.

Of course it was in German. Irritated that the Aryan Goddess couldn't at least write in English and hence make my job just a touch easier, I went to the site that offered translations, cut and pasted, and sat back. Bam, there it was. I started reading. All pretty much harmless drunken Shakespearean chitchat: A mutual friend of theirs was "a mountain without a tree," for everything "stout ales dilemma fixed," she also was quite sorry because she'd had no idea his "treasure was over thirty, quite a burden doubled," how to deal with such "an old basket of eggs," and "niceness was seeing him day other."

Oh, no. No, she didn't. An "old basket of eggs"? She called my eggs old? My eggs might have been aging, but they weren't old! They still worked, I was pretty sure. *And I am not over thirty! I am thirty!* I wanted to kill her. She must be a *baby* to view thirty as ancient. A baby with no wrinkles, no cellulite, and no flippin' clue. This was what I got for getting involved with a twenty-five-year-old. Of course his recent past involved *children*. Wait. I read that last part again. Niceness was seeing him day other?

Amid my confusion (What day other? How had she seen him if she lived in Germany? What was she doing here? Could he have gone to Germany? Why hadn't he told me he'd seen her? Why in secret? What had happened?), I felt the overwhelming urge to puke. Puking is my natural response to any kind of anxiety or emotional turmoil and, in addition to my neurotic need to act, was one of the main reasons I could never be a paramedic or a cop or in any other profession that deals with stress. While others valiantly step up to the plate and perform heroic rescues and feats, I would arrive on scene, promptly keel over, puke, and for the rest of the day need to be fed saltines and ginger ale at hourly intervals. And now, having just read that my boyfriend had seen the Aryan Goddess the other day, keel over was exactly what I did—just as soon as I'd hurled myself into the bathroom. Congratulating myself for having bought such a soft bathroom rug—my best and most appreci-ated purchase—I stared at the water in the bowl and cursed myself, Wilhelm, the Aryan Goddess, spyware in general, and, for good measure, Hugo Boss.

After a while I regained my composure. I had to deal with this. I couldn't curl into the fetal position, play dead, and later awake to find none of this had happened. No, this involved action. Unfortunately, Wilhelm had said he might return that night, once he'd saved the day at work, so there was no telling how much time I had. *Lord, give me strength,* I implored. *Give me the strength I need to read the rest of his e-mails.*

I took a few severely deep breaths, almost passed out, and then returned to the computer. Heart racing, I searched through more of his recent e-mails, but found nothing that would explain the Aryan Slut's existence or intentions. This situation, I knew, was why one should never snoop. No matter how I spun it, I was pretty much guilty. I couldn't exactly phone him at work and say, "Hi, honey. So, with the best of intentions I man-aged to get your e-mail password and was checking your e-mails to, uh, see if I could get any hints for what to buy you for your birthday in eight months, when I came across an e-mail from some sweet girl in Germany who mentioned she saw you the other day, and I just wanted to know WHO THE FUCK SHE IS AND WHY YOU FUCKING KEPT HER A SECRET." Nope. I could safely rule out that approach.

Naturally this was a job for psychics. I had to hand this over to the professionals. So I called Erlin, who smoothly told me not to worry, she was just a friend. At first I felt better, but then something inside me clued in to the fact that "Don't worry" was all he ever said. In order to believe someone when they say you shouldn't worry, they sometimes need to tell you that you *should* worry. At the very least you need to know they're *capable* of telling you to worry. Was "Don't worry" what he told everyone? A stock response? Was he not paying attention here? *My boyfriend's got an Aryan mistress!*

After spending almost forty bucks to learn that Erlin would most likely tell me not to worry even if I were sobbing about a man in my living room with a maniacal glint in his eye and an AK-47 in his arms, I knew I needed a second opinion. My trusty "Psychics I Like and Why" document in hand, I scanned my options and picked two more. Of course, both had vastly different takes on my future. This, I noticed, tended to be a trend when I was freaking out: Every answer was maddeningly different. It was almost as if the universe couldn't concentrate with me down here on earth being such an entertaining mess, perhaps couldn't come up with a straight answer because my moaning or crying or wailing was just too flipping funny. And alas, if there weren't a psychic consensus, I was pretty much on my own. I had to think of something.

Sarah Lassez

And that, of course, was right when Wilhelm called to tell me he was on his way back. I surveyed the living room; the couch's pillows haphazard and flung around, tissues crumpled and scattered, my list of psychics spread out on the floor to allow for easy viewing. Everything was a mess. I didn't want him to come over. I was nowhere near done freaking out. I had at least another two or three hours left in me.

And then inspiration struck. "Hey, Wilhelm," I said casually. "I was just on the phone with Gina, and she mentioned she saw you driving the other day."

He laughed, oblivious. "Really? It's amazing what a small town L.A. is."

"Yeah, totally. Anyhow. She said you were in the car with some girl."

"What? What girl?"

I must say, he sounded genuinely surprised. *Shit.* "I don't know. That's what I was wondering. You know, I was just curious. It's not a big deal. It's just funny."

"I have no idea. I wasn't in the car with anyone. Are you sure it was me she saw? Or was it someone like me? What was I wearing?"

Oh, for crying out loud. "Never mind. I'm sure she was confused. She gets like that. What with being *in love* and *so happy.*"

He told me he needed to stop at the store for some baby potatoes, and that was it. He was on his way, and I was at a loss. For damage control I called Gina and brought her up to speed. "I saw him driving with another girl?" she asked.

"Yes, you did."

"Okay. Just in case he wonders, what'd she look like?"

"Like your typical Aryan whore."

"And that would be six feet tall, blond, and gorgeous?"

"That would be it."

"Got it. Hey, know what you need to do?"

I said nothing, since I did know what I needed to do. I needed to fly to Germany, find this girl, kidnap her, and enlist some CIA-type tactics—no, scratch that; *Republican Guard*-type tactics—to figure out exactly what she was up to with my boyfriend. That and I needed to hook Wilhelm up to a lie detector and start the inquisition. Oh, and while I was at it, I needed to forever ban him from the Internet, the postal service, and the telephone.

"You play psychic."

"Excuse me?"

"You guys have talked about this stuff; he believes in it. So you pretend like you had a dream about him, about him and some other girl. You tell him all about it. Pretend you're really upset—"

"I *am* upset."

"Fine, so be upset and make him think you psychically knew of Nadja's—"

"Don't say her name."

"Of *the Aryan Goddess's* existence—"

"No. She's no longer the Aryan Goddess. She's the Aryan Whore."

"Okay, okay. So you essentially bring up *the Aryan Whore* without admitting what you did. Which, I must say, was very bad."

"I know; I'm aware."

"This worked for me once, when I found out a bunch of info

on some guy I had a date with. It turned out one of my friends worked at the same company he did, and she told me all this shit, which of course he didn't know I knew. So on our date I got a bit tipsy and decided to mess with him. I told him I was psychic and started rattling off all these things about him, down to the fact that he'd recently been on house arrest."

"You went on a date with a guy who'd been on house arrest?"

"It was during my bad-boy stage. He used to be a model and was absolutely gorgeous. It was just the one date, though, which was just as well, 'cause he obviously wasn't relationship material. He even had a tattoo across his lower stomach that said 'Pervert.'"

"That's pretty spelled out."

"I know. Point is, though, he totally bought it. He flipped out. He thought I was psychic. Of course I scared him off and never saw him again, but I went overboard with the predictions. I was *trying* to freak him out."

"That's an interesting first-date tactic."

"Yeah, then I got him drunk and painted his nails pink. In general guys don't have nail polish remover at home, so he had to go in to work like that." She laughed. "My bad-boy stage coincided with my angry stage."

Play psychic. It wasn't a bad idea. How else was I going to confront him? Of course, having just asked about the mystery girl in the car, I couldn't exactly claim to have also had a dream about a girl. He'd get suspicious. I'd have to give it some time.

I made it till the next morning. As I watched him sleep, so peaceful, so innocent, a small puddle of drool on his pillow and his sparse hair locked and in the upright position, I debated over approaches. Would I tell him the dream freaked me out? Made me mad? Scared? Sad? The words "old basket of eggs" streaked through my mind. Damnit. I was pissed. I got out of bed and went to the kitchen, where I furiously paced till I heard Wilhelm staggering down the hall.

"Hi, honey," I said, my words laced with a top note of sweetness, a middle note of challenge, and a base note of pure fury. A smile plastered on my face, I opened the refrigerator door. "Do you want some *eggs*? I have some, but they might be *old*."

"Are they rotten?"

My eyes narrowed. "No. They're not *that* old."

"We don't have to have eggs; we can have something else."

I slammed the door shut. "Fine."

"I can make au gratin potatoes?"

"Yeah. You do that."

I watched him peel the potatoes, then start to slice them. What remained of his hair was still upright, though a few strands had ventured sideways. Poor guy hadn't even had time to take a shower before I'd accosted him and forced him to cook. I had to calm down. *Calm*, I thought. *Use the Good Dog Voice.* "I'm sorry, honey. I guess I'm in a bad mood."

He nodded. "I know. They're just eggs. Who cares if they're old?"

I smiled. "That's sweet. Not necessarily true, but sweet."

"Are you okay?"

"I'm fine. I just had this horrible nightmare last night. I think it's still with me. You know how your dreams sometimes affect your moods? In it there was this girl in Germany who was in love with you."

He laughed.

"Yeah, it was crazy." I rolled my eyes as if to say, "I know, I'm just so wacky" and then said, "So there was this girl who lived there, and I guess she really liked you because she was upset we were together. And then I found out that you guys talked all the time. God, what else? There was something else." I paused, staring up at the ceiling as if trying to jog my memory. "Oh, right. You e-mailed each other."

Now he looked up at me, his smile gone. "Huh." Then, without saying anything more, he went back to work on his potatoes, sliding the slices to one end of the chopping board.

"And then," I continued, "I found out you two were involved."

"Involved? Like romantically?"

"Yeah. Strange, huh? It *was* a romantic involvement. Ha." I said this in an absurdly flippant tone, as if remarking how silly an F5 twister was when it wiped out an entire town. "And then it got *really* bizarre, because I found out you saw her recently."

Now he put the knife down. His eyes were wide. "Okay, Sarah, this is strange. I do have a friend back in Germany I talk to. We're just friends, though, nothing more, but we *do* e-mail to each other, *and I saw her recently.*"

"You did?"

"*Yes. My God!* I cannot believe you dreamt that!"

"Me either!"

Shaking his head, he resumed his slicing. "Just last week she was here, too, visiting California with her boyfriend. That is so strange."

Her boyfriend. She has a *boyfriend.* Suddenly the image I'd conjured, the two of them cozy and speaking in their mother tongue over white wine and oysters, morphed into the two of them plus her boyfriend, all with café lattes in a bright Coffee Bean & Tea Leaf. Maybe they'd had blueberry muffins, but they certainly hadn't had oysters.

I don't think I'd ever felt relief like that. It was more comforting than shade on a hundred-degree day, more exciting than discovering an employee at a skin-care counter who ached to give out free samples, more welcome than a spotless restroom on a road trip. In short, I'd worried for nothing, and relief flooded over me with such force I felt the need to lie down in the middle of the kitchen and start giggling. "She has a boyfriend?"

He nodded. "They've been together for a year? Maybe less. He sounds like a great guy, but a bit dull."

Sounds like. Sounds like. Sounds like? "So wait, you didn't meet him?"

"No. Not this time. They were on different flights; he got in later than she did. I met her at the airport and took her out for the afternoon."

Okay, breathe, Sarah. I needed to fixate on something. Stare at something, take it in, think of nothing else, be calm. *Breathe.* My eyes locked on his widow's peak. I watched it. The skin beside it was shining. The hair was haphazard. I swear it was becoming more defined by the second. I blinked. "That was nice of you. What day was this?"

"Last Wednesday? Thursday? No, Wednesday." As if realizing, for the first time, that this could get him in trouble, he quickly added, "I worked that evening, so it was a short visit. Very short."

That was it. That was all I got out of him. As we ate our au gratin potatoes, I had to concentrate on chewing in order not to scream, "Why didn't we all go on a double date? That's what FRIENDS do! And why have you still not mentioned that she was one of the girls you kissed? That her name was NADJA? And why, oh, pray tell, did you not tell me?"

I made it my mission to hunt down every single e-mail that Nadja the Aryan Hussy and Wilhelm the Suspicious had ever shared. Right away I noticed he replied to only a fraction of the e-mails she sent him, a fact that left her extremely nonplussed but that lent me a lovely sense of superiority. *Ha!* I thought. *You're in love with him, but he's mine! MINE!* But then, a few e-mails later, any and all superiority I felt was replaced by seething anger: Along with complaining about his sporadic communication, Nadja the Vicious had become skilled at subtly weaving in bitchy comments about his "L.A. treasure." Well, this L.A. treasure was not going to sit idly by and endure digs behind her back. No, this L.A. treasure was going to ask how her boyfriend felt about the whole situation, by calling Erlin!

"He doesn't care about her. You need to believe me on this. She may be in love with him, but he's in love with *you.*"

I smiled. *Take that, you Aryan spawn of Satan.*

"To him," Erlin continued, "she's nothing more than a fly buzzing in the corner of his vision. It's you whom he sees."

A fly? A six-foot-tall blond, gorgeous *fly?* I think not. Nonetheless, I tried to embrace the sentiment by repeating in my mind *Nadja is a fly, Nadja is a fly.* The crucial thing to remember was that he didn't care about her. Most likely, I figured, he had no idea how she felt about him. Okay, that last one was hard to sell, even to me. Though men are notoriously clueless about all things to do with women, Nadja was so glaringly obvious with her feelings and intentions that she might as well have been sending him e-mails with a subject line that read "Hi, Wilhelm! I love you and am trying to break up your relationship!"

But it was clear from his sporadic responses as well as from what Erlin had said that Wilhelm did not share Nadja's amorous intentions. Ultimately, when I really thought about it, what had he done wrong? If anything he'd been trying to spare me needless worry. He couldn't help it if she was in love with him. He had no control over her feelings. And honestly, I myself was still friends with guys I'd kissed. Was that a crime? No. Of course, I knew myself and knew I could be trusted around those guys, but then again, what evidence did I have that proved Wilhelm wasn't trustworthy? All I had was proof that he barely kept up a friendship with a girl he'd once kissed, and to prevent any unnecessary worry, he'd omitted it. That was it. There was nothing to worry about.

Unfortunately, his behavior wasn't helping me forget about the Aryan Fly. Perhaps sensing something was amiss, he became distant, his romantic talk of our future muffled once more into silence. What the hell? Only a month before, he'd been spouting plans for our life together, had taken me to Hawaii and babbled endlessly about how much I meant to him. Now it was as if I were simply a lump on the couch, a frilly annoyance that didn't match his Lucite decor. Nadja. I knew it had to do with her. With renewed vigor I threw myself into monitoring his e-mails and prowling the depths of his apartment, determined to find any and all evidence of Nadja–tivity.

One morning, after he'd left for work, I logged on as usual to check his e-mails. There in the subject line was a confirmation from American Airlines. Hmmm. Are we taking a trip? Maybe the distance I'd sensed was in fact secret vacation planning? Sure, we'd just gotten back from vacation, but American Airlines is, well, an airline, so it's usually safe to say plane tickets are involved. *Click.* There was his name, and the details for a flight to Frankfurt in just a couple of weeks.

Germany—to meet his parents! My heart began to pound. I scrolled down. And down. And down. Then I could scroll no more. That was it. My name was nowhere to be found. I went back to his in–box, searching for another, perhaps separate, confirmation, but the only other e-mail that day was one from Dustin.

I tried to breathe. What had happened to his promises that the next time he went home he'd take me? Didn't he still want me to meet his parents? Was this . . . was this to visit *The Fly?*

Determined to learn more about this trip, I began reading other e-mails. All other e-mails. I got to the one from Dustin, which was, of course, in German, and was actually a reply to an earlier e-mail I'd somehow missed. Not a problem. By now I was well practiced in this little routine, so within seconds I had it translated and ready for perusal. I immediately scrolled to the bottom and began reading the original e-mail, from Wilhelm to Dustin. Okay. Blah blah blah, chitchat, yadda yadda, all normal guy stuff made slightly cryptic by what must have fallen through the gaps in the bridge from German to English . . . and then I saw my name. I skipped to that part. "You by now must be in knowledge of the reunification of Sarah and I. Weakness was my battle, and now we are together paired." Weakness was my battle? Getting back together made him weak? I kept reading, and that's when I saw, in torturously clear, concise English, the last line of his e-mail: "Did I make a mistake?"

Oh. My. God. Quickly I scrolled up and read Dustin's response, some lame quip about how it was never a mistake to kiss Julia Roberts. That was it. Though I hate being compared to Julia Roberts, I must admit I said a silent blessing for Dustin's existence, since I suppose he had indeed taken my . . . or Julia's . . . side. Whatever.

It was undeniable. I was screwed. Why, why, why, why don't I learn my lessons? After finding The Insect's e-mails, I should've *known* that snooping was bad and could only lead to unanswerable questions. So there I was, yet again filled with questions I could never utter aloud but would instead be forced to drill into Wilhelm's head with my deadly and penetrating stares. Never could I scream, "You begged me to take you back, so where the hell do you get off thinking it was a mistake only a month later? And why are you just now telling your friend we're together? Were you ashamed? And why are you going to Germany? WHO IS IN GERMANY? And don't say your parents!"

I had to address this. That night Wilhelm came over. It was late, he'd just gotten off work, and I could tell he was tired. He sat down to take off his shoes and I bided my time, waiting for the right moment, waiting, waiting, waiting . . . waiting till he got one shoe off.

"So. I guess your friend Dustin isn't very good with the whole e-mail process."

"What?"

"Dustin. E-mails. The two don't go together. Why, you ask? I'll tell you."

"Okay."

"Okay. So he went to reply to an e-mail you sent him, but when he did he accidentally *sent it to everyone in his entire address book.*" I don't know where I came up with that; it just hit me in the moment and flew out of my mouth.

"What?"

Stay strong. Strong and confident. "Uh-huh. So Gina goes to check her e-mails and there's one from Dustin, apparently intended for you. She saw my name, and not knowing what it was, forwarded it to me. So tell me, Wilhelm, did you decide whether or not it was a mistake to get back together with me? Or is kissing Julia Roberts a good enough reason?"

I must admit, I felt a touch bad. The poor boy was frozen with his hand on the heel of his shoe and his eyes filled with immobilizing bewilderment. *Do not feel bad.* I charged forth. "Well?"

A few things helped sell my grossly convoluted story. One, he was tired. Two, he was confused. Three, he was unsuspecting. Never would it have occurred to him that I was really as insane as I was. Though I gathered by what came next that he was beginning to skim the surface. "Wasn't that e-mail," he said, his voice deepening, *"in German?"*

I couldn't go on the defensive. I had to continue, strong and on the attack. "It was about *me*, Wilhelm; I saw my name. I had every right to translate it."

"I see. You *translated* it. And you didn't find that to be an invasion of privacy?"

I must say, I didn't care for his tone. "No. The e-mail was *sent* to me, and was *about* me. Don't try to turn this around to mask what you did. The only subject we need to address is *what the hell you meant by questioning getting back together with me.* That really hurt me, you know."

He shook his head. "I wasn't serious. It's how we talk. Look. The last time I was with Dustin, you and I were apart. The whole time I spent crying in my beer about *you.* So this, what you read, was just macho speak. It wasn't serious."

I stared him down. In support of his claim, I *had* seen him and Dustin interact, and in general it had involved German-accented impersonations of plastered frat boys who blabbed for hours about absolutely nothing of importance. It appeared to almost be a rule, a mandate of sorts, not to broach real subjects, to steer clear of anything of significance, and to display not one emotion other than drunken oblivious joviality. "So, you weren't serious?"

He laughed. "No. I'm *happy* to be back with you. I'm not *questioning.* But," he said as he started down the hall to my room, "there is one thing you won't be happy about."

I followed him, my nerves prickly with panic.

"I have to go back to Germany to renew my visa. I know I said I'd take you when I next went, but it's not the right time. It's in two weeks. I need to go alone now. It won't be a long trip."

I sat on the bed, heartsick. How could I argue? I wanted him to want to take me, and clearly he didn't. Sure I could force my way on the plane, but I've never been fond of tagging along. I need to be the center of attention, not an afterthought bringing up the rear, not the unexpected guest who eats all the Brie and then turns a lovely dinner into a cramped, elbow-jabbing, knee-bumping culinary catastrophe. And besides, getting upset about *this* could incite him to revisit the story of the e-mail and its complicated path to my in-box. No, the best course of action right then was to do nothing.

"Well, if that's how you feel, then I understand."

Wilhelm's eyes went wide. "Really? You're okay with this?"

Oooh, too suspicious. "Well, no, of course not. I'm actually really hurt because it was a promise. But if it's not the right time, it's not the right time. I can't argue with that; I basically have no choice but to understand." I smiled, and patted the bed. "But I bet there's a way you can make it up to me."

He nodded as he undid his belt buckle, his trousers barely skimming the floor before he scooped them up and hung them neatly on a hanger. "I already thought of that. You know those chocolates, the nougat ones you somehow found in my closet and ate all of?"

I smiled seductively. "Who could forget something so *orgasmic*?" And honestly, I hadn't been able to forget those chocolates. For the past week I'd been dreaming of them, and just the other day I'd craved one (fine, one *box*) and as a last resort had ended up buying a Hershey's bar and then verbally abusing it for not living up to its chocolate potential. It was disturbing. Those German chocolates he'd so cruelly—and futilely, might I add—hidden from me had ruined me for life.

He folded back the covers and slipped into bed. "I'll bring some back for you. Maybe even a couple boxes." He sank deep into the bed under the layers of blankets. "Mmmm. You got new fabric softener. This is heaven."

From the corner of the bed I watched him. He closed his eyes, his smile lessening only slightly as he turned on his side and pulled the covers around his face. Then, just like that, he was asleep, drifting off into downy soft dreams of mountain springs. The bastard.

One thing you don't do is send your boyfriend off to visit an Aryan whore with a bad taste for relationships in his mouth. Essentially, I realized, that was the situation I'd created. So before he left, I tried to be cool, sexy, fun, and undemanding. I figured while the sneaky wench was preparing an arsenal of evil comments about Wilhelm's "L.A. treasure," this L.A. treasure would engage in a preemptive strike by increasing her own worth. For everything she might say, I bestowed upon my dupe of a boyfriend an action that would help form my defense. "No," I envisioned him countering, "she's not a nag! Just last week I didn't call for an entire day and she didn't care! And she actually said she'd like to make enough money so she could support me and I wouldn't have to work! She's amazing!"

Though my newfound coolness seemed to have a positive effect on him, I still sensed distance. Now and then I'd catch him staring off at nothing, and in my mind it was an alternate life he was viewing, one without me and my neuroses. *But,* I'd remind myself, *I wouldn't have these neuroses if he'd been honest about Nadja in the first place.* If he had told me about her, then when I'd found the first e-mail from her, it would've simply been evidence of her already spelled out existence. I would have told myself it was nothing I hadn't already known, chided myself for being so ridiculous, and moved on. *He* was the one who'd created the situation with his secrecy; *he* was the one who'd given me reason to freak out.

And freak out was what I did. The second Wilhelm told me he was boarding the plane and had to shut off his cell phone, I called Erlin. The battle began.

"You don't need to worry, Sarah. He's faithful. He'll spend time with her, but as a friend. Nothing more."

This was what he'd been saying ever since I'd learned of the trip, but I needed daily reassurance that the future hadn't changed. After three days with Wilhelm off in the land of temptation, I called in more troops. I figured if four more psychics concurred with Erlin, my trust would be fortified, and then, maybe, I could relax.

Three agreed that Wilhelm had no interest in the Aryan Temptress or her cunning ways. And whereas that's certainly the majority, the truth is, it only takes one, one hairline crack in the crystal, one attachment with a virus, one moth let loose among cashmere . . . one psychic who makes a claim that haunts you. And that one, the dissenter, the rebel, the mutineer, was none other than sweet, soothing Southern Misty Mystical.

"Something needs to be *healed* in their relationship." (Sumthin' needs to be hee-eeled.) "There's like this unfinished business with them? A connection, something almost karmic. I just—I don't know what to tell you, hon. There's no goin' forth with this wound so open."

Misty was my mothering psychic, the one whose lap I wanted to crawl into, yet her words had basically flung me to the ground, her once calming rocking chair now crushing my outstretched fingers. What was she saying? My voice splintered with fear. "Are you serious? Is it something romantic that needs to happen?"

"It's hard to tell. I mean, the romance is there for sure, on her part. She's completely in love with him."

Fabulous. "Well, what—what does he think about that? How does he react?"

There was a short silence, during which time I managed to chew through all the nails on my right hand and then start in with those on the left.

"I can't say for sure. I just can't." (I jest cay-ant.) "I can feel his *intentions*, to be good? But it's hard for him."

"So, you think I should be worried?"

"If *you* think you should be worried, I'd say you're right on with that instinct."

Way to sugarcoat it, Misty. I tried to think of another question, one that would open the door for Misty to proclaim, "Well, of course you'll still marry," but in the silence of my pause I heard a rooster crow—which, in Los Angeles, is actually very normal. Still, I read it as a sign of her betrayal and tearfully hung up the phone, no longer sure whom I could trust.

My one source of comfort, oddly enough, was Wilhelm himself. He called religiously, every day, and sometimes even twice. *He missed me.* Only on Wednesday was there silence, a collection of long dark hours when my mind went wild. But the next day I heard from him, and the next, and the next. There was nothing to worry about; he'd just been busy. Then, one afternoon he completely put my mind at ease by bringing up the Aryan Vulture all on his own.

Sarah Lassez

"All I dealt with today was my visa. The whole day. I was supposed to have lunch with Nadja but had to cancel to deal with red tape."

"Nadja?" I asked innocently. I was frozen, filled with fear of whatever he'd say next, as if a piano were teetering on a window ledge and I was the innocent schmuck standing on the sidewalk below.

"Yes. My friend from Germany who visited in L.A."

Friend. He's calling her just a friend. All is fine. Of course, he'd never officially admitted that his "friend from Germany" who'd visited in L.A. was indeed the Nadja he'd admitted to kissing way back when, but there was no bringing this up now. "Oh, right. That's too bad. So, you're not gonna get to see her at all?"

"No. I already saw her, so it's not a big deal. It just made me mad that my whole day was spent with this visa."

He'd already seen her. But if there were something to hide, he wouldn't have brought her up on his own, would he? Of course not! "That does suck. How's her boyfriend? Did you finally get to meet him?"

"No, they broke up. He got a little crazy at the end; she had to walk away."

Oh, right, they broke up. Naturally.

I attempted to laugh, and said jokingly, "Oh, no! Wilhelm, remember that dream I had? What if she's in love with you? What if now that she's single she's gonna make her move?"

To this he laughed as well, though just for a second. Then he wisely snapped into prevent-girlfriend-from-going-crazy mode. "Don't worry. We're just friends. Nothing more. I don't feel *anything* romantic for her. Not at all. And anyhow, I won't have time to see her again. The rest of the trip is family, family, family."

Thank God.

With that conversation a huge weight was lifted. I believed he was honest and faithful, but what was more comforting was that even if he weren't to be trusted, it didn't matter, since he wasn't going to see the hussy again. All was fine! In fact, it was better than fine. The worst thing that could have happened did: He'd been alone with a boyfriendless Nadja, and yet he'd passed the test. From here on out I had nothing to worry about, no reasons to doubt, nothing left to snoop for. I was free! Just three more days till he came home, till life became wonderful once again.

A week of German food—everything boiled, involving cabbage or ending ominously in "wurst"—put Wilhelm in the mood for sushi, so the second his plane landed, we made plans to meet up at Chaya, our favorite restaurant. Enticed with visions of my magnificent boyfriend and spicy tuna rolls, both equally alluring, I was out the door in minutes and speeding toward the west side.

Beneath a beautiful Japanese painted ceiling, we were reunited. Wilhelm, being the thoughtful boyfriend he was, bestowed upon me a bag of gifts, the most important being the chocolate I'd coveted and prayed for almost as much as I'd prayed that the Aryan Cow would slip and tumble off the planet. Everything was ideal. I had my boyfriend back, I no longer had to worry about his loyalty, I had my chocolate, and now I also had a plate full of sushi. As I mashed wasabi into my little bowl of soy sauce, I asked how his trip had gone and listened to the tales of all his family outings and the nightmare he'd endured getting his visa renewed.

I chewed and smiled and made the appropriate commiserating sounds. Then he said the word "Nadja" right as I accidentally ingested a glob of pure wasabi. My nose shot with pain as if a nail were being hammered into it, and my eyes became tearing sinkholes. Water wasn't helping, and all the ice was stuck at the bottom. Furiously I waved my hand in front of my mouth—the ridiculous and universal reaction to eating something fiery, as if somehow the miniscule breeze I was creating would have any sort of impact on the fact that my head was ablaze.

"Tell me about her," I managed to squeak out once I'd found the ability to open my mouth again. I must add that I said this without a trace of jealousy, with genuine interest in this friend of his, actually happy that we could now talk freely and openly about her. I must also say that I expected only a few words about her—a brief overview of what they'd done—and then for him to move on to another topic.

What I got, however, was a distressingly detailed description of the time they spent together, an account that started with them meeting at her place in the city, where he left his car. Then they ventured off together in her little Audi. Gray, with black interior. She needed to buy something for her mother, so they went shopping together and found the perfect scarf. Gift secured, they slung back a few drinks at the bar where her sister worked, a place with an outside beer garden and rickety green chairs. Afterward they journeyed to dinner, where Nadja had coq au vin—which, may I just add, translates to "cock with wine"—and he had a salmon filet in a ginger emulsion sauce. They shared a slice of strawberry Grand Marnier cake.

As he described the cake—the most heavenly thing he'd ever had, with strawberries so flavorful that there was no way it could ever taste as good in the States, because fruits and vegetables in Europe are far superior—it occurred to me that it must have been getting late in the day, and his parents lived an hour from the city. But he didn't go home then. No, some friends of hers met up with them, and the group then headed off to another bar. *Okay.* More drinks were had. People danced. And then, he said, because it was so late, he stayed at her place and left the next morning.

Maybe it was that my hand, still holding the chopsticks, was frozen in midair. Maybe it was that I actually hadn't moved in quite a while, and one might also have deduced that I wasn't breathing. Whatever it was, Wilhelm quickly realized that the last detail might not have been wise to share.

"In separate beds, in separate rooms," he added hastily.

Suddenly the shock I'd been in wore off. My heart started back up and began beating so loudly I wouldn't have been surprised at all had the man at the table next to us leaned over and said, "You there! Keep that pounding to yourself!"

I took the last sip of water, and of course now was when the pile of ice at the bottom of the glass freed itself, and shot into my face. Calmly, eerily calmly, I patted the drops of water with my napkin, and then smoothed the linen on my lap. "In separate rooms?"

"Well, sort of."

Sort of? Sort of, in a situation like this, didn't cut it. I was about to inform him of this when he began describing the layout of the room, a description that's usually not necessary if there are indeed *two separate rooms.* But apparently, in the case of all things Nadja, it wasn't that simple. No, he then started actually drawing the floor plan of the room on a napkin. An L-shaped room, a wall here, a wall there. The bed was from the seventies, he threw in, and beneath it was another bed that slid out, very cool. Then the dresser was here—

"Wait. You spent the night, in the same room, in a bed that was attached to her bed?"

"No. Not attached. We moved it to a different part of the room. And the room was mostly two rooms, because of the L." Then with a deep breath he firmly added, "Sarah, I was *drinking.* I could not drive home."

This last statement was intended to end the conversation. I was supposed to be thankful my responsible boyfriend hadn't put his life and others' in danger. It certainly wouldn't have been appropriate to say, "I don't care if you were drunk. You should've been a good boyfriend, gotten behind the damn wheel, and hightailed it outta there!"

For a second I think he figured he'd wrestled himself free. But honestly—when I pictured them sliding a bed from beneath her bed, and then going to great lengths to move it to another part of this crazy-shaped room—I wanted to laugh. There was no way that happened. Besides, if it was understood they were just friends and there truly *was* nothing more, they wouldn't have *needed* to move the damn bed to a secure location. Hence, if they needed to keep the beds separated from each other, it was to avoid temptation, in which case a few feet of carpeted floor wasn't much of a barrier, especially not after a night of bottomless steins of Bitburger and endless shots of Jägermeister.

Yes, clearly the Aryan Huntress had set a trap, one that involved a sketchy L-shaped room and a crazy bed from the seventies. I felt sick. I didn't say anything; I didn't move. I had to wait till the urge to puke passed. Wilhelm, meanwhile, observed me with concern, and then, perhaps thinking the danger was over, resumed eating.

"But," I finally ventured, "you must've known you'd spend the night there, because you left your car at her place. It was planned."

The skin around his widow's peak caught the overhead light, shiny and smooth. *Mr. Burns*, I thought, *what have you done?*

And that was when I left my body. Suddenly I was hovering beside myself. This horrible mealtime conversation was happening to someone else, to that poor girl who looked just like me and was sitting in front of a half-eaten spicy tuna roll that had at some point been stabbed with chopsticks. I heard the distant claim, "We're just friends." I thought of all the e-mails he'd kept secret, all the bitchy comments she'd made about me. I noticed that Mr. Burns was talking again, but now all I heard was Misty Mystical, questioning his loyalty.

Until, that is, I heard the words "one-night stand."

I snapped back into my body. "What? Repeat what you just said."

"I said, we're just friends. She's someone I slept with *once*. Nothing more. Ever since, we've been nothing more than friends. That was a long time ago. Okay? Nothing happened recently. This is not a big deal. I'm with *you*."

Now my heart was back to furiously pounding. I bypassed the water and went straight for the sake, surprised the thumping didn't knock it right out of my hand. Okay, so way back when, they'd had *sex*. He'd told me they'd just *kissed*. Call me old-fashioned, but I actually consider the two activities to be different.

Somehow, I realized, I was speaking. "What one, what day that you spent the night there, this time?" Was I making sense? "On this trip. Which day."

He paused, then said, "Wednesday."

Wednesday. The day I never heard from him. The collection of dark hours. The night my mind went wild. No longer could I talk over the pounding in my chest, which had spread to my head and become a dull, throbbing sensation, so I sat there and sipped my sake. Refilled my sake. Sipped my sake. Was he really trying to say that *spending the night* with a girl he'd lied to me about—a girl he had kept secret and actually had sex with, a girl who'd shown her hatred for me in e-mail after clandestine e-mail, a girl he'd spent all night drinking with, on a trip that I as his girlfriend should've accompanied him on—*wasn't a big deal?*

If there were cool girls out there who could have handled that, I was not one of them. He'd gone too far. Whether or not anything had happened between them was irrelevant. I felt betrayed and disrespected. The fact that I would always wonder was enough; the fact that I was even *able* to wonder was enough. I needed someone I knew was honest, someone I could trust without doubt, someone with whom I didn't live in fear of what I might uncover. Wilhelm, I realized sadly, was not that person.

Right there, beneath the beautiful Japanese painted ceiling, I broke up with him. I told him it was over. I told him why. I told him I felt disrespected and betrayed and would *not* be treated like that.

His expression was that of suspicious disbelief, as if he were convinced someone had a video camera on him and soon there'd be the big revelation, the big "Ha! It was a joke!" Despite everything I'd just said, he wasn't getting it. Until, that is, I stood up. Then he quickly began talking, justifying his actions, telling me this was crazy, asking me not to go.

Calmly I collected my presents—because, damnit, I'd earned them—and turned and strolled out the door. It turned out that even crazy codependent girls have their boundaries, and Wilhelm had just crossed one of them.

9

And She's Down for the Count!

SOME PEOPLE HANDLE BREAKUPS WELL. I IMAGINE they're the same strange souls who get their oil changed every three months, have their annual physicals annually, and don't rear-end the car in front of them because they happened to be cutting their split ends while driving. Gina, for example, is one of those people. The second the words are uttered and the tearful good-byes are said, she's spurred into action, embarking on a methodical search-and-destroy mission that involves removing any and all pictures of the ex and any and all evidence of the ex. House sufficiently ex-proofed, she cleans, *for hours*, and then drives to the store for the proper breakup accoutrements—tissues with aloe, food, wine, smokes, and chocolate bars—essentially preparing to hibernate in comfort. Once all is neat and tidy and the jagged edges of fond memories have been filed down, then she's ready to mourn and grieve in her own little Virgo way. At this point she allows herself to collapse in tears. "Allows herself" being the key words.

Me? I'm a bit different. I break down because I have no choice. I break down in a messy house, and it gets messier by the second. I break down alongside photographs of my ex and end up wailing and clutching those photographs to my chest as if illustrating to the universe just how my heart had been broken. I break down wearing clothes he gave me, or wrapped in a sweatshirt he left behind, and I refuse to change for days. I don't spare myself pain, I *embrace* it. It would no longer be appropriate to call me a human being. A "useless mass of pain and raw nerves" would be far more fitting, and this is only in the initial breakup stage, when my emotions are still somewhat muted by shock.

So, no, I didn't handle the Wilhelm breakup well.

Three days into it and I was embracing my pain from the floor, though I had no idea how I'd ended up on the floor, since one delightful aspect of my states of extreme misery is a lack of consciousness. Not that I pass out, no; I'm simply not present at times. My crying jags are like supernatural events, essentially abducting me, and when I stop, when I finally manage to breathe without heaving, I find myself in situations of which I have no recollection—perhaps clutching a shoe or lying in the bathtub. So at this particular moment I'd just found the ability to breathe again and was on the floor with my head on a stack of magazines. In my hand, for some reason, was a little gold Buddha statue. With no motivation to move, I simply stared at the fibers of my Pottery Barn rug. *Hello, old friend,* I thought. *Here we are again.*

When the phone rang, I rolled my head slightly in the

direction of the noise. I refused to answer. So far I'd only told a couple of people, including Gina, who'd offered to come over and clean, though even that I'd refused. My apartment was beyond repair, but it was fitting, it matched my mood, and I knew her energy would be wasted. The second she left, or even while she was there, I might be overcome with the urge to heave the couch cushions across the room or rip the flowers from a vase and hurl their shreds at the wall. Besides, being social wasn't something I wished to attempt. Forming sentences was asking too much. I couldn't even call *psychics*—which is when you know it's bad—partly because of the inability to form sentences, and partly because I honestly didn't think I had a future.

The phone continued to ring, and finally my machine picked up.

"Sarah, it's me."

I swallowed. I hadn't moved, yet somehow I began sweating. Wilhelm—otherwise known as the Antichrist—should no longer be allowed to use the "It's me" phrase. That right was revoked the second he spent the night at the Aryan Whore's house. He was no longer "me." He'd never be "me" again. In fact, he shouldn't even be "he." He should be "it." It should be it.

"I cannot believe you're serious about this," it said. "Vot's the big deal?"

I stared at my dresser, as somewhere up there was my answering machine, the source of the ridiculous and defensive words. I don't know why, but suddenly its German accent was strong. Had it always been like that? How had I not noticed before? Not only the accent, but the way it spoke:

level, controlled, cold, and devoid of feeling. Exactly the kind of man who would break your heart. I hated him. It. Whatever. But I also loved him. I *definitely* hated that I loved him. *For the love of God, just make him go away.*

"I did nothing wrong. It's not like you're my *wife*. I'm young; I can do vot I please."

And then he hung up. I blinked. Some things, I must say, are just not necessary—like shooting someone in the toe after you've already stabbed them twenty-three times, ripped out their vital organs, and severed their head. Or like this phone call. *I'm not his wife?* Thank you, Wilhelm. I just adore it when people mash salt into my wounds.

Two more days passed, a fact of which I was aware only as the proof hit my door. Literally. I was lying on the floor in my living room, crying softly, when something slammed against my front door. I sat up. The shock stopped the tears. I made my way down the stairs to inspect, knowing it was one of two things: Either a crazed and blind pigeon had just met its maker, or Wilhelm, dying, had used his last bit of energy to get to my house and knock on my door, and was now slumped on the front steps with a letter pinned to his shirt explaining that a new and exotic disease had made him behave like an imbecile and that in truth he *did* love me and would do *anything* to get me back, but alas it was too late.

I opened the door. The newspaper. The Sunday paper. Which meant only five days had passed since the breakup, and also that it was currently around four a.m. I looked up at the sky. It was actually dark. Why was I awake? I went back inside, dumped the paper on the floor, and flopped into bed, where I continued to cry until I somehow, mercifully, fell asleep.

When I finally awoke, it was to one of those something-happened-what-was-it moments, one of those horrible moments when you wake and your eyes adjust to the light and everything feels right and good but for a slight nagging sensation, and you think, *Hmmm, something happened, what was it?* And then, then whatever it was you'd been trying so hard to forget slams into you like an eighteen-wheeler driven by a man named Travis who doesn't do so well on whiskey but has just polished off a bottle of Southern Comfort—and once again you want to die.

So yeah, I wanted to die. And another thing I noticed was that my room was *really* bright, painfully so, but unfortunately the damn curtains were all the way over by the windows, and the windows were all the way over on the wall. Slowly I got out of bed to kill the light, but on my way there I happened to see my closet, which was much closer and already dark, so into the closet I went. Without much grace I curled up beneath some dresses and pulled the door shut. For the first time I noticed a very dirty tiny arched window. It didn't let in much light, but unfortunately it let in just enough that I could see the fabric of one of the dresses that hung by my nose . . . a dress I'd once worn to the Cannes Film Festival.

It hit me, as I sat crouched and crying in my closet, that I had once had a life. I'd gone to Sundance. I'd gone to Cannes. I'd been a working actress. I'd had a future. I'd worn lipstick and styled my hair. Hell, I'd *washed* my hair. Now? Now I was unemployed, I was unshowered, I couldn't stop crying, and I had a rather sharp ski boot buckle digging into my ass. Since when did I own ski boots? I looked around, sniffling. *So this is where Onyx lived for all those years.*

And that's when I saw it, flung into a dark corner, the bag of gifts Wilhelm had given me. Okay, I admit that having kept the gifts meant part of me had hopes we'd reconcile, in which case having tossed everything he'd so thoughtfully picked out would've been bad. But now, now that he plainly was not going to see the error of his ways—after all, he was *young* and could do *vot he pleased* and I wasn't his *wife*—now I could safely destroy it all. I grabbed the bag. *Mmm. Chocolates.* I'd destroy everything but the chocolates. I tore into a box and started chewing. Dare I say I was in a mild state of happiness—until, in the bag, I spotted the ugly rose-shaped stud earrings he'd also given me, earrings I immediately decided would look good only if they were protruding from his bleeding neck. Heh–heh.

The chocolate gave me the energy I needed to get up, throw out the rest of the gifts, verge on being human, and check my e-mails. Fine, fine: check Wilhelm's e-mails. Ever since I'd determined his password, checking his e-mails had become so routine that I'd checked them before I checked my own, and in fact now and then—when we were still together—had even read e-mails *to me* in his sent folder before I'd found them in my in-box.

I typed in the magic "HugBoss" and sat back, waiting to be horrified, prepared for the worst. Visions of e-mails from Nadja with the subject line "Hooray! You finally ditched the old basket of eggs!" tripped through my mind. God I hated her.

Once everything was refreshed and up to date, I leaned in. A

Sarah Lassez

few sale notices from Loehmann's, a lot of spam informing him of great deals on ink cartridges. Other than that, nothing new.

Good. Maybe he's too miserable to write anyone. Just to be sure he was suffering, I decided to ask a psychic. I admit, the fact that I'd made it six whole days after the breakup before having a reading, had nothing to do with willpower . . . but still, my inability to speak coherently had probably saved me a lot of money. Therefore, after the first reading failed to comfort me and once I'd had a few more chocolates, I figured I deserved the treat of four or five more readings.

And just like that, what little functioning I'd had in the world was gone. I didn't leave my house. I barely changed. I hardly ate. I'd wake, cry, check Wilhelm's e-mails, check my own e-mails, cry, call half a dozen psychics, cry, check his e-mails one more time, cry a bit more, have an Erlin night cap, go to sleep, and then start the process again. Let me tell you, I made up for those six days without readings with a vengeance, essentially embarking on a psychic binge to end all psychic binges. It would be an understatement to say that I was worse off than I'd been the first time we broke up, though I suppose one prime difference was that after round one I'd been sad and in disbelief; after round two I was sad and toying with mental instability.

The only thing that changed from day to day was the amount of crying I did. Eventually the tears lessened, which I saw not as a sign that I was getting better, but as a sign that my readings would be much more efficient now that I was no longer paying to hear myself sob.

Many psychics confirmed that yes, Wilhelm had cheated on

me. Though those readings left me momentarily vindicated, they also flung me into a tailspin of utter sadness that forced me to seek out *another* reading to be assured that no, he was faithful and had always loved me and had never cheated. No longer did I have any clue what I wanted to be told, and soon the definitions of "good reading" and "bad reading" became interchangeable. Still, I continued to call, convinced that each psychic was in competition with the last to make me feel worse. Did they perchance know each other? Were they taking bets to see how fast I'd lose my mind? Erlin, by the way, still insisted Wilhelm and I would marry.

It goes without saying that I couldn't afford these readings. The issue of my massive debt and barely-there unemployment checks versus my tendency to spend *a lot* on psychics was one I knew I had to address, but the problem was that stopping just didn't seem to be an option. No. I had to think of something else, and was thus quite pleased with myself when I discovered the free three minutes that Psychicdom and a couple of other sites offered. Yes, apparently when resting your future and your wallet in a psychic's hands, all you need is three minutes in which to test and deem the psychic worthy. Technically each caller is supposed to get only one free call, but me, being the crafty and determined mentally ill girl I was, I decided there was no such thing as *only* one free call. I called from my home phone, from my cell phone, and then from the cell phones of any and all friends who made the mistake of visiting me to see how I was. "Fine," I'd tell them, "I'm fine. But can I borrow your phone? Be right back."

And the funny thing is that I really thought I'd duped them.

Me, the obsessed girl in sweatpants with the unwashed hair and the wild glint in her eye, I thought I'd pulled one over on the machine of the psychic industry by collecting free minutes. I was quite proud of myself. The catch, of course, was that a future cannot be told in just three minutes, and since the psychics knew they were being tested, their prime concern was getting callers to love them—and that didn't always involve telling the truth. Saying, "No, it really *is* you. He can't stand the sight of you, and yeah, he *did* notice the twenty pounds you gained," is not going to lead to repeat business. They need to get paid; they're not stupid. That's why when I pretended to be a new caller in need of my free three minutes and was told Wilhelm had never cheated on me, that he loved me and would come around within a couple months, I was disbelieving. Such a rosy reading was highly suspect, and therefore I'd been forced to call another psychic, one from my stable of regulars, pay for the call, get upset, and thus call someone else.

My system was flawed, to say the least.

Three weeks into the breakup—three weeks of calling psychics and crying and checking Wilhelm's e-mails—I decided to spice things up. I was going to *leave my house.*

My car was in dire need of an oil change, even though I never went anywhere, and since I had no food except for a dangerously dwindling supply of chocolates and my requisite heartbreak meal of Pad Thai noodles, a trip to the grocery store was also urgently needed. Of course I could afford neither activity, so I instead opted to pay for a live psychic reading.

This was a huge step for me, as it involved both leaving my

house and driving to the Valley, where the psychic lived. Leaving my house for the first time was already difficult, but leaving it in order to head to the Valley was a little like an agoraphobic deciding her first venture in public should be a day at Disneyland. As the land became flatter, the sky grew smoggier, and the temperature rose by about fifteen degrees, I seriously began questioning my sanity. I hated the Valley. Even the people who lived in the Valley hated the Valley, and were notorious for trying to disguise the location of their homes by saying things like "I live in Sherman Oaks," which to the untrained ear sounds like "I live in Sherman Oaks," but to the true Los Angeleno it sounds a whole hell of a lot like "I live in the Valley."

At any rate I was desperate, and desperation will make you do crazy things like drive to the Valley to meet a psychic. More than anything I just needed to hear that life would once again be okay, but this psychic also came highly recommended, and she practiced psychometry, the art of reading by way of holding a personal belonging. No matter how severe my heartbreak, a new form of fortune-telling was impossible to resist.

An hour later, sweating from the grueling heat, I arrived at Carol Ann's house, a single-story slab of stucco with windows, a door, and a street address that was six digits long (another delightful feature of the Valley). No time was wasted with pleasantries, and with barely a word I was led to a kitchen that smelled so strongly of Pine-Sol that I suspected she hadn't been cleaning with it but had instead opted to use it as a room spray. Was she high on the fumes? Would that affect my reading? Or was it what made her psychic? Perhaps she employed some strange cleaning-agent-fumes portal into the future?

In a charming I'm–on–the–other–line–what–do–you–need–and–make–it–fast manner, she asked to hold my personal belonging. I'd come prepared and was wearing my antique Victorian gold moonstone ring, a ring I loved and had bought for myself (no big surprise there) years ago. Without another word she took the ring and held it in her fist, her eyes closed. She was silent. And silent. And silent for so long I began to wonder if she was fighting to stay conscious and not succumb to the fumes, but then I began to wonder if perhaps she was confused by receiving information on the ring's *original* owner's life. *What, what's this?* I imagined her thinking. *On your trip to the cobbler you'll meet a gentleman in a fine pair of top boots with something they call a* zipper? *Rejoice, for he is a good Protestant? What's this now about taking care while chewing the mutton tonight?*

Finally she set my ring on the table and glared at me. "There are so many *holes* in your aura that it's impossible to read you."

"Oh." What?

She shook her head. "You've had too many readings. Ideally you need six months after a reading before you get another one."

I laughed.

"*At least* forty–eight hours. The way it works is that every time you get a reading, the reader taps into your energy to receive the messages. When they do this, you're left with a hole in your spirit. You," she said, pointing to me in case I didn't understand who she was referring to, "look like Swiss cheese. You're all holes. Come back in six months."

And that was it. I was hustled out the door, herded back into my car, and sent on my cheesy way. I must admit, I did feel like there were holes in my spirit, but in my humble opinion the drill at fault had had a German accent. It had *nothing* to do with psychics or readings. Was there anything wrong with my aura? No. She was probably just incompetent as a psychic. Her Pine-Sol powers had failed her, and she'd blamed *me*. Other psychics could read me just fine—and to prove this I called a few the second I got home.

All right, I admit it. Her words stuck with me. At this point I was averaging at least half a dozen readings a day, the worst I'd ever been, and even I was pretty sure that wasn't right. As Benjamin Franklin said, the definition of insanity is doing the same thing over and over and expecting different results. That was what I did. Day after day after day. And by the way, when a crazy person begins to question her own sanity, you know she's got problems.

I'd hit rock bottom; I knew this. This wasn't just your garden-variety heartbreak. This was everything I'd gone through before, multiplied times ten and woven with a despair and hopelessness I'd never known possible. I was lost. I had no direction, no purpose, and the only things that kept me going were the words of people I *paid* to talk to. All the built-up pain from ten years of Hollywood's rejection and all the failures of my relationships had finally taken their toll, and at last my nerves simply gave out.

I'd reached a dead end. I was single, over thirty, and a failure, and on top of that I had evidently lost my mind somewhere along the way. With horror I noticed I wasn't even cute anymore. I looked as though I were a heroin addict who'd just gone cold turkey, my body far too thin, my gaunt face now sporting strange reddish patches just beneath my eyes.

In a plea for help I broke down and called my parents. I'd been avoiding them for a while. I knew they'd sense something was wrong, and I hadn't wanted them to worry. And, sure enough, just as I'd figured would happen, my father was immediately on to me.

"Are you okay?"

"No, Papa, I'm not okay."

I heard him say something away from the phone, and within seconds my mother jumped on another extension. With both of them listening I came clean. Okay, I omitted the part about checking Wilhelm's e-mails, which I knew they'd be appalled by, but I did confess my psychic sins. Neither scolded me, neither yelled. They both calmly listened to everything, then told me we'd get through this.

"Remember *fluctuat nec mergitur*?" my father said, trying to sound strong, though his voice split with concern.

"It tosses but it does not sink." This, this Latin motto of the city of Paris, made everything inside me lurch and my eyes sting. My father always said that these words reminded him of me, because like a ship on the high seas that's rocked by storm after storm, I continued to stay afloat. But now I couldn't fight anymore. It was too much. I couldn't pretend to be okay.

"I know," I finally said, "but this time I'm sinking."

My father was silent, and I knew I'd upset him.

"Don't be ridiculous," my mother said, always practical. "You're not sinking. You're my daughter! We'll help you!"

I relished their comfort, their words and vows. The Three

Musketeers, my father used to call us. And just thinking of that phrase, our nickname, made me feel better—a feeling that was promptly ruined when they made the most wretched of wretched suggestions: Add up how much money you spent on psychics.

I didn't want to do this. I knew the number was big, and as far as I was concerned that was as much as I needed to know. But my parents, both mathematicians, apparently had penchants for big numbers and continued to insist I add everything up. To get them off my back I agreed, and logged into my account at Psychicdom.

The strange thing about Psychicdom was that they actually listed, month by month, the breakdown of calls and just how much you'd spent. To me that was a little like a drug dealer handing over a baggie of coke along with a printout of the customer's monthly usage. I was shocked that they didn't try to hide this information, for surely seeing it in big bold print would dissuade people from calling again . . . but then again, anyone consumed with readings would most likely be too busy to add up all those pesky little numbers. And seriously, seeing how much I'd spent just made me want to get a reading to see if there was money in my future.

I started adding. And adding. And adding. It took a while; I had to tally each month and then move on to the next. Finally I had numbers that were staggering—and yet still I had to add *them* together. Hands shaking, I punched each month's tally into the calculator. I hit enter.

Holy crap.

I don't know what I thought it would be, maybe in the high

hundreds? Well, I was wrong. It was, as Gina pointed out when I told her, *more than the value of her car*. I had shelled out thousands (plural) of dollars to essentially make myself miserable and torture myself on a daily basis. Though I've never been the queen of logic, this impressed even me as not so wise.

I vowed to stop calling. My parents, God bless them, understood the magnitude of the problem—or perhaps didn't buy my weak promise never to call again—and immediately came up with a plan. Though my father had to work, my mother would hop on a plane and come stay with me.

The deal was, if I broke down and called, I paid her five dollars. This worked for about a day and a half. I don't know if my mother noticed, but after that my showers were much longer and the phone was never where she'd left it. I also tended to forget things in the car, random items I had to run downstairs to get right away, and I had to do this with my cell phone, in case, God forbid, there was an emergency in the driveway. What can I say? Old habits die hard.

We finally called off the deal when I tired of the feats of deception and simply handed her a twenty (one I'd borrowed *from her*, as Lord knows I didn't have cash, and she didn't take credit cards) before curling up on the couch to make some calls. I obviously wasn't going to change overnight, but now that I knew how much money I'd spent on psychics, I made every effort to curb my calling. And when I did call, I picked the cheap dollar–a–minute psychics, psychics who used stock photos of clouds and rainbows and aurora lights as their photos. Could they not afford to have their pictures taken? After calling a few times, I was soon convinced that it had nothing to do with money but everything to do with dedication. These cheap psychics weren't nearly as committed. With longing I thought of my carefree former life, the good old days when I'd called expensive psychics who'd cared enough to go to Sears and get their pictures taken with turbans on their heads or wings strapped to their backs.

Before I could completely relapse, my mother whisked me off to our ranch in New Mexico, a place they'd bought upon leaving the East Coast. Going from a cramped apartment in Los Angeles to a sprawling ranch in New Mexico involves a certain amount of welcomed adjustment. For instance, if you look up in the sky? There are stars. And not the kind that drive big black SUVs and are so skinny you can see through their earlobes. No. We're talking the celestial kind, and the sky is chock-full of them. Also, whereas in L.A. you could step out your front door, whisper "I'm going to slash the tires of your Prius," and within seconds about thirty neighbors would be calling the cops in an effort to protect their Prii, that would never happen at the ranch. The ranch was completely isolated. Our nearest neighbor was a good half hour *drive* away.

If I was ever going to find the ability to recover from my addiction to psychics, it was there. Just seeing my father's face (he pretty much looks like me, but with a beard) made me feel better, and soon I realized I'd stumbled into a rustic rehab, complete with a handful of dogs as a support group. Billy, Annie, Shadow, Attila, and Tyson all gathered around to listen to my stories. Tyson, a black pit bull my father had saved from being shot by some cowboys, was my favorite. I'd pour my heart out to him and he'd take it in, gazing at me with big brown soulful eyes, and I swear he'd nod his head at what I'd said, agreeing in his own little doggy way that *Yes, Wilhelm is the Antichrist.*

Part of the recovery process involved *Law & Order* episodes. Many episodes. It was my and Tyson's favorite show, and my stint at the ranch rehab happened to coincide with a marathon or two. Curled on the couch together, we watched so many episodes that soon the sound of the judge's gavel—*DMM-DMMMmmm*—became relaxing, as soothing as a meditation chime. For hours we'd be snuggled under a mohair blanket, settled in and refusing to move. My parents would bring us food, but we couldn't be distracted from our cases. I felt with the utmost conviction that I *had* to be a member of the Special Victim's Unit. On TV, of course. In addition to the real-life job not paying nearly as much and being a tad dangerous, I also had that instinctual reaction of puking when stressed, a reaction that really wouldn't be fun for anyone.

Of course, to get on the show I'd have to audition. Auditioning meant facing rejection, and I honestly didn't know if I could handle more of that right then. Though at the time it paled in comparison to what I was going through with Wilhelm, only months prior I'd been signed by another agency and then promptly dropped. I had a theory that they'd signed me simply so they *could* drop me. Maybe it was some rite of passage for young agents: Sign an actress, give her hope, then crush her very soul. There, now you're ready to be a Hollywood agent! Honestly, I'd had such heartbreak with my career that I simply couldn't fathom putting myself out there again. I was *tired* of putting myself out there, tired of the rejection, of auditions. It seemed like that was all I did, audition. Audition for acting roles, audition for agents, then audition men for the role of soul mate. What about *me*? When would I land the role of Sarah Lassez, a woman with a *life*?

Maybe it was the altitude—eight thousand feet above sea level can make one slightly lightheaded—but a week later I started planning my wedding. Not to Wilhelm, of course, but to a nameless, faceless groom who had yet to be cast. Truth be told, he wasn't that important. This was about the wedding itself. The point was, I was going to get married, and the ranch was where the festivities would take place.

On long nature walks with my mother I perfected the vision. Cowboys would play fiddles as my father and I rode in on an antique horse–drawn carriage—the one sitting in the barn, left over from the ranch's glory days, clearly destined to be a part of a wedding—the smell of hickory and sage in the air, bunches of wildflowers gathered in pails and placed on long tables amid candles and wine. Beneath hundreds of stars people would dance, the dogs would bark, and I would look positively smashing.

In fact, I decided one day as I filled my mother in on the plans, "We'll rent out the entire motel in town to make sure all my friends come!"

My mother stumbled and tried to hide her alarm.

The funny thing was that this was the first time I'd envisioned my wedding. Oh sure, I'd debated over wedding dresses and engagement rings, but that was because I like fashion and diamonds. But the wedding itself? That had never been my thing. Too conventional. The appealing part of marriage was actually the security aspect, the part about never being alone and always having someone to wake up next to—basically, someone being contractually bound to be with me.

But now I was kind of into the actual wedding. While we were walking, I narrowly avoided walking into a prickly pear, which naturally made me think of Wilhelm. "It's not like you're my wife" ricocheted in my mind. Whatever. Back to planning. I had much to decide, like what kind of shoes to wear in this rough terrain, how I could wrestle the dogs into tuxes, and where I could find a good catering company in the middle of the Chihuahua Desert.

My recovery wasn't flawless, as the damn ranch did have a phone. It wasn't really my fault, though. I mean, I was left alone in the house, completely unattended. That should *never* happen at a rehab. But there I was, all by my lonesome, with a phone, on an afternoon when my parents had gone out to get supplies. Getting supplies, by the way, is what you do when you live on a ranch, versus life in L.A., where you end up at the grocery store because you're *bored* and figure you'll kill time by studying the carb content in tofu or selecting the perfect teeth whitener.

At any rate, they were buying supplies and I was eyeing the phone. The store was so far away it'd be nightfall before they returned, and I knew I couldn't spend the entire evening in a face-off with the phone. Well, I could, but I shouldn't. To distract myself I flipped on the TV and was about to settle in on the couch when I spotted a book on the coffee table about my great-grandfather, Louis Marcoussis, a rather well-known cubist painter. Hmmm. Curious, I flipped it open, and then froze. There before me was a chapter on a series of works that he'd done, called "Les Devins"—which translates to "The Fortune-Tellers."

My first thought was, *Holy crap, it's genetic.* No wonder my mother didn't seem shocked when I'd told her about my addiction to psychics—the predisposition runs in our family! I've got the gene! I tried to remain calm, though I seriously felt exhilarated, comforted, and strangely justified. Honestly, I must not have stood a chance.

The etchings were amazing. Each one represented a different form of divining: the interpreter of dreams, the crystal ball, the palm reader, the séance, the medium, the card reader, and several others. In fact, in one of them my great-grandfather portrayed himself as the numerologist, and, as the author mentioned, out of all the numbers that filled the etching, only one was repeated: the number twenty-two. As if my great grandfather were predicting his own death, he later died on the twenty-second of August.

I read more and realized that these were his last artworks, that he'd done this series while hiding from the Nazis in Vichy during the German Occupation. *Huh,* I thought. *Look at that.* We both have an interest in fortune-telling and we've both suffered at the hands of the Germans.

Well, that was all it took. I had Germans and fortune-telling on the brain and a phone that I *swear* was pulsating on the table behind me. Before I knew it, I was talking to Lady Lily.

Lily, a card reader, informed me that she was shuffling and that I should focus my energy on the cards. Duh, as if I were new at this.

"This first card," she said at last, "is going to represent your situation."

"Mmm–hmm."

"Oh! The sorrow card."

I sank into the sofa. "Go on."

She tried to buffer her words just a bit. "The sorrow card's not always bad, though. Anyway, it's more about this sense of *upheaval* in your life I'm getting. Emotional or physical. Something has caused a disruption. Does this make sense?"

I thought of the breakup, which had evidently caused a disruption in my sanity. "Yeah, I get that."

"Sarah," she said, "I don't usually do this, but I'm going to put the cards down. I don't think I need them right now. Psychically I'm feeling your energy *very* strongly, what you're going through. This doesn't happen to me often. But it's really strong. I'm being told that this time in your life is *necessary*. It's a time to sort out your problems and allow for progress. Does that make sense?"

I said yes. I mean, I didn't know about sorting out my problems, but I certainly had discovered a lot of them. I guess my next goal should have been to sort them, and then do that whole progress bit. Still, if she was getting strong psychic wavelengths, I wanted to know about Wilhelm, not about me. "But can you tell me how Wilhelm's feeling?"

"Love," she said right away, "makes people do crazy things."

Oh my God! Yes! Tell me about it!

"He was confronted by something wonderful," she continued, "and his worry was that he didn't deserve it. I feel he doesn't always think he's deserving. Does this make sense?"

I pictured him window-shopping at Ross. "It *completely* does. Yes."

"So there you were, and the intensity of his feelings scared him, because in a way he thought he'd lost you. But those are *his* issues. Those issues and fears, I feel they go back into his childhood. Does that make sense?"

He'd never spoken of issues with from childhood. In fact, he'd never spoken of his childhood at all. He'd glazed right over that portion of his life as if it had never happened. Right there, I figured, that said there were issues. "Yeah, that makes sense."

"Okay. So he must confront the idea of losing you, of life without you. And he *will* do that if he hasn't already. He loves you. That much I'm getting really strongly. It's just a matter of *when* he'll come around. My feeling is by Christmas you'll hear from him. He'll be back in your life before the stockings are hung."

The reading was amazing. Just hearing he'd come back to me and that he still loved me made me feel better, which, I have to say, pissed me off. I mean, did I even want him back? Why would his loving me make me happy? I didn't want him! Or did I? Maybe I just wanted him to want me. That's normal. Or maybe I did want him back, just so I'd not have to face being alone, or, God forbid, have to go blindly through another maze of a relationship? *The evil you know is less scary than the evil you have yet to meet.* Maybe that was it. I didn't want him back, but at least I knew him. I knew the extent of the pain he could cause me. With someone else my pain could be endless. *Or*, I thought with irritation, *maybe I did just want him. Period.*

Back in Los Angeles, a month and a half after the breakup, I was again faced with the horror of the Hunt for a Job. This would help my recovery, my mother insisted, as no longer would I have time to call psychics if I was actually working. And although this was true, the real motivating factor was the arrival of my last unemployment check. That came, and I started making calls.

It didn't take long. Soon I was working as a personal assistant for a rich Beverly Hills woman who didn't mind when, in the interview, I declared I'd need time to go on auditions. (Not that I *was* going on auditions, but I had fond memories of days when I had, and I liked saying the words.) Really, my new job wasn't that bad. Of course, while other people my age were already doctors and lawyers, their days filled with importance, my days involved such tasks as going to Prada to get the handle on a handbag fixed. But you know what? Getting paid to go to Prada was just fine by me.

Soon, on my daily excursions to stores I couldn't afford, I got the hint that the holidays had arrived. Whereas cheaper stores accost customers with holiday cheer, higher-end boutiques are subtle about such observances, and very easily one could miss the single red tie on a suit's hanging display, or the white fiberglass sculpture vaguely shaped like a wreath behind the front counter. Meanwhile, at cheaper stores off in the land of malls and other such gauche shopping complexes, tinsel abounds, Santa music blasts, and reindeer antlers sprout from employees' heads.

All this was why the holidays had crept up on me, essentially ambushing me when I left the clean sanctity of stores such as Chanel and Christian Dior and stepped out onto a Rodeo Drive that had suddenly been adorned with yuletide décor, trees tied with stylish matching red ribbons, and tasteful and well-groomed poinsettias placed lovingly in center dividers. The holidays had officially arrived, but this lead to another, more upsetting feature of the season. Where, oh, pray tell, was Wilhelm?

There was no sign at all to indicate that Lady Lily had been right. My phone was silent and there was nothing of promise in his e-mails. Yep, I still checked them. The thing is, I couldn't *not* check them. Checking his e-mail was a habit, a custom, like morning coffee, just a part of my daily routine . . . very similar to how the readings were. Adjusting my life to calling only two psychics a week had been hard, but that had been an emotional and financial necessity. But checking his e-mail? I was fine, and it was free. So why not?

But, as I said, there was nothing of interest in his e-mails, and from what I could gather, he'd still not told friends nor family we'd even broken up. That, I figured, was because it was still such a sore subject for him. Besides, if he was planning on getting back together—as Lady Lily had said—informing people of a minor split would have been pointless.

I tried confirming this with Gina one night at her house. "Right? If he hasn't told people we've broken up, maybe it's because he's banking on it not being permanent?"

"Are you *still* checking his e-mails?"

"Maybe." I eyed Mark on the other couch, my expression that of "Don't say another word. We can't let him know how crazy I am." Mark, however, was completely engrossed in a football game, his eyes tracking a guy in orange and blue racing across the field, and I realized he wouldn't have noticed me even if flames had been blasting from my head. "Should we go in the other room?"

"Nah. He's seen it."

"The game? It's not live?"

"No, it was on two days ago. He saw it then."

Clearly men and women have their own special versions of crazy. "Okay," I said. "So back to me. I just don't get it. Lily gave me such a great reading. I mean, it should be coming true. It's almost Christmas."

This last fact was confirmed by the Christmas tree Gina and Mark had bought, one tastefully adorned and glowing beautifully by the window, one with a silver ornament shaped like a bell that said GINA & MARK, FIRST CHRISTMAS, an ornament that was literally like a sword in my heart. I wanted one. I wanted to have a first Christmas with someone, and yet somehow it seemed like I was always having last Christmases with people.

"Maybe I should call Lily," Gina said.

"What? Why?"

"For a reading. You know, to see how good she is."

"You mean to *test* her."

"Why not? She's getting her four dollars a minute, what does she care?"

"Dollar. I'm only doing dollar psychics now."

"Even better." She turned to Mark. "Honey, Sarah and I are going into the bedroom to call psychics."

He nodded, the images of full-grown men jumping on each other flashing in his eyes.

It was an interesting idea. If Lily were right in her reading about Gina's life, then surely I'd hear from Wilhelm soon. "Wait," I said as we made our way down the hall. "I just thought of something. I don't even *have* stockings to hang. What if she was talking about some future Christmas? Like I hear from him Christmas 2008, when I have stockings? She didn't say *which* Christmas."

"Oh, good God. Just give me the number."

She called Lily, and I sat on the bed kneading a pillow. "She's on," Gina eventually mouthed. "Hey, Lily, do you mind if I put you on speaker phone? My neck's been bothering me. Oh, and I'd love to hear your theories on when that's gonna get better."

With that, Lily's voice sprang from the telephone. "Gina is it? I'm shuffling and I need you to *really* concentrate and focus your energy on the cards, okay?"

"Okay."

"Now this first one," she said, "this is going to represent your situation."

Gina rolled her eyes. "Okay."

Lily took a deep, audible breath. "Gina, I got the sorrow card."

"I'm sad?"

"Not necessarily. And the sorrow card's not always bad. It's more about a sense of *upheaval* in your life I'm getting. Emotional or physical. Something has caused a disruption."

I looked at Gina, who shrugged. I was having a slight sense of déjà vu, but ignored it. I was too busy racking my brain to identify Gina's upheaval, her disruption. Mark *had* just moved in, did that count? She now only got three quarters of her closet?

"Gina," Lily continued, "I don't usually do this, but I'm going to put the cards down. I don't think I need them right now. Psychically I'm feeling your energy *very* strongly, what you're going through. This doesn't happen to me very often."

Now I was off the bed, hovering above the phone, glaring.

Lily went on, oblivious to the fire in my eyes. "But it's really strong. I'm being told that this time in your life is *necessary*. That it's time to sort out your problems and allow for progress. Does that make sense?"

I couldn't take it anymore. I'd like to say I screamed, "No, Lily, it doesn't make sense, because you're reading from a script! You're a cheat! You're a scam!" But alas, I still had that fear of psychics putting curses on me, so instead I very angrily, and with much force, hung up the phone.

Gina looked amused.

"What she just told you?" I said. "That was word for word what she told *me*. She was reading from a *script*."

Then, like inspiration from above, Astral Astrid's name coursed through my head, Astrid being a blind psychic I'd had a quick reading with upon my return from New Mexico. *She* wouldn't be reading from a script, I figured, unless they made those scripts in braille too, which I kind of doubted.

I forced Gina to call Astrid. The great thing about Astrid was that she didn't waste time reading cards, because she couldn't, and thus callers tended to get more bang for their buck. None of that shuffling business, no spreads or meanings.

"Gina," Astrid said, "recently you've been given an amazing opportunity in your career. I see this as a window before you, and it's now up to you to *shine* through this window. You must seize the opportunity, take it and don't look back. Your employers are watching, and they gave you this chance because they see you as a rising star."

"Okay," Gina managed to say, right before she clamped her hand to her mouth to squelch the laughter. Not only had she *not* been given an amazing opportunity, but it was just dawning on her that she would most likely never be given an opportunity unless she managed to morph into a frat boy with a shaved head who burped and played golf with the partners.

Giving her one more chance, Gina then asked about Mark, and was told that the distance she feels with him is because he's worried he might fall victim to layoffs at work. "He's a provider, and he's worried he won't be able to provide. What you're feeling from him is stress and pressure, but it's *not to do* with his feelings for you."

"Astrid, thank you so much for your amazing reading. Unfortunately, I just remembered I left a turkey in the oven, so I'm gonna run. Thanks again." She hung up, and turned to me. "Do you think it's Opposites Day?"

I sighed. "Tell me."

"Well, for starters I'm going *nowhere* in that company. You know that, I know that, and the partners know that. To them I'm a shape at a desk, I'm the reason a phone stops ringing. That's it. Nothing more. And she used the word 'career.' I don't *have* a career. I have a *job*. There's a difference. Second, I feel *no* distance from Mark. I mean, he just moved in. We're completely in love. And third, Mark just got a huge *raise* this week. *This* week. A *raise*. We're talking a thirty percent raise. They love him there, and the company's doing great. Astrid was high."

I was teetering on complete and abject depression, though was slightly comforted by having recaptured my tarot cards when Gina wasn't looking. So Lily was a fake . . . and perhaps Astrid was just *off*? Surely psychics had bad days. The bottom line was, it was hard to accuse a psychic of being wrong, because until you dropped dead there could still be a chance they'd be right. For all we knew, Astrid was picking up on events that would occur in Gina's life years later. Timing, I'd learned, was the most difficult aspect of a prediction to get right. Of course, this way of thinking was exactly why I was snared in the psychic trap; it essentially strung me along indefinitely.

I needed the opinions of others who believed, so the second I got home, I pored through the feedback on Psychicdom. Some user names I recognized, people who rated and left feedback for just about every psychic they'd spoken to, which, by the way, was *a lot*. Perfect. I figured, they're addicts like me, psychic connoisseurs.

The first thing I noticed was that these callers now seemed miffed. For instance, KatyKate922, who used to leave glowing feedback for Erlin and many other psychics—all of her comments interspersed with smiley faces and LOLs—seemed to be . . . well . . . possessed. I wondered what the hell her problem was, and then found one particular rant/feedback concerning Erlin that seemed to convey what was on her mind.

You've LIED to me. How much have I paid you? And for WHAT?! For WHAT, I ASK YOU? You are a SCAM! For the last *three months* you've had me waiting for him to dump his girlfriend, and you know what? He hasn't! I'm still waiting! You told me we'd be together by Thanksgiving, but T-Day's over and I just found out he's taking her on a cruise to Mexico!! To what, break up with her? I THINK NOT. People don't go on cruises to dump people! Once more I will be alone and BROKE on Christmas while the man you said I'd be with is dancing on the deck of some ship I HOPE SINKS with his GIRLFRIEND. Have fun counting MY money, you FAKE!!

Geez, I thought. She'd only been waiting three months for this prediction to come true, and she was this angry? Talk about overreacting. Three months is nothing. Hell, I'd been waiting for some predictions to come true for *years*!

I paused.

Years. I had been waiting for years.

When a belief system starts to crumble, it's like being thrown off a raft. You hit the water, there's a shuddering chill, and then there are choices to be made, directions to go. But at first? At first there's a whole hell of a lot of panic.

That was me. Flailing in the water, trying to figure out what to cling to if not my belief in predictions. I didn't know how to face the unknown. I didn't know how to deal with uncer-tainty. I didn't know how to surrender control. For years, if I was confused, I called for an answer. If I was scared, I called for comfort. If I was nervous about rounding a corner, I made a phone call to find out what was on the other side.

But now I had nothing. Without my readings, I had only myself.

The next few days were spent reading through pages and pages of notes on past predictions. I don't know what I was looking for. To believe again? To find proof that things *had* come true, that there was still something in which to rest my faith?

Sure, sometimes psychics were eerily accurate, but it was sinking in that they weren't *reliable*. To anyone else this might have seemed obvious, but to me the realization was as shocking as when a friend told me that no, the national anthem did not begin with "Jose, can you see." (In my defense, I *was* an immigrant, and from an immigrant's point of view this interpretation makes perfect sense.)

But this realization, that psychics weren't reliable, really hit home once the government got involved. Okay, it's not nearly as exciting as it sounds. My mother, in a very sweet attempt to understand what the hell her seemingly intelligent daughter was going through, ended up doing some research online. With happiness she e-mailed me an article she'd found, one she thought would make me feel better. With horror, I read it. It seemed that our own government had spent around twenty million dollars employing psychics as part of some Pentagon defense intelligence program. However, and here's where the horror kicked in, they scrapped the program when they finally realized that the psychics were accurate only around 25 percent of the time. Twenty-five percent! That's practically the same, I figured, as an educated guess! Maybe it was even worse than an educated guess? I had no idea. All I knew was that these government psychics must have come *very* highly recommended. Their feedback must have been stellar if they'd been handpicked by the Pentagon. And yet, if *they* had only a 25 percent accuracy rating, what did that say about the psychics at Psychicdom?

Still, even with this knowledge, I couldn't stop calling. I knew psychics weren't reliable, I knew they weren't the answer, but I simply couldn't stop calling. Only twice a week now, Thursdays and Saturdays, but I could not give up those calls. They were my treats for having endured all the other days as a phone-less questioning overwrought mess. Knowing Thursday was approaching helped me make it through Tuesday, and lent me relief and comfort on Wednesday, similar to if I'd known I was nearing a picnic at the top of a mountain, the thought lightening each grueling uphill step.

I knew it wasn't right, the obsessive calling and checking of e-mails, and yet I couldn't stop. I had no idea how to fix myself, but I knew I wasn't getting the job done on my own. It was time to turn myself over to a professional. Not commit myself, of course, but make an appointment with the psychotherapist I'd seen once or twice over the years. She wasn't cheap, and her swank office proved it, but I'd liked her and didn't really have the energy or funds to audition new doctors. Though really, what was I talking about, not thinking I had the money? Money seemed to emerge from cracks in the floor when I needed to call psychics. And when I broke it down, my expensive psychotherapist was about two dollars a minute. Erlin was at least double that.

Before I could think twice, I counted up what was left of my paycheck and made the call. There. Appointment set, I felt much better. Almost like I needed a treat for being so healthy. Granted it was only Monday, but really, what was the harm of one more reading?

10

Internet Warfare

YOU KNOW YOU LOOK BAD WHEN A THERAPIST—A person trained in disguising alarm—*gasps* upon seeing you. I guess I still resembled a junkie, and not of psychics, but of actual hard-core drugs. This was something I'd not been aware of. I thought I'd gotten past that stage. Sure, I still couldn't keep food down, wasn't sleeping properly, and was an emotionally frenzied and fragmented mess, but no one had said I *looked* bad. Then again, the only people who ever saw me were my Beverly Hills employer and the employees on Rodeo Drive, and in all likelihood my gaunt, skinny, unhealthy appearance made me look just like any other Hollywood starlet after a night out. To them there was nothing shocking about my appearance. In fact, it probably made me look successful.

Oh, and I saw Gina as well, but when she told me I looked really thin, it had actually sounded like a compliment, and she'd said it with a certain amount of longing, perhaps the residue of her anorexic high school days. After all, this is the girl who claimed life would be perfect if only scientists could invent and breed a cute and adorable tapeworm, the perfect pet who would accompany you everywhere and allow you to eat anything and everything. Seriously, the girl was twisted, and I really should've known she wasn't a proper judge.

In my therapist's professional eyes I didn't look good. And, I must say, I was shocked to see my therapist. Whereas the last time I'd seen her—years before, during a spell of couples' counseling with an ex who was actually willing to work on things—she'd had short brown sophisticated hair, now she had long gorgeous fiery red hair, perfectly styled in that bed-head sort of way. I also noticed eyeliner, applied in a fashion I myself still had trouble with. What the hell? My therapist was hot.

I soon identified what had sparked the transformation. She was, it turned out, the resident therapist on a popular reality show. Not only was my therapist now better looking than I was, but she was on a TV show *and I wasn't.*

I bypassed the sofa and went straight to the leather club chair in the corner. With the news of my therapist's acting career, it was as if a trapdoor had opened up and dropped me into an even lower level of rock bottom. Where I now dwelled was a musty cavern with no light and no way out, yet in this cavern were two big projection screens, the first one cheerfully playing montages of my predicted life—images of love and happiness and roles on hit TV series—and the other one slowly and excruciatingly playing my real life—images of a frightening-looking girl clutching a phone, essentially *paying* for hope in a tornado-swept room, or scraping the dregs of a jar of apricot jam for dinner. The latter montage stopped with a shot of me in my therapist's office, realizing that not only did she put me to shame looks–wise, but she also had an *acting career*, while I spent my days searching for discontinued pink nail polish and quilted Gucci dog coats. Then the film looped back around and the fun started all over.

"All right," Olivia said, forced to sit on the couch. "Tell me what's going on. It's been a while since we've seen each other."

In a few sentences I recapped the chain of boyfriends since the one who'd accompanied me to couples' therapy. The fact that I was able to just flippantly list them off like that was both intensely disturbing and enormously comforting: Each relationship had felt *monumental* at the time, their demises so injurious that I'd questioned whether I'd ever be able to love again. And yet there I was, feeling nothing as I reduced them to a few select words. Would I one day be able to do that with Wilhelm? To laughingly refer to him as "that bizarre metrosexual German sous–chef I once dated"? God, I hoped so. What a truly glorious day that would be.

After bringing Olivia up to speed with my love life, I mentioned my issues with psychics and a certain ex's e–mails.

"Describe to me a typical day for Sarah. You wake up, and then what?"

"When it was bad, or now?"

"Whichever you feel you should tell me."

Ah, there we go. Typical infuriating therapist banter. "Okay, well, I guess I'll tell you about when it was bad, because now I'm only calling psychics twice a week, on Thursdays and Saturdays, which is pretty normal."

At that, I noticed one of her eyebrows twitch.

"Right. I said that wrong. Maybe not *normal*, but a huge improvement. Okay. So here it goes, when it was bad." I rattled off my daily events: the e-mails, the translations, the tarot cards that had crept back into my life with arthritis–inducing fury, the intensive split–end cutting, the crying, and, who could forget, the psychics. "Oh, and I have a job working for this rich woman, so I do get out of the house, which is good." I smiled proudly, as if that one little factor made all the difference, then added, "Sometimes I do online tarot card readings at work. But only the free ones."

Olivia didn't look shocked at all. On the contrary, she was nodding as if this were typical for many people. With a smile, I watched as she made one more little note on the pad of paper in her lap, then looked up at me and said, "You need to be in intensive therapy."

My smile disappeared. *Shit.* That was so not what I wanted to hear.

"I can recommend one of my associates who works on a sliding scale. But in the meantime, I highly recommend that you join a twelve–step program."

My brain was reeling. I'd gone there to be cured, but had basically just been told I'd be the way I was forever. My brain was reeling. I'd gone there to be cured, but had basically just been told I'd be this way forever. Intensive therapy? And twelve steps?! Was she kidding? I didn't have time for *twelve* steps. I need *one* step. One! *No, no, no, no, no, no . . .*

I took a deep breath. I needed to communicate this with my therapist. I needed to be clear and rational, needed to make her respect me and my concerns. I opened my mouth, but what came out was the "No, no, no, no, no" I'd thought had been confined to my head.

"Sarah? Tell me what you're thinking."

Okay, here it goes. Be calm. Be cool. Don't frighten the therapist.

"It's just that I don't have time for intensive therapy. I'm a mess *now*. And twelve steps? Are you *kidding* me?" Uh-oh. I felt the roll I was on and knew I was about to fall victim to the building momentum. "Not only are there *eleven steps* too many, but *which* twelve-step program do you want me to join? Because I looked. Believe it or not, I looked. If I were lucky enough to be addicted to heroin, I'd be at a meeting right now, but I'm not! I'm addicted to *psychics*. And though there are a *million* twelve-step programs out there, *they are for everything else*. Like Messies Anonymous? Yeah, you should see my apartment; they'd welcome me with open arms. Or Debtors Anonymous; I bet my thirty grand of debt would buy me a seat in *that* meeting. Or what about Love Addicts Anonymous? I want love, so maybe that *is* me, but then of course that brings us to Sex Addicts Anonymous, which *also* could be me, because my stupid ex-boyfriend *wouldn't* have sex with me, so I *obsessed* over it, so maybe I *am* a sex addict now and maybe we *should* add that to my list of dysfunctions, but I'm telling you right now that if you put me in that meeting and there's some guy who just wants to have sex with me, I'm going to *fall in love with him*, and I honestly don't think that's good for me right now, and after all that, *you know what? I'd still be addicted to psychics!*"

Olivia nodded. "Another approach would be drugs—"

"I'll take them!"

She smiled. "What you have is classic obsessive–compulsive disorder."

I took a deep, relieved breath. *Yes.* I have something with a *name.* That means it's curable. I wanted to do a dance of delight, a pirouette of happiness, a jeté of joy. I wanted to twirl around her office and knock down all the degrees from the walls; I wanted to stand on top of the coffee table and sing, "The sun'll come out, to-morrow! Bet your bottom dollar that to-morrowwww . . . there'll be sunnn."

"I'd recommend Zoloft; that would be a quick way to . . ."

When I'm stuck with a DAY, that's GRAY, and low-ow-ownly, I'll just stick out my CHIN, and GRIN, and SAYYYY . . .

Drugs! It was so easy. It was immediate, it was painless, it was perfect. I tried to pay attention to what she was saying, but the sense of hope I felt got in the way and essentially blocked her out, presenting me with images of Sane Sarah, a girl who could look at food without cringing from heartbreak, who could pass a phone without itching to pay for a call, who could use her computer for normal, healthy things like out-of-control shopping. I was *sold.* This Zoloft stuff would be my new best friend. I just knew it. Never had I been into Western medicine. I'd always preferred the holistic route: vitamins, herbs, homeopathic remedies and teas. As a matter of fact, I'd always been staunchly *opposed* to antidepressants—which I'm sure I'd always needed—partly because of the fear that if I took them, they could affect my acting, and one overwhelming element of being an actor is the ability to fully feel tortured. But this was a new me. A desperate me. A me who would gobble down any kind of pill if it would make the deep pain I felt go away. A me with no acting jobs in sight.

But alas, I realized once I was in the car, I had no health insurance. My bubble of impending sanity burst, and I fixated on how I'd get my drugs, determined to get them *today*—and fleetingly I noted, *Why, yes, look at that, I am obsessive*—as I knew I'd never be able to think of anything else until I could rest assured my brain chemistry was successfully being altered. Then, of course, I began to obsess over my obsessiveness. It was a vicious, vicious cycle.

What was I going to do? When all I could think of was ordering the drugs from Canada (too expensive) or venturing off to Mexico (too risky), I called all my friends to see how they went about being mentally ill. To my dismay, everyone acquired their antidepressants through their insurance, and I realized that in order to afford mental illness one also had to be able to hold down a full-time job with benefits. Somehow that didn't seem right.

Speaking of jobs, I realized as I pulled into my driveway that I'd forgotten to go to mine today. Somehow, in all the excitement of the therapist's office and my new disorder, I'd totally forgotten to call my boss to tell her I'd be late, and then I'd totally forgotten to be late and had instead just been *not there*. She was going to kill me. I yanked up the parking brake, turned off the ignition, reached for the door handle ... but couldn't move. I sat there, fingers curled around the handle, and yet I simply couldn't get out of the car. I couldn't even open the door. Nor, I realized, did I want to. It was actually nice in there, warm, like a sunny spot on a carpeted floor.

Was this what being numb was like? Had I finally gone numb from all the stress and worry, or was I just really tired and now suddenly cozy and peaceful? I stared at the peeling paint of the garage door. It looked like at one point it had been turquoise. A bright turquoise garage. I kind of wished I'd been there for that. I took a nice, long, deep breath, appreciating the air freshener I'd stuck in my car's console—a scent that normally drove me crazy because it smelled exactly like a scratch 'n' sniff sticker I'd had when I was young, yet for the life of me I could not figure out which one. Usually, when in my car, I'd smash the air freshener against my nose and furiously breathe in while driving, racking my brain to identify its place in my childhood sticker album. Yet I was only ever able to conjure the joyful bubblegum machine (Looking Good!), the grinning caramel apple (Stick to It!), or the bashful slice of pizza (Hot Stuff!).

Now I let it sit there. Now it didn't torment me; now it was just absolutely lovely.

Maybe I was numb, but my composure was beginning to worry me. I should be a lot more freaked out. I was officially afflicted with something that had a name, and yet I couldn't afford to make it go away. It was like the curse all over again. Okay, now I was freaked out. I was afflicted, and I had no way to get better.

Before I lost it, I had to call my boss. Lip quivering, I dialed her number. *Just make it sixty, maybe ninety, seconds, Sarah, that's it. Then you can lose it.* She picked up and I started speed talking, lasting a total of about fifteen seconds before my lip did one final quiver and it was over. In my parked car, in my driveway, with my seat belt still on, I began weeping. As if this in and of itself wasn't already a fabulous way to impress one's employer, I then managed to explain, through gasps for air, that I was mentally ill and needed Zoloft.

And to this she said something remarkable. She said, "I'll see what I can do."

All at once it hit me, the reason she was so rich, the source of funding for her far too numerous Gucci and Prada requests: She was married to a doctor.

"Sarah? So you promise you'll be in tomorrow? As soon as I wake up, I'd like you there. I really need you."

As soon as she woke up meant one o'clock in the afternoon, but to be safe I got in at twelve forty-five. Immediately one of the crew of housekeepers informed me she was still sleeping, so quietly (not that she could hear anything with a bedroom approximately four thousand square feet from where I was standing) I made my way to the kitchen for some orange juice.

I kid you not—there on the counter, held magically in a ray of sunlight from the skylight above, were *boxes and boxes of Zoloft*.

I ran to them. I picked one up, held it lovingly, and admired the little cartoon smiley-faced bouncy ball with the lone tuft of hair. How had she done this so fast? She was a wonderful, wonderful woman who must have really, really needed something done today. I tore into the box and hastily determined how many were in there, multiplied that by all the boxes, and with delight learned I had months' worth. Jackpot! Best get started! I poured myself a glass of orange juice and popped two little blue pills into my mouth, imagining them smiling their way into my bloodstream, gleefully tickling my brain, and laughing joyfully as I promptly became the contented person I longed to be. *There*, I thought, *I feel better already.*

Unfortunately, the feeling better part was short-lived, as soon I became crazily jittery, a fact that made sense when my boss finally strolled into the kitchen, silk robe flowing, and told me I was to start off with half a pill a day for the first week. *Oops. Oh well,* I thought, *perhaps I've just given my brain chemistry a jump start on the process. I'll be better in no time!*

I was religious about my pills. Never had I been a good pill taker, especially not when it involved remembering to take something at the same time everyday, but this was different. Each pill was one pill closer to peace of mind, and I urgently, dreadfully, *frantically* wanted peace of mind. So there I was, each morning, ready with a glass of water and my little blue happy pill, just waiting for the clock to strike ten. Ten o'clock and down went the pill. Then I'd wonder, would *this* be the day? Would this be the day my long-lost friend Sanity returned? I pictured the little smiley bouncy ball turning into Pac-Man and coursing through my brain, gobbling up little demons of obsession, making a right turn and then a left and gobbling up some more.

Sadly, progress was slow. I managed to eradicate my Saturday call, but Thursday still involved a phone, my credit card, and a dollar-a-minute psychic. And Wilhelm's e-mail? Sometimes I could go a whole day without checking, then there I was, first thing the next morning, popping my blue happy pill and typing in "HugBoss."

One fateful Saturday, I'd made it through the day without a reading (despite an incredible urge to call Erlin, scream at him for his failed predictions, and then ask if maybe Wilhelm was miserable without me) and had *almost* made it without checking his e-mail, but then something—perhaps my being alone on a Saturday night or my own rusty intuition—*something* commanded me to the computer and made me log into his account.

At first glance I didn't see anything unusual, so I clicked on sent mail. There, the third e-mail down, was one addressed to *me*, which I'd not yet received because it must have just been sent.

This was it. I was certain. The plea to give him another chance, the revelation that he'd been suffering and missing me and that these last two and a half months had been the darkest he'd ever known. *Click.*

> Dear Sarah,
> I wanted to let you know I will not be in L.A. much longer. I
> secured a job with one of our partner hotels in San Diego, and will
> be moving at the end of the month. Thanks for the good times.
> —Wilhelm

Okay. Clearly this wasn't the big push to give him another chance ... but more important, "Thanks for the good times"? *Thanks for the good times?* Great. The heads-up that soon he'd no longer be infecting my city with his presence was nice, but "Thanks for the good times"? I found that disturbing and insulting, akin to having barely survived a plane crash with someone, only to get a note from them with the words "Thanks for the fun flight!"

Thanks for the good times, my ass. Now let's check out the e-mails he sent after mine. Click.

Greta—I'm finally off work. Let's celebrate. Meet you at the
hot tub.
Yours,
Willy

It was strange. One of my first thoughts, after reading this note
that clearly indicated the man I'd thought was the love of my life
was dating other women, was, *Wow, I don't feel like hurling myself off
the balcony. How strange.* The Zoloft, I realized, was *working.* Granted,
I was still horrified, my heart was still pounding, and I still sort
of felt the need to puke, but I also felt slightly removed, as if my
life had turned into some strange soap opera I was watching on
TV. And, oddly, I was sure that if I tried hard enough I could
change the channel. Before there'd been only one channel. One
channel and no volume control and no knobs on the TV. But
now, now I had a mental remote. I was getting *better.*

But alas, I wasn't ready to change the channel. I mean, Greta?
Greta? Was he purposefully picking women with names he knew
would torture me? Greta, in my still rather frenzied mind, was
a beauty queen hailing from the land of ABBA and IKEA, a
stunning Swede with long blond braided hair, a crazy white fur
cap, and a pair of wooden clogs that with my luck would turn
my demented ex *on* and morph him into the sex fiend I'd
always longed for him to be. Briefly I pictured Greta and Nadja
battling it out, blond pigtails pulled, lederhosen tearing,
Swedish meatballs sailing, steins smashing. Strangely, I realized,
I was now rooting for Nadja. This Greta chick had crashed our
party, and I wanted her *out.*

Wait, though, back to the hot tub. What was he doing in

there with this girl? Who was this girl, where had he met her, and did he have his arm around her? Oh, and most important, *did he not know about mourning periods?* It had been just over two months since we'd broken up! That was way too soon! And what, I had to ask, was he doing referring to himself as "Willy"? That was just wrong.

I couldn't think about Greta the Swedish Slut any longer. I was about to go lie down and smother myself with a pillow when I decided, again rather fatefully, to check that one other sent e-mail. After all, maybe it was Wilhelm e-mailing Dustin, saying something like "Hey, Dustin, Grandma Greta's in town and hurt her back, so I gotta help her into the hot tub. Oh, and it's her birthday, so we'll be celebrating with a tasty bundt cake. Join us if you want, but don't get freaked out if she calls me Willy. You know grandmas."

All right, even *I* didn't think it was really going to be like that, but I certainly didn't think it would be this:

Miss Simons,

It must have been fate to run into you again on one of my last nights in Los Angeles. Many evenings I would drive by the bar hoping to see you outside, leaning against the wall smoking a cigarette. In fact, I went back to the bar the night after we met, looking for you. Many times I would think of you and your beautiful smile. Well, my dear, you are even more beautiful than I remembered . . .

I stopped. I couldn't read any more. I didn't have to be told there was no way Miss Simons was his grandma. I didn't have to be told he was moving on, or that he was dating, or that he was kissing girls who weren't me. The knowledge pushed against my skin; it twisted my stomach, stung my eyes. There was something else too, something else I felt that was quickly surfacing, climbing, climbing, climbing, rising like a torpedo. . . .

Ah. Anger.

Lovely, happy, wonderful *anger*.

This Miss Simons had gotten an all–out love letter, and I'd gotten "Thanks for the good times." I was still recovering, and he was dating. I was still reeling from all the false promises he'd told about our future, and the secrets he'd kept, while he had Greta in a hot tub.

Suddenly I felt calm. I knew what I needed to do; I was on a mission. My mental gearshift had kicked into stealth mode, and all of a sudden I possessed the methodical mind and steel heart of a secret agent. I scanned the last line of the e-mail to the smoking, wall–leaning Miss Simons ("Please call me, for I long to see you before I leave"), copied the entire thing, opened up a new e-mail in his account, typed in Greta's address, then hit paste and send.

Next mission. I created a phony Hotmail account, hit the write message button, and started typing.

Dear Miss Simons,
You don't know me, but I feel the need to write you. I've been dating Wilhelm rather seriously and he accidentally sent me the e-mail below . . . one that was obviously intended for you. Not that you have any reason to listen to me, but I wanted to warn you that this guy is a major player, and a lying, cheating, untrustworthy jerk. Oh, and he gave me crabs.
—A friend

I stared at what I'd written. My mind was beginning to come out of stealth mode and was debating whether this was wise or healthy or perhaps just wrong—though my hand must still have belonged to the secret agent, because it ignored everything and simply hit send. *Oh no*, I thought once the e-mail was gone, *I should've been more specific*. She might not realize that when I referred to his giving me crabs, I'd meant seafood, as in sautéed soft-shell crabs, fried king crab legs, and imperial crabs! I mean, Wilhelm *loved* to cook crab. *Bad Sarah, that was very unclear of you*. Heh–heh.

I sat back. I could practically feel the e-mails spiraling their way toward the Swedish beauty queen and the beautiful, smoking, smiling Miss Simons. Surely they'd be miffed, especially Greta, who'd realize that as she was turning into a prune in the hot tub, good ol' Willy was writing e-mails to other girls, and not doing a very good job addressing them either, I might add. But you know, e-mails get sent to the wrong people all the time. These things happen. Greta, I'm sorry he was so careless. May I hand you a towel?

The great thing about the meds, I was learning, was that in a situation like this they held me upright, whereas unmedicated I without a doubt would've been reduced to a heaving mass on the floor. But now? Now I was sane enough to fully explore my insanity.

I figured I'd have some time to kill before the shit hit the fan, so I went to the kitchen and poured myself a glass of wine. Upon my return I noticed that Wilhelm had a new e-mail. Greta. Apparently she hadn't left for the hot tub yet and had just received Willy's latest e-mail.

I opened it. I leaned in. Boy, I noted right away, that Greta sure had a temper. It was truly beautiful. She mercilessly railed against him for being so stupid as to send her an e-mail intended for another woman, made catty comments about the girl with the beautiful smile, and then demanded to know just how he could be so cold as to be romancing more than one woman. *Yep,* I thought, *I'm with ya on that one, sister.* But then I kept reading and discovered, with dismay, that at the end she actually apologized for being angry, saying she realized she had no right. No right? Was she serious? I wanted to shake her. I wanted to scream, "He's got you all lined up for the hot tub while he e-mails other girls! Just how low is your self-esteem that you don't think you deserve better?"

Greta was pathetic. I checked my phony account, but of course Miss Simons hadn't replied. And why would she? She was obviously a very beautiful woman; there was no reason she'd be at home, alone, drinking wine and checking e-mails on a Saturday night. *Sigh.*

Over the course of the next few days I was gifted with endless entertainment at the hands of Greta and Wilhelm. With something I could describe as fevered joy, I'd race to the computer for updates several times a day, thrilled to catch up on the latest drama, the newest installment in their saga. It seemed that what Greta had meant in saying she had no right, was that she had no right to ask Wilhelm not to see other women *since she herself was married.* That was a twist I hadn't expected. Also, within a matter of time her I-have-no-right attitude quickly disappeared and instead she became simply *mean*. Her poor husband. Not only was he being duped, but from what I could tell, he was married to a very bitchy woman. Still, her evil comments and digs gave me great pleasure, as Wilhelm had obviously been in need of having a lesson pounded into him.

On the fourth day my fake e-mail account had a reply from Miss Simons. I admit, I was shocked at her response. I thought for sure she'd be angry or suspicious or even just dismissive, but instead she was grateful. She was touched that I had gone out of my way for a total stranger, and went on to say she doubted she would've seen him again anyway, but hoped one day she could return the favor. In fact, she added, she was a great listener and would be there for me if I wanted to talk about "that loser."

I wanted to cry.

Miss Simons was really, really nice. I liked her and knew, with a sinking feeling, that what I'd done was *very* wrong . . . but as a matter of fact yes, yes I *did* want to talk about that loser.

I hit reply.

Thank you so much for your kindness. It's just hard, because he'd promised marriage, you know? Perhaps I shouldn't have bought his promises hook, line, and sinker, but I did, and I really thought we'd be together forever . . .

I wrote and wrote and wrote, my hands flying across the keyboard as my brain struggled to keep up. When finally done, I grabbed the mouse and moved the cursor to the send button, the little hand now hovering over its target. What was I doing? It was amazing I'd thus far escaped unscathed from my cyber-acrobatics. What was I thinking, taking such a risk by calling myself Bridgette (hey, if everyone else got sexy names, I wanted one too) and pouring out my heart to a woman Wilhelm was trying to date? What was I doing trying to strike up a friend-ship based on lies, just so I could vent? Though I may not have been completely sound yet, it was as if I'd finally grabbed the edge of sanity, my fingers scraping to get a grip, nails digging, and I knew this opus I'd just created was counterproductive. Sending this would render my grip even more tenuous, like a steel-toed stomp on my unprotected hand.

I clicked the *X* in the corner of the e-mail, and agreed that yes, I did want to discard the changes. There. Done. Miss Simons had been spared.

To mark my first major step toward sanity, I decided to put an end to the Internet shenanigans. Truthfully, I was beginning to tire of the drama between Greta the Adulteress and Wilhelm the Immoral. The two just went at it nonstop, and they didn't seem to be making any progress in addressing and working out their issues. This, I decided, wasn't healthy for either of them, nor, I had a suspicion, was it healthy for me. Knowing what I had to do, I created yet another phony e-mail account and popped off a quick anonymous note to Greta, informing her that if she didn't end things with Wilhelm pronto, her husband would be informed. *There,* I thought with pride, *I just saved a marriage.*

Of course just because I was no longer playing Anti-Cupid didn't mean I stopped checking his e-mail. In fact, I checked it even more, now that I knew he was capable of dating, and it *hurt*. I lived in fear of what I'd find, torturing myself by reading his words, keeping the wound fresh and open. I had to stop, but I needed help to do it.

When I finally mustered up the nerve to ask for assistance, I dialed Gina's cell phone, completely forgetting she'd be at work. I guess not everyone was at home on a Tuesday afternoon, in their sweatpants and checking their ex's e-mail. Still, this was important, so I told her she needed to take five minutes to help me.

"Okay, but no more than five, 'cause we've got a staff meeting in the other room right now. Not that I was invited, but you know, if they run out of bagels, they're gonna need me."

"I want you to perform Operation HugBoss."

I heard her adjust the phone. "Sarah, what have I told you about TV marathons? They're dangerous and they mess with your reality."

"No! This isn't marathon-related. This is serious. Operation HugBoss, aka change Wilhelm's e-mail password so I can't get into his account. 'HugBoss' is the current password."

"*Ah.* I see. And I must say, I approve." There was a pause. "But wait, then he won't know the new password either. He won't be able to get into his own e-mail."

"Yeah, well, certain sacrifices must be made."

I recapped the past week's shady dealings. Whereas most people would have scolded me for such underhanded sneaky business, Gina was thrilled. "That is *brilliant,*" she whispered. "I love it. I mean, it was bad, but I love it. I swear your talents are being wasted as an actress. You should seriously be working for the CIA."

I admit it, I was proud. I had in fact sabotaged his affairs from the comfort of my own home, essentially short-circuiting two of his budding relationships via remote control. I'd been like an evil wizard, pressing buttons and pulling levers and— *No, Sarah, this is not something to be proud of.* "So you'll do it? And remember, pick something I'll never figure out. Because I'll try. You know I will. And I'm good."

She promised, and I waited nervously for ten minutes before attempting to log on. I typed "HugBoss," held my breath, and hit enter. "You have entered in an invalid password. Please try again."

I sat back in my chair, slightly nervous and slightly sick, as for the first time in years Wilhelm was going to exist without me. I'd be free, but I'd be in no way a part of his life. The man I'd loved, the man I'd thought I'd marry and be with forever, that man who'd meant so much, was going to continue on, trudging down a path of his own, becoming more and more distant until one day our world together would be but a fading memory. One day I'd be so used to life without him, that in passing I'd reduce him to nothing more than a few select words.

11

I See Dumb People

WHAT DOES ONE DO WITH ONE'S TIME IF NOT obsessively calling psychics, reading tarot cards, or checking an ex's e-mail? Daytime, I must say, was much longer than I'd thought it was. *When*, I wanted to know, *would that pesky sun finally set?* What does one *do* when it's still light out? Had there really always been *this* many hours in a day? I felt as if for years I'd been standing with crutches in the midst of a stadium and just now someone had yanked them from under my arms. Surrounded by what seemed like miles of nothing, I was wobbling and wondering what the hell to do.

What I needed was to become friends with that caller who'd left scathing feedback for Erlin. *She'd* know exactly what I was going through; *she'd* help me feel not so alone, so crazy. As much as I loved my friends, they didn't understand my addiction, *couldn't* understand my addiction. Though they each had their own issues and their own bouts of insanity, psychic addiction was new territory for us all. Never had anyone encountered such an issue, and though they were supportive, they couldn't *relate*.

But KatyKate922, she would understand, she would relate. One lazy afternoon I gave myself a mission: Study KatyKate922's feedback for clues and then find her. Already I fancied myself as something of a covert agent, so I deemed this an easy task and began scrolling through hundreds of messages. I searched and searched, yet all I saw was praise and flattery. KatyKate922's rant was nowhere to be found. Had it . . . had it been *removed*?

Now, I admit I can be naïve. And though it might seem obvious to others that the powers behind Psychicdom most likely weren't the pillars of morality, I was truly shocked. Feedback was the very essence of what had convinced me to trust the site, the supposed candor and honesty was what had sold me in the first place, and to learn that comments were being manipulated was as horrifying as if I'd just spent a fortune on a diamond, only to be told the authenticity report had been conjured in a drunk Russian's basement and the stone actually involved the words "cubic" and "zirconia." It was all a fraudulent, unfair game, and I was *appalled*.

I decided to check the feedback on all my favorites, starting with Misty Mystical. The Psychicdom monitors must have taken an ill-timed break, because there, right at the very top, was a brand-new and very irate comment. PrincessPlum had written:

WARNING! She gave me FALSE HOPE!! I've been waiting for TWO YEARS for my man, my "twin flame," to leave his wife. She told me his wife was VERY SICK and would die soon and he'd be free to be with me. As of today his wife is STILL ALIVE and they're STILL TOGETHER. I've wasted thousands of dollars on Misty and have started a support group online for callers of Psychicdom. COME THERE SOON, as I'm sure Psychicdom will erase this as soon as their SPIES catch it!!

Wow, did I want to be part of a support group led by a woman who was waiting for someone to *die* so she could have her man? *You bet.* I desperately wanted any kind of support I could get, and that I'd actually found a group for people like me, psychic junkies, was like learning I wasn't the only one on a very lonely planet.

Unfortunately, I soon learned I'd be alone on that planet for one more night, because apparently it took twenty-four hours—twenty-four grueling, nail-biting, floor-pacing hours—before I would officially be a member and could access the site. It was torture, but finally the hour of my rescue arrived. Though there were only twenty members, there were over three hundred and fifty posts, each story horrifyingly similar to either what I had gone through or what I *could* go through if I didn't break the addiction soon. With a cup of coffee, and then another, I read each and every one, story after story, saga after saga, until I saw something that made me stop: Erlin's name.

Though the proposal hadn't happened (and yes, part of me still added "yet" onto that sentence), Erlin had been right about enough that in my mind he'd become the last vestige of my belief. If people said he wasn't reliable or accurate or right, where would I be? What would that mean for the years I'd spent searching for the path he'd promised?

But this was what I needed, the shock of cold water, the pinch of reality. I clicked on the post and noticed it had been started by a Psychicdom insider, someone with the scoop on all we'd trusted. I forced myself to keep reading. And I saw it. Erlin, my savior, my debonair gentleman who'd always left the ballroom to ease my mind, the man whose words had gotten me through the day and in whom I'd confided my most precious dreams and deepest fears, this same man was said to express his view of his callers, the source of his incredible wealth, by wearing a T-shirt that said I SEE DUMB PEOPLE.

Something inside me shifted.

It was over; everything was over. No longer would I blindly believe in people who had been so wrong, people who saw us, their faithful, their followers, as laughable. No longer would I spend my life reaching for the carrot, my eye on a prize always slightly beyond my grasp, close enough to keep me going but never close enough to be caught. No longer would I live life waiting for a better day. No longer would I wait, always wait.

After I read the last post, I composed my own. I detailed my experience, said how happy I was to have found this group, how comforting it was to know I was not alone. At the end I decided to list the psychics I'd called the most during the Wilhelm saga, and counted, with sorrow, seventeen. *Seventeen psychics.* Those weren't even all the ones I'd called, just the ones I'd called the most.

From that day on the support group claimed the extra hours I'd not known what to do with. We compared notes, prophecies, and results. We tried to encourage one another not to call, partially by detailing the unreliability of certain lauded readers, pulling the curtain aside and exposing them as nothing more than a waste of money. Eventually a blacklist emerged, one that kept growing as again and again psychics failed to be accurate and were placed on the growing do-not-call list. And though we had the best of intentions, our group did have a rather grim flipside—similar to how I imagine AA could be a great place to meet a drinking buddy. If someone had a *great* experience, if perhaps they extolled the virtues and wonders of a new psychic they'd found, our site tended to experience something of a mass exodus as everyone abandoned their computers and practically flung themselves on their phones, determined to be first in line for a reading. So yes, in this aspect the "support" backfired, eventually culminating in the outrageous and alarming invention of Psychic of the Month. Let me tell you, whomever that psychic happened to be, they struck gold by tapping into us.

But then something horrible happened. . . . As more and more addicts came, so *came the psychics*. Let me tell you, they were not so happy with us. Before we knew it, our happy home had been infiltrated by the enemy, and the psychics joined in droves. All hell broke loose; accusations were made, addicts cried, psychics screamed, curses were cast, tarot cards went flying, and crystal balls were smashed. It was a complete melee, a clash of angry, upset, and *very* expressive forces.

Being irritated with failed predictions was one thing, but being personally attacked by an agitated horde of psychics was another. The site was caught in a downward spiral, and nothing—not even my attempt to restore peace by taking over as moderator—seemed to help. There was just too much drama, and soon even I began to pull away.

When at last I emerged from my cyberwar of battling psychics and addicts, it struck me that not only had Wilhelm skittered to the outer edges of my mind, but also something wonderful was about to happen: Gina was about to turn thirty. Not that I wished others to experience such trauma, but it's comforting not to be the only one on a sinking ship, you know? She'd join me on my flailing boat, and together we'd scowl at young twentysomethings on passing ocean liners, attempt to hide from the damaging sun, and compare our burgeoning wrinkles in the shade.

The one thing that confused me was how on earth we'd both gotten so old. Years were now scattered behind us, and yet what had we done with our lives? My mother and all my friends' mothers had been married, owned houses, and had children by our age. And here I was, single and living paycheck to paycheck in an apartment with a sloping floor. Sure it was a different era, but damnit, I wanted to live in that era, not this one with its million-dollar shanties and single women forced to keep a frenzied eye on the expiration date of their eggs.

Gina, strangely, seemed unaffected by her advancing years. I'd say things such as, "This is your last week of being in your twenties," or "Did you ever really think you'd be thirty?" yet she just wouldn't crack. She was calm; she barely cared. According to her, this was because she was not an actress and thus was not convinced that turning thirty meant a possible weighted journey to the bottom of Puppy Lake. Still, Mark, being the wonderful and rare boyfriend he was, anticipated something of a breakdown and decided to distract her by throwing a dinner party at a restaurant in our neighborhood.

That night, I readied for the evening (my rare venture into a social environment), got in my car, and within three minutes was at the restaurant. After another fifteen minutes spent looking for parking, I passed through an old wood gate and into a stunning, glimmering courtyard wrapped in white lights and glowing with candles. The courtyard also, I noticed right away, was chock full of absolutely gorgeous men. We're talking well groomed, polished, sophisticatedly hunky men who looked as though perhaps they'd decided to get a bite to eat after finishing up with their Banana Republic and J.Crew photo shoots. Unfortunately, we're also talking men who might as well have been wearing T-shirts with the phrases DO NOT TOUCH! or OFF LIMITS! as Silver Lake was a predominantly gay neighborhood, and thus only window-shopping was allowed. The gorgeous men were, unfortunately, all getting a bite to eat with one another.

Once at Gina's table I put my hands on her shoulders and leaned in. "Tell me again why we live in Boystown? It's *torture*. Oh, and happy birthday."

She smiled and grabbed a chair from the table behind us, sliding it in next to her. "Sit. Well, for starters it's cleaner, safer, and more artistic, and there's a cheese shoppe. Shop spelled s-h-o-p-p-e."

"But where are all the single straight men?"

"Hermosa Beach. With all the annoying girls who think 'evening wear' means a black bikini."

"Right."

I paused. There was an excitement in her face that I'd come to know meant trouble, and she was grinning like a fool. What the hell? I was about to ask what was going on, when suddenly she lifted her hand and I saw it—a beautiful, sparkling, radiant *diamond*.

I practically fell over in my chair. Sure, the ring was impressive, but mostly I was in shock. When had this happened? I was completely thrown. "Oh my God," I managed to say, then hugged and congratulated her and ferociously guzzled champagne.

Mark, I realized, was one incredibly smart man, as he hadn't allowed her even seconds to bitch about her age before providing her with one hell of a sparkling distraction. And though I was truly and absolutely beyond a doubt happy for her, it was just that, well, she'd jumped ship. She'd joined me long enough that her feet had barely touched the listing surface of my deck before she'd immediately been thrown a line, and just like that had been pulled onto a yacht pointing toward the sunset. I was again alone.

The next morning I pampered myself with a passionflower bath, a bubbly floral attempt at cheering myself up, and had just stuck my foot in the tub when the phone rang. Tracking one watery footprint into my bedroom, I answered, and was immediately sorry I'd done so.

"I'm in Home Depot right now," Gina said, "and I swear you would die if you saw the *fire* in this rock. Who knew Home Depot would have the perfect diamond-viewing lighting?"

Now I got completely into the water, aware that drowning myself would be one way to end the conversation. "Yeah, that's crazy."

"That was a side note. I'm actually calling because I think you need to start hanging out here. Home Depot is *filled* with men; everywhere you look there are men, and these guys all know how to build things or tear things down. It's a jackpot. I'm seriously getting an eyeful. Oh, just be sure to avoid the indoor plant section, 'cause those guys don't play for our team."

I thanked her and made the rather odd promise that yes, in the next couple days I'd get all dressed up and head off to Home Depot.

Immediately after I hung up, the phone rang again. I stared at it lying on my blue bath rug next to a damp footprint. I swore if this was Gina calling back to give me a sparkle update, I would indeed go to Home Depot later this week—but *with* her, and tragedy would strike in the lumber section. I picked up.

"Hey," someone said. "I have good news for you."

Most likely it was a telemarketer calling to inform me of a great deal on some riveting publication like *Fisherman's Weekly*, or to inform me that if I just wasted a day of my life watching a video, I'd get a free all-expenses-paid cruise to Mexico, my only costs being plenty of outrageous random charges and a plane ticket to Antarctica, from where the ship would depart in early January. I was about to hang up, when I figured, you know, good news is always good, right? Besides, at least I didn't have to hear about diamonds, and Gina was spared a pine-scented death. "Who is this?"

"It's Holly, your manager. Remember me?"

"Oh," I laughed. "Vaguely. What's up?"

"You just got offered a role. The director from *Until the Night* wants you to star in his next film, *Mad Cowgirl.*"

I didn't even need to hear the description to know I'd be perfect. I *was* a mad cowgirl. Well, when I'd been at my parents' ranch, I'd been a mad cowgirl. Now, back in L.A., I was just mad and a girl, but still I was perfect. As she went on to describe the part—a young meat inspector who's obsessed with red meat and is having an affair with a televangelist and then slowly begins to lose her mind to mad cow disease and becomes convinced she's a kung fu action star—I was in pure passionflower and career bliss.

I was going to be in a movie.

I was going to be the *star* of a movie.

12

If You Can't Beat 'Em, Join 'Em?

THINKING BACK, I CAN SAFELY SAY THAT THE LAST day of school was always the best part of summer vacation. On that final Friday everything was still possible, each minute spiked with an unrivaled and buoyant anticipation. Nothing had yet interfered with "summer," that golden shiny barbeque-scented, sand-beneath-your-feet, purely divine word. The days were unencumbered, bright, and spread out in lazy bliss, as if school would never ever happen again.

But alas, then rolled around the first free Monday, and the countdown to the dreaded first day of school officially began. Just like that the end was inevitable and looming, and from then on summer was a slippery waterslide downhill.

Similarly, the best part of doing a movie is when you still have yet to do it. *Mad Cowgirl* wasn't slated to start filming for several months, and thus I was blessed with plenty of time to anticipate how wonderful it would be, and plenty of opportunities to utter such things as, "Me? What am I up to? Oh, you know, preparing for my next role. Is it a big role? Well, it's the starring role, the title role, so yeah, I guess so. Oh my, look at that, I'm late for my kung fu lesson. We'll chat later! Ciao!" And though perhaps it wasn't very wise, I promptly quit my job as an errand girl to the rich. The way I saw it, I'd been given an opportunity and I was going to take full advantage of it by studying up for my role and relishing in my ability to claim I was a working actress.

The only downside to so much time before filming was that the psychic junkie within me was being seriously tested. Like a smoker in a cigar shop or a sex addict at a strip club, I was facing a monumental trigger. The only activity that could rival (and surpass) an acting job as a psychic-calling inducement was dating, which, thankfully, I suppose, I was in no danger of doing. Still, what I was facing would be tough. The old Sarah, the Sarah whose brain was held hostage by psychics, would be calling for at least two or three readings a day to ask how production would go, if the film would make me a star, or if it would get into Sundance, Cannes, Berlin, or Deauville. There were so many questions, so many unknowns, and since I refused to call psychics, the questions remained jammed and trapped inside my throat.

Okay, that's almost true. I did call a couple psychics, but I don't count those calls because my heart simply wasn't in the readings. I just no longer believed. I knew psychics were some-times right, but who was to say *when* those times were? Needless torture was what most of the predictions were, and right then my life was glowing, so why would I want to dull it with mean-ingless and possibly frightful words? Yes, even I was shocked at how rational I was becoming. Though, when dealing with an addiction, rationale and logic are all fine and dandy, but habit is the enemy. Despite everything, I couldn't shake the habitual pull to call or bust out my cards for a spread.

As if all that free time with countless questions and a world made of phones wasn't already a challenge, I then got a call from my friend Gordon, an event planner, that made me wonder if perhaps God had grown bored with my recovery and was longing for the good old endless entertainment of Sarah high on psychics. It turned out that, over a year ago, in one of my piques of psychic ecstasy, I'd promised Gordon I'd read tarot cards at a bar mitzvah. Getting out of the evening wasn't an option, as not only was it too late, but the job was going to pay me three hundred dollars in cash. Oh, I should've added the words "independent film" onto the part about being cast in a movie. Hence, three hundred bucks wasn't something to refuse.

As the date approached, I questioned my newfound and supposed sanity. I mean, would it be wise for an alcoholic to play bartender for a night? Or an opium fiend to tend a field of poppies? *No, Sarah, you can do this*, I told myself. *They're just* cards. *They're not to be feared.* Yeah, sure, that's it.

The day of the event, Gordon called to tell me I'd freak when I saw the estate where the festivities were being held—a sprawling mansion on a bluff overlooking the Pacific—and to request that I arrive early enough to change into my costume.

"Costume?"

"Oh," he said distractedly, clearly in a state of pre–event chaos. "Sorry. Thought I told you. It's a haunted–house–themed bar mitzvah. You're the Bride of Frankenstein."

Okay. First, I'm the *Bride of Frankenstein*? And second, just who is this rich and twisted thirteen-year-old? Before I could voice any of this, Gordon was yelling at someone in the distance. "No! The kids can't *touch* the dry ice! Do you want them to lose their fingers?" He took a deep, audible breath. "I'm losing it. Sarah, sweetheart, can I see you here soon, please?"

I promised I was on my way, and then collapsed on my bed. I was going to spend an evening with the instigator of my psychological downfall: the dreaded tarot cards. And, now, on top of that, I was voluntarily humiliating myself. Clearly I was a masochist. A danger to myself. A threat. A menace. I should be locked up or under constant supervision.

No, Sarah, you are the Bride of Frankenstein and now you must drive to Malibu.

I stared at the ceiling.

An hour and a half later I had a geisha whiteface and a three-foot-high black beehive wig with a white skunk stripe smack down the center. As for clothing, I donned a white sheet (one I prayed had never been used, though I found no reassuring crease marks) cut with tiny slits through which I was forced to jam my arms and head. I was uncomfortable, irritable, and itchy, and I looked ridiculous, but Gordon was too busy to field my wardrobe concerns.

"I don't look like the Bride of Frankenstein," I tried telling him as I followed him through the enormous backyard. "I look like Marge Simpson possessed by demons."

Gordon told me I was his favorite person in the whole wide world, pointed out a table by the pool, draped in black velvet, that was to be my "station," and pushed me in its direction. I obediently sulked to my spot, adjusted my hair, and took a seat in a chair whose legs were a far cry from being even. Just *lovely*. Beside me were my neighbors, Frankenstein and Dracula— Dracula being the lucky bastard who got to lie around in a coffin all day.

Swaying in place, I shuffled my cards and watched as a flock of preteens and barely-teens burst from a set of French doors and into the yard, heads swiveling as they took in the sights. Their nonchalant comments about the dance floor, which had an incredible view of the Pacific and was bigger than my apartment, and their remarks about the sushi bar, made me reminisce about my own childhood, a childhood where party décor had been comprised of such uncouth things as balloons and streamers. This décor included fake fireflies like those from the *Pirates of the Caribbean* ride at Disneyland, and props rented from the actual Addams Family movie. Upon hearing what appeared to be a ten-year-old proclaim, "You know, I'm not such a fan of unagi," I feared I was in for a long, long evening.

Very soon I was descended upon by a gaggle of kids. "Your wig is funny," they cried. "Who're you supposed to be?" "Are you dead Marge?" "Does Ricky like me?" "Will I get into Crossroads School?" "Will I be a pro skater?" "Will I have my own band?"

I relaxed. This was easy! They were *kids*. In this case everything truly was for entertainment purposes only. I could tell them anything! They were so far from real life it would actually be good for them to dream big and hope high. And honestly, would any of them even remember what that strange dead-looking Marge had predicted at the party? No, they had MTV and lip gloss on the brain. They aspired to morph into Britney Spears or the next Tom Brady. What dent would my words make?

I pulled cards until, without warning, the kids around me disappeared, flocking to the other side of the dance floor to join a disturbed child who'd discovered the fun that could be reaped from poking and harassing the mummies. Fine, at least I got a break. Wobbling back in my chair, I told myself all was good. I could do this. Everything was okay. Wow. Suddenly, just like that, as if brought about by the power of my positive thoughts, a tray had been placed before my eyes, one filled with root beer floats and a very tiny and very well-hidden glass of clear liquid. *God?* I thought. *Did you just bring me a shot?*

I looked up, into the face of a very hot bartender. *Why, hello, God.*

"Vodka," he said. "They won't smell it on you."

Drat. Gay. I should've known. Quickly I slung back the shot, thanked him profusely, and made him promise he'd return with more liquid kindness. He winked, clearly in agreement that I was in need of whatever mercy he could afford, and was gone.

Seconds later a little wallflower of a girl emerged from the crowd of Britney Spears wannabes, her ponytail slightly crooked, her glasses a bit too big for her face. When she spoke, I had to practically lie across the table to hear her, her timid voice no competition for Justin Timberlake's "Senorita," the song blaring from speakers taller than most of the partygoers. "Come around to my side!" I told her, smiling broadly, much friendlier on hard liquor. "Sit next to me!"

I confess I was nervous about what she'd ask, worried she'd

inquire about popularity or boys or any number of things I myself remember being obsessed with at her age, any number of things I had a sinking feeling were bound to disappoint. *Stay positive, Sarah. They're only cards.* "Now, what would you like to ask the magic tarot cards?"

She looked at me intently, as if trying to decide whether or not I was real. *Smart girl,* I thought.

Finally, very seriously, she said, "Will Sophie and I be friends forever?"

Ah, how adorable. I shuffled, concentrated on her friendship, and laid down a card: Death.

Shit. I quickly scooped it back up, hoping she hadn't seen the sinister skeleton morbidly dancing with his scythe, ready and eager to hack into her dreams. Why hadn't I taken the creepy cards out of the deck? I could practically hear the fuming call I was bound to get from this poor child's parents. "Our daughter is convinced the grim reaper's after her! We've had to put her in therapy! And she can't watch her favorite show, *The Simpsons,* anymore, because she thinks Marge is the devil! What did you do to our daughter?!"

The poor girl was sitting quietly, hands folded in her lap, waiting for an answer.

"What was your name again?" I asked.

"Rebecca."

"Rebecca, are you feeling that you aren't seeing Sophie as much these days?"

She looked at her hands, fiddling with a little gold bracelet on her wrist. "She's not really hanging out with me anymore."

She's not really hanging out with me anymore. That was a sentence

I myself could've uttered every year of my childhood. I knew the pain well. "Okay." I glanced around, then leaned in closer. "I'm gonna tell you a secret. Normally I'm not supposed to reveal these things, but here it is. Right away I *knew* you were going to grow into an amazing, amazing woman."

A little hesitantly, as if something had tickled her, she smiled.

"Seriously, you're going be very happy with your life. But, here's the thing. To become who you're going to be, there will be changes. There have to be; otherwise in twenty years you'd be exactly as you are now, no taller, no different, just still sitting in this chair. So the changes are good, but sometimes they'll be hard to go through. And friendships are one of the things that change. For *everyone*, friendships change. Sometimes we outgrow them and make new friendships. It's just a normal part of life."

To this she nodded solemnly. "Thanks. I gotta go."

Great, I thought as I watched the short glittery crowd swallow her, *I've just ruined her life.* Psychics suck.

Nelly's "Hot in Herre" started up, and I was afforded a little break, as all the thirteen-year-olds and preteens within sight abandoned their drinks and food and fun to hit the dance floor, inspired by a song about stripping, to bust moves that would make me, a grown woman, blush. On the outer edge of the floor a prepubescent boy gyrated alongside a little girl in a half top. I looked away, at the chocolate fountain in the distance, and wondered what the hell had happened to the world.

Throughout the evening I kept an eye out for my little wall-flower girl, searching the room for signs of distress, perhaps clumps of people comforting a crying child or gathered around the still body of a recent suicide. When finally I did see her, she was hurtling toward me at an alarming speed.

"Hi," she said, breathless and excited and practically still skidding to a halt. "Does Ryan like me?"

Oh, boy. In the course of the evening I'd heard that same question about Ryan from about six mini Britneys. With those girls as her competition, poor little Rebecca didn't stand a chance. I nodded toward the crowd. "Which one is he?"

She went to raise her arm, but I stopped her.

"No! Don't point! Just tell me. That's a lesson in life: Don't ever point."

"He's at the sushi bar."

I squinted. All I could see was a boy's back and, unfortunately, that he was surrounded by what looked to be a fawning entourage. Without a doubt Ryan was a member of the übercool, and I wanted to dash across the room, grab his arm—and a few spicy tuna rolls—and take him aside to have a long chat about the power he possessed and the hearts I feared he'd break. Instead I forced a hopeful smile for Rebecca's benefit, and shuffled. I figured I'd pull the Disappointment, Sorrow, or Futility card—cards I myself knew too well—and thus would be obliged to come up with some speech about boys and crushes and how just because your heart gets broken doesn't mean you won't go on to experience the wonderful bliss of a *lying pink-shirted metrosexual German sous-chef.* Yeah, the uplifting love speech could be tough for me. In order not to scare her, I'd have to go against all my instincts and ignore all my true feelings. After all, screaming "If you think you know pain now, just you wait!" to a thirteen-year-old just wouldn't be right.

Okay, here we go. I pulled the first card: Happiness. Huh, good start. Now just two more. Second card: Attraction. Wow. I snuck a peek at Rebecca, who was grinning widely. Crap. Just hold on, Rebecca, don't get too excited, there's still one more. And lastly: Love.

The cards were lying. I knew this, with sinking certainty. A psychic had once told me that sometimes the cards told you what you needed to hear, even if it was not the truth. At the time I'd figured the psychic had just been covering her ass for having been so wrong with her past readings, but now I knew. Sometimes you *do* need to hear something. I looked up at Rebecca, who was now leaning forward with such excitement that I worried even one word from me would serve as a sort of release mechanism, and off she'd go, springing toward Ryan, knocking him over and taking out the sushi bar in the process. I had to be careful. I couldn't toy with her heart, but clearly the cards wanted her to believe in herself.

Remembering my own experiences with boys at that infuriating age (though, who was I kidding, boys are infuriating at any age), and that a girl could measure how much a boy liked her by the intensity of his torment, I tried a different tack, one that could work if he didn't like her at all, as well as if he did.

"So," I said, still smiling, "what the cards are telling me is that he does like you, a lot. However, and this is something you've got to remember, sometimes boys don't admit things like that. Sometimes they even act just the opposite. So he may never admit that he likes you. He may even act like he doesn't. But don't worry. Secretly he does. A lot."

She beamed at me and then was gone, floating across the

dance floor and sneaking furtive glances at übercool Ryan. Ah, what the hell. I figured, she's thirteen. It's not like what I said was going to keep her waiting around for a proposal. I had given her hope and confidence, and that was a good thing, right?

Before long another little girl—one obviously from the Britney camp, with an exposed midriff, perfectly applied eye shadow, and a Gucci purse I knew, with jealousy, was real—made her way to my table. I prayed she wasn't going to ask me about the resident heartthrob as well, but then sized her up as more of the career type. Many kids wanted to know what they were going to be when they grew up, and hours before, I'd made peace with inventing wonderful and exciting careers for them. Why not? There was no way they'd track me down in ten years to give me an earful, so if a girl wanted to be a fashion design-er, she'd be a fashion designer. *Poof!* You're a fashion designer.

This one, a girl who was thirteen going on twenty-five, looked like the type who'd want to work in the entertainment industry. Then again, for all I knew, her dad owned a studio and she *already* worked in the entertainment industry. I was about to ask her what she wanted to know, when faster than the speed of light Gucci Girl spat her question. I blinked.

Her chin rose just slightly. "I *said*, will I ever see my father again."

The way she resisted lifting her voice at the end, refusing to turn her words into a question, told me we both knew the answer. In her eyes was the truth: Despite her bravado and pol-ished facade, she was a scared thirteen-year-old girl who missed her father.

"When was the last time you saw him?"

She didn't break my gaze. "Five years ago. No one knows where he is."

I nodded, desperately wanting to get up—to hand Gordon my cards, scale the nearest ten-foot perimeter wall, and jump back down into a world where I wasn't responsible for anyone but me. This girl didn't need a not-so-successful actress in a beehive wig pretending to be a tarot card reader; she needed a therapist. What could I say? "No, you may never ever see your father again, but I do see a bright future for you as a movie producer"? None of this was right. And where was that hot gay bartender when I needed him?

I had to give her a reading, so I pulled some cards, making damn sure I approved of them before I laid them on the table. There was no way I'd slap down the Death or Disappointment card in a case like this. And though nothing frightening appeared, neither did anything hopeful. I needed to be encouraging, but I didn't want to doom this girl to years of waiting by the window.

"To be honest, I don't know if you'll be seeing him soon. The cards aren't telling me that, but what they *are* telling me is that he wants you to know that he loves you. He thinks about you all the time. You should always remember that, even when he's not here, that doesn't mean he's not thinking about you, or missing you, or wishing he was with you. Always remember that your father loves you. That's what the cards are saying."

Though her chin was still tipped upward, barely, just barely, I did see her nod.

"Thanks," she said as she got up. "I like your wig."

What happened to only fun and glitter mattering to people this young? I stood up, about to voyage to what I feared was a spicy-tuna-roll-ransacked sushi table, when a couple—in their midforties, impeccably groomed, and exuding the word "rich" down to their no doubt buffed and manicured toes—appeared out of nowhere and announced that they wanted a reading on their marriage.

I sat back down. I *really* didn't want to read adults. Adults cared. That I knew, and I'd been hoping to get through the entire evening without journeying into such dangerous, mine-laden territory.

"Is there something in particular you'd like to ask?"

They looked at each other, smiled, and shrugged. Of course not. A question would be too easy, too fast; they wanted an entire reading. They wanted me to be left with just the mounds of ginger, gobs of wasabi, and chopsticks I could do nothing with—other than stab myself over and over in an attempt to end my misery.

I decided to do a general relationship spread—a spread I'd mastered over the years, though sadly had had no reason to use as of late—just to see what surfaced. What surfaced was the Three of Cups, otherwise known in my deck as the love triangle card. Great. My wig was itchy, I was tired, I was denied sushi, and now this? Adultery? Then again, if it was in the cards, maybe I was meant to tell them? Whatever. I decided I was just going to be honest. I'd say what I saw and let them take it how they would. For a second I pictured the table uprooted, cards flying, man and wife screaming, designer clothes ripping, and children running. The bright side of such an outcome, I figured, would be that I might get fired, escorted out, and be wigless on my couch within the hour.

Here went nothing. "Are you aware ... of a third party?"

There was silence, and I braced myself for an earsplitting scream or the wet slap of a drink hurled in my face.

"Yes," the wife said, her eyes wide. She squeezed her husband's hand. "It's okay. I know about the third party. Go on."

Oddly, her husband looked excited, and he too nodded me on. I stared at him in silence, affording him a chance to regain his sanity, to try to change the subject so we weren't all forced to dwell on his infidelity, but he quickly added, "It was during our separation. We just got back together. Sorry, it's just amazing that you picked up on that. But yes, please go on."

So on I went. And the rest, I must say, was actually a breeze, all good fortune with only a few obligatory bumps along the way. By the time I'd finished, they were exhilarated, gazing into each other's eyes, and commenting on little things I'd said, completely impressed with the reading and their future.

Two hours and one measly California roll later, I was finally packing up my tarot cards to leave when the husband approached my table. The wife, I noticed, was nowhere to be found.

"Can I just ask you a quick question?"

I nodded and smiled as visions of couches and food, any kind of food, danced in my head.

"I'd like to know," he said, then looked over his shoulder quickly, "if I did the right thing leaving my girlfriend, or if I made a mistake getting back together with my wife."

I was tired, I was hungry, I wanted to go home, and now, on

top of all that, I was just *done* with the entire species of men. I mean, was he kidding me? There he'd been, all lovey-dovey with his wife, holding her hand and gazing at her as if she were the most beautiful woman in the world, and yet now, just two hours later, he was asking me, a perfect stranger, if getting back together with her was a mistake?! I literally wanted to leap across the table and beat him with my wig. I took a deep breath. Why was I this upset? Suddenly I heard the question again, only this time with a German accent. Right. Wilhelm asking Dustin if he'd made a mistake getting back together with me. *Men.*

"I don't even need the cards for this," I said firmly. "I feel it very strongly. Absolutely, without a doubt, you made the right choice going back to your wife."

The next day, as I counted up my twenties, I thought of that man's question. There he'd stood in expensive Italian shoes, his suit perfect and pressed, a man with a watch that had cost more than I'd made that whole year, a man who no doubt had a very important and respected job, and who was friends with the owners of that estate—that mansion with a view of the world—and yet he'd stood there asking me, a girl often not responsible enough to pay her bills on time even when she did have money, if he'd made the right decision or if his heart had led him astray. Never had I fully understood the control psychics had, the trust people placed in them, or the opportunities to abuse that trust and influence. Sure, I'd been on the other side, I'd been the one asking the questions and believing and imploring, but the understanding of the *power* really only sank in when I myself had become the maker or breaker of dreams.

And when he asked if he'd made the right choice in going back to his wife, what was I to say? I'm human. All I'd had to go on were the looks of love I'd caught them sharing, my instinct, and my own personal feelings on the matter. What was psychic about that? Absolutely nothing. Sure, it was strange that the Three of Cups had popped up when there had indeed been a love triangle, and there were a few other times when the cards had been eerily accurate, but for the most part there was nothing psychic or strange about what I'd done. I'd simply spoken whatever had come to mind, just hunches and feelings and the advice I would have given a friend.

And that's when it hit me.

I could do this. I could read cards. I could give advice.

I could work as a psychic! I'd go undercover at a psychic hotline and wield my tarot powers for good! I understood the power psychics had. Callers would be safe with me, because I'd never abuse that power! Instead I'd tell people to trust their instincts and stop calling!

Right away I found a want ad for readers, and within ten minutes was waiting for my "interview" phone call. My interview was, of course, a reading, so my preparation involved sitting on my bed with my tarot cards and staring off into space. I was actually trying to clear my mind, trying to not worry that Angelique, my interviewer, would see right through me and realize I was a sham of a psychic, nothing more than a bored girl in her bedroom trying to save the world one caller at a time. Yet all I could think was, *Why have I never painted my apartment?* I'd been there for years. Did I not care about these things? At one point the walls had been white, but now they were that strange dusty age-sooted white, some corners and spots mysteriously darker than the rest and adorned with fossilized spiderwebs posing as cracks. I couldn't for the life of me think of a fitting name to describe the hue of the walls within which I'd been living, as even the diplomatic "off-white" was too kind. No, my walls were simply "not-white."

I needed to do something about my apartment. The home that lived in my mind looked so different, a shocking comparison: clean and decorated with plants, fine rugs, painted walls, candles, matching plates, and curtains. I mean, *curtains*. I had curtains only in my bedroom, and those were purely for function and certainly not for appearance, while the living room was practically a greenhouse, all windows through which neighbors and stalkers could monitor my every move.

Granted, my future home was a *house*, not an upper-level living-room-floor-sloping apartment. But when would that future begin? Why force myself to live in an agonizing interim? I would have loved to buy a house, and I would have loved to live with someone, but was I really going to exist like this, just skimming above the surface of functionality until that mysterious time of love and success arrived? What was I waiting for?

Okay, we know damn well what I was waiting for: a man. With Wilhelm, any amount of investment into my own style would have been futile and wasted, as his tastes overrode mine. But *why* had I thought that? Why had his sparse, boring, sterile style become more important than my own? Sure, if either of us were going to throw a tizzy fit over interior design, it would've been him, but still, I'd rolled over and played dead. I'd been so determined to keep him happy that I'd conveniently forgotten that *I* had style too—and style that I actually liked. And now, now that I was single, I'd somehow continued to forget about myself as I put my entire life on hold waiting for a man who might never come.

I thought of Gina joyfully passing up the shoes she'd been coveting when she'd discovered an oak mission–style bookcase that was "the perfect size to fit in that corner that just needs something." Yes, as a woman obsessed with decorating, she had *corners* that needed something, while I had an apartment that needed everything. Before she'd met Mark, we'd all accused her of nesting—the if-you-build-it-he-will-come theory—and had liked asking her what she'd do if her future man didn't like her style. She never gave it a second thought. "Then he won't move in, will he?" And while that attitude could certainly have backfired, in her case it hadn't. Mark arrived, fell in love with her and her couch, and never left.

I'd buy curtains, I decided. I'd find the money; I'd make it happen. I was debating over color—sage green would be soothing, white would be versatile—when the phone rang. Oh, right. I'm a psychic.

I shuffled the cards and concentrated. Angelique wanted to know about work, not love, as apparently she wasn't happy at her job. That right there blew my mind. Her job was *testing psychics and getting free readings all day long.* Um, hello? How can I get your job? Immediately I decided that she was unappreciative and undeserving—though it did occur to me that testing psychics most likely involved getting readings from bad psychics, and I knew that even if a psychic was proven inaccurate, it was very difficult to forget their words. Poor Angelique. Within her brain must have been swarms and swarms of conflicting readings, all driving her batty. Then again, I had those swarms too, and yet I'd paid for mine. Yeah, no more feeling bad for Angelique.

I tried not to worry about what I was saying. I simply told the story of the cards and whatever else popped into my mind. I talked and talked, and when finally I was done, there was silence. I waited, nervously. For all I knew she'd set the phone on her kitchen counter ages ago, and was off doing laundry or polishing silver. Had I just wasted thirty minutes of my life?

"Wow," she finally said, her voice a bit wobbly. "That was amazing. You were right on. I definitely want you on board. Can you start today?"

Thirty minutes later my e-mail in-box was flooded with forms, and I was horrified at how easy it had been to get a job as a psychic. Granted, there's no Psychic University from which to graduate, or psychic internships to be had, but getting this job had been as easy as when I'd gotten my first job at Baskin-Robbins. No experience? Great, we'll take you.

At any rate, I printed what they sent me, including a confidentiality agreement (hence I will be referring to said nameless psychic hotline as "Said Nameless Psychic Hotline") and pages and pages and pages of a code of conduct. I'd stumbled upon a self-proclaimed "moral" psychic hotline. Endlessly they rambled on with their claim that the goal was not to keep the caller on the line longer than necessary, yet then, hidden as a footnote, was the information that our average call length determined our pay schedule. Huh. I assumed it worked like this for most hotlines, and flashed back to the many times I'd called psychics only to encounter an inordinate amount of shuffling or excessively long prayers to guides and the universe. The bastards.

I was no longer Sarah; I was Mirabel. *Yep*, I thought as I leaned back on my bed and flipped through a J.Crew catalog, *I'm Mirabel. Mirabel the Psychic. That's me.* Now, for my first prediction as Mirabel: An actress, who still hasn't gotten paid a dime for the movie she's filming in a month, will spend an unreasonable amount of money on a pink cashmere sweater with sparkly rhinestone buttons, and will then tack on a pair of chocolate-brown high leather—

The phone rang.

I sat up. Shit. People really believed I was a psychic? I took a deep breath and plastered a perma-grin on my face. Not that anyone could see me, but I wanted them to *hear* me smiling, and perma-grins somehow come with sound effects.

"Hi! And welcome to Said Nameless Psychic Hotline! My name is Mirabel. Who's this and what's on your mind today?"

"Hi, this is Tisha. I want to ask about John. How's he feeling about me?"

Without wasting time (money), I pulled the cards, my fingers flying. "I see that he's very attracted to you, but he's struggling with something. He's feeling a lot of anxiety, like he's torn in two. Does that make sense?"

"Uh-huh," Tisha said, sounding bored. "He's married. So, will he leave his wife?"

More than anything I longed to scream, "No! And damn you for even hoping for that, you evil husband stealer!" But alas, I'd been instructed not to judge the callers. Tisha, I'm sure, wanted to hear "Yes, he'll leave her and you'll be together, and now let's do a reading on your big bright future with him." Truthfully, that's what most psychics would say because that's what would keep her on the phone. Then, convinced John would leave his wife, she'd wait for that to happen. Then she'd wait some more, and call another psychic, wait, and call many more psychics.

Tisha's emotional well-being was in my hands. Essentially, I was responsible for the next few years of her life.

"Well, Tisha, to be honest with you I don't know if he'll leave his wife. But maybe it's time to ask what *your instincts* are telling you. And maybe it's also time to ask yourself if you deserve to be with a man who's available. Don't you deserve that?"

And in response to this, in response to my attempt to spare her pain, to divert her from a psychic noose and to lead her down a much healthier, rewarding path, the little hussy hung up on me. Fine, don't face reality. Whatever.

The phone rang again, and then again, and then again. Angelique had warned me this would happen, that everyone rushes to test out the new psychic. Whereas other readers might capitalize on this, I used the opportunity to spread my trust-your-own-instincts mantra, a mantra, I might mention, that wasn't so well received.

Soon my brain was fried and I was mentally and emotionally exhausted. I felt as if I'd taken on the weight of all the callers' problems, and I literally ached from the strain.

The phone rang again.

"Hi. And welcome to Said Nameless Psychic Hotline. My name is Mirabel. Who's this and what's on your mind today."

"Uh, yeah, this is Gina, and I'm wondering what Mirabel did to my friend Sarah?"

"You're tying up my line. I'm a psychic."

"No, you're not."

"Yes, I am. I'm Mirabel the Psychic and for the last two hours people have been telling me their problems and then hanging up on me."

"What an awesome job."

"I have to do it. I'm on a covert mission."

"Ah. Mirabel the *Undercover* Psychic?"

"Yes, but no one wants to hear that they should stop calling and just listen to themselves. I'm making *no progress* and am totally exhausted from trying to be nonjudgmental, sympathetic, and rational, and at the same time save these people from themselves."

"So this means you don't want to go bowling tonight?"

"What is it with you and bowling?"

"What is it with you and your *unacceptance* of bowling?"

"I gotta go. I'm taking one more call and then a three-hour bath."

I hung up and stared at the phone. One more, just one more. *In fact,* I thought, *I'll start running the bathwater now, and then, with my pathetic water pressure, the tub might be full in forty-five minutes.*

Right as I cranked the hot water, I heard the dreaded ring.

Drying my hands on my bedspread—starting *tomorrow* I was going to care about my apartment—I did my hello and welcome bit and prayed for a call that wouldn't be serious. I might even be able to handle a "Did my sister sleep with my boyfriend" call, as long as there was no crying. But really what

I wanted was a simple call like "What colors should I have at my wedding" (something Gina had been tormented over since the engagement), or "Will I be forced to wear an ugly bridesmaid dress" (something I'd become tormented over once I'd realized that Gina saw her wedding as a chance to decorate, and couldn't have cared less about fashion).

Unfortunately, I was to have no such luck in the simple call department. Joanie, from Virginia, started off with the not-so-encouraging-yet-not-so-awful question of "Will things improve between me and my daughter?" I figured I could handle this, until Joanie then continued with, "She's going out with a *woman*, which is just wrong and a sin, and I can't have that in my house. She asked if she could bring home this woman from college for the weekend, and I said no. No way was I gonna let that happen. Now we haven't spoken since. Been about eight months."

I heard my bathwater running. I envisioned my stress-relief bath soak. *Just get through this call,* I thought. *Just this one call.* And though I wanted to yell at Joanie for being homophobic and then inform her she was a horrible mother, I couldn't do that. That wouldn't help anything. Basically, I had only minutes to completely change this woman's attitude and salvage her relationship with her daughter. What a way to end a day.

"Joanie, how old is your daughter?"

"She'll be twenty-two next month."

I was racking my brain for clever approaches. "Okay, so she's young. She's not going to settle down with anyone—man or woman—for a long time. And, actually, I feel that she *may* have a relationship with a man next, but if you don't accept her for who she is now, she'll never forgive you and the damage to your relationship will be permanent, which I see leading to years of unhappiness for you both. So tell me, why are you *really* upset that she's with a woman? Because I do see pain around you, but it's temporary pain, pain that can be worked through. Tell me how this hurts you."

"I don't know. It's just *wrong*. It's a sin, and I can't wrap my brain around it." Joanie gave a slight huff, and I swear I practically heard her shaking her head with scorn as she stared out the window of her double-wide.

Changing her views on morality was unlikely, not in ten minutes and not by a perfect stranger on whom she could just hang up. I had to be innovative. I had to find a way to basically sneak acceptance into her, perhaps by playing on her (well-hidden) mothering side. "Well," I started with, "let's look at the benefits of her being with a woman, shall we? She won't get pregnant before she's ready."

"That's true," Joanie said reluctantly. "She needs to finish college. I've been telling her that since day one."

"Right. So she'll be able to finish school and won't get *pregnant*." "Pregnant" I verbally underscored as if it were the same as possession by the devil, which, in Joanie's mind, it may have been. "Oh, and another big positive is you won't have to worry as much about AIDS."

Okay, I admit, I scrambled on that one. Though it seemed like transmission from woman to woman would be rare, I really wasn't sure, and was pretty much banking on the strong hunch that Joanie had no clue about statistics, or science in general.

"AIDS'd be bad," Joanie said. "That's true. I don't want her to get that. Maybe you are right. I never looked at it this way."

"I am right. The *guides*," I said, putting emphasis on "guides" because that word got people to pay attention, "are telling me very strongly that you need to accept your daughter's relationship."

Remarkably, we talked for another twenty minutes, and when we hung up, not only did Joanie have a new perspective, but my bath was also perfectly full and the ideal temperature—which, by the way, is a very tricky science.

Maybe it was easier for psychics who didn't care as much about their callers, or psychics who didn't take on the responsibility of their callers' lives to the extent that I had, but this wasn't something I could do every day. The mere thought of doing it even one more day made me want to cry from exhaustion and pressure. That last reading had been like the call that broke the psychic's back, and though I barely had the energy to dump the entire jar of aromatherapy stress–relief bath salts into the water, there was practically a spring in my step as I went back to my room, grabbed the phone, and dialed Angelique's number. I thanked her for the opportunity, said I just wasn't cut out for the job, and quit. There. Done. No more.

Sinking into the tub, I couldn't smell a thing, but honestly did feel stress relief like never before.

14

(Come on, would I really have a Chapter 13?)

Laser Beams and Curtains

MAYBE BEING HAPPY IS THE NORM FOR OTHERS, but for me happiness is a sign that something is different. An acting teacher once described me as "damp" and needing to find my "joie de vivre," and though when he said this I was traumatized (and vowed to perfect the expressions of happiness and joy), years later I understood what he meant. Happiness is not my norm. Sadness is my norm, and being on the verge of tears and afflicted with constant worry is my natural state. Therefore, when it strikes me that I'm happy, it's as shocking as if I'd discovered that overnight my brown eyes had turned blue.

Driving home from kung fu practice, two weeks after my short-lived career as an undercover psychic, I was in a rush to get home and get ready for a special screening of *Until the Night*, when I realized I was happy. Actually, initially I identified the sensation as "feeling strange," and then I pinpointed that I *wasn't worried about anything.* Then, once

I went so far as to conclude I was in a good mood, it hit me: I was happy.

The last time I'd realized I was happy was long ago, on an exquisite day spent with Wilhelm discount-store window-shopping and then dining on lobster imperial, a day that had rendered me completely joyous. Yet the moment I'd identified my happiness, I'd fixated on the idea that it was only a matter of time before things went wrong, and I was immediately filled with an insurmountable sense of impending doom and disaster—at which point I promptly had an anxiety attack. But now? Now I was happy and wasn't even *worried* about being happy. Was this a result of the endorphins from exercise? Was it the Zoloft? Or was it that I was two weeks away from filming, from being the star of a movie? Or, perhaps, it was the screening that night? Wow. It hit me I had a lot to be happy about. And I couldn't even remember the last time I'd called a psychic. Maybe it was a few weeks back, but for me that was eons ago. Of course, thinking about how long it had been since I'd called made me crave a reading, but still, the point was I was improving.

To add to this strange feeling of pleasure, it occurred to me that it had been a year since I'd broken up with Wilhelm and, shockingly, I was over him. Not only was I over him, but I was *so* over him. Rarely did he sneak into my thoughts, and when he did, I no longer felt that top-of-the-roller-coaster leap in my chest. I no longer had sad flashes of my life as a lounge singer or wistfully reminisced about our days at Ross or T.J. Maxx. Even my future house was void of Wilhelm, and I realized that for a while he'd been nowhere near my infinity pool—nor had he been mixing a drink in the cabana or strolling along the bamboo perimeter. He was, officially, off the premises.

My good mood continued into the evening. Only once during the movie did I have a mild sense of panic, but I figured that was normal since it was sparked by viewing myself topless on a ninety-foot-wide screen. Let me just say, regardless of how self-assured you may think you are, that confidence hasn't been truly tested till your nipples have been front and center—and about one foot in diameter—in front of an audience of everyone you know, all of them chomping on popcorn and getting an eyeful.

I simply took a deep breath, and then another one, and then before I knew it the movie was over and I was making my way to the lobby, basking in the glow of praise and good wishes and questions, to which I was able to joyfully respond, "Why, yes, funny you should ask. I *am* actually about to start shooting my next movie in two weeks. Oh, and what a coincidence, it's the same director! Why, thank you, thank you, yes, he does have good taste."

Everyone was extremely complimentary, though I admit I could've done without the strange little man who sidled up to me and murmured "Nice tits" before scurrying away. The only other blight on the evening was that, having had very little reason over the previous months to wear high heels, or shoes for that matter, my feet were no longer cut out for being social. Already I could isolate six spots where blisters were forming, and my back had started aching to the point where I no longer cared about the movie or crowd or acting or anything. I only cared about a chair. Right then, sitting down was all that mattered in life.

I spotted an oasis across the room: an empty chaise against the wall and a waiter with a tray of champagne. I beelined and had almost made it there when a woman with electrified curly blond hair stepped into my path.

"Sarah Lassez, right?"

Drat. Only two feet from my oasis. As I agreed that yes, I was Sarah Lassez, I shuffled around just slightly, backed up a bit, and dropped my purse on the chaise, claiming it as my own. Then I smiled politely, knowing relief was just inches behind me, and waited for something like "I loved the film," or "Great job," or "How come you don't work more?"

Instead, the woman leaned in, as if about to kiss me, and whispered, "You worked at Said Nameless Psychic Hotline, right? Mirabel?"

To say I freaked out would be an understatement. It was as if two worlds I'd desperately wanted to keep separate had just collided, and somehow I'd been standing in the middle and gotten seriously plowed over. How did she know? Had word of this somehow gotten around? Were people now aware that Sarah Lassez was not really a steadily employed actress, but was actually working as a psychic? That she was actually a freak?

She must have seen the look of terror on my face. "Don't worry. I didn't mean to ambush you. I'm Gloria; I do the books there. I really didn't mean to startle you with all this, but I recognized your name as the girl who worked for just one day."

"One day *undercover*. For a role." I don't know what possessed me to say this, but I'd suddenly felt the urge to seem a bit cooler than I was appearing to be.

"Really? What role is this?"

Shit. I couldn't exactly get into detail about a nonexistent role, so I proceeded along as if she'd never spoken, a strategy I'd always admired in others. "Have you heard of psychic addiction?"

Like before, Gloria quickly leaned in, though now, knowing she was an employee of the enemy, I was struck with a momentary fear that she was about to head butt me.

Of course she did no such thing. Instead she quickly glanced behind her, perhaps to make sure the entire crowd hadn't snuck up behind her to listen in, and whispered, "My husband is a cameraman. He's why we're here, but *he's* a psychic addict. I know all about psychic addicts. We've had customers at Said Nameless Psychic Hotline spend fifty thousand dollars on readings. Because of that? We have a policy that says you can only spend up to three thousand a month."

For a few seconds I wondered how she'd grown taller, then it suddenly dawned on me that I was actually now sitting, and sitting on my purse, for that matter. Three thousand dollars in one month? And that's a limit they had implemented because people spent *more* than that?

"I mean, we're small and actually pretty new, but we make upwards of four hundred thousand dollars a month—so, yes, addicts I know *all* about. That's actually mostly what I do, talk to addicts. Well, talk to people who've reached their limit and beg for one more reading."

Somehow I managed to find my footing again, and stood, a bit wobbly, as she regaled me with a few quick and very alarming stories. When someone tapped me on the shoulder, I turned, so enrapt with the tales that I'd almost forgotten where I was and why.

"Sarah, right?" a man said. "It's Ted! Ted from Sundance!"

I feigned recognition of this man, whom I'd evidently met years ago at a festival filled with thousands of people. Then I turned to introduce Ted to Gloria, but already she was across the room, her arm linked with that of a shorter man with sparse hair and a round face, a sweet-looking man whose life, I knew, was not so different from my own.

A week later Holly called. Knowing I hadn't had any auditions lately, I heard her voice and immediately figured she'd been roped into being the bearer of bad news. Would they not be ready to film in a week? Had the director died? Had they decided I was all wrong for the part? Were they not happy with my kung fu? *Was I out of a job?*

"There's this big music mogul," Holly said, "who's throwing some shindig tonight. I thought you might want to go. Open bar, food's supposed to be great. I think there'll be some interesting people there, along with your typical producers, agents, et cetera. Do you already have plans?"

Do I already have plans? That's like asking a vegetarian if she'd planned on ordering the braised lamb or the delightfully tender veal. The answer is no, a big resounding *no*. I stopped the bathwater, put away my Mistral Linden Lettuce foam bath, my latest bubbly craze, and agreed to go.

After all, there are two things you don't turn down: one, an open bar with great free food, and two, an invitation from your manager to hang out. And by "hang out" I mean go to a work-related function with business opportunities, which is the least work-related activity a manager or agent is capable of and so is, relatively speaking, their version of hanging out. I knew from past experience that being on Holly's radar was like securing a spot at the top of Santa's list, so I took this opportunity very seriously and within seconds was standing in my closet—well, not so much standing as *balancing* on top of all the junk I'd shoved in there. A music industry party. What does one wear? For some reason my brain reversed into the eighties, and I pictured everyone in black leather pants and shredded T-shirts. Surely that wouldn't be the case; at least I hoped it wouldn't be.

After twenty minutes I had on an outfit I was happy with, one I topped with my grandmother's vintage leather Christian Dior coat with mink collar. I had a hunch I'd be the only one at the party wearing something that belonged to her grandmother, but still, I looked sophisticated and successful—or like I *should* be successful—and I *was* wearing leather in some form. Satisfied, I was out the door.

Now, I've never been one to drool over cars, but when I hopped out at the valet and spotted a midnight blue Audi TT Roadster pulling up behind me, I admit it; I stopped. I stared. I had no control over myself, because I wasn't just looking at a car, I was looking at *my* future car. I wanted it, and when I want something, I fixate. I stood there and the world fell away, leaving just me and my car, though I decided I wouldn't buy it in blue after all, maybe silver. I was trying to figure out if I'd keep the black leather interior or opt for something lighter, when all of a sudden the driver stepped out and turned in my direction.

Laser blue eyes. I *knew* those eyes. I didn't even have to see the rest of the face to know who it was: Matthew, otherwise known as the Hot Successful Actor with Laser Blue Eyes.

Approximately ten million years ago, we'd worked together. So as I watched him hand his keys to the valet, I figured he'd pass me by, another victim of Success Amnesia, a horrible disease that claims those who've risen to the top, by erasing all memories of the little people they once knew, and taking with those memories any and all understanding of the value of a dollar. A victim of Success Amnesia will often be overheard uttering the words "I'm only getting paid two hundred and fifty grand for this, so you *know* it's not about the money," and can be spotted walking like a horse donning blinders, ignoring the smiles and waves of some poor soul nearby who in truth might have no pull in the entertainment industry but who once shared his SpaghettiOs back when life was a bit rougher.

And then his eyes were upon me. I stood straight, trying to gather as much confidence as possible before it was destroyed by the unrecognizing and uncaring gaze of the blue laser beams. But then something shocking happened.

"Sarah!" His voice was loud enough that everyone in line for the restaurant turned, then, seeing who'd made the outcry, they all proceeded to seek out this Sarah creature, determined to locate the object of the Hot Successful Actor with Laser Blue Eyes's delight.

Inside me was a little girl impressed by movie stars and popularity, a girl who was jumping up and down, screaming, "He remembers me! He remembers me!" The outside me, the adult me, was aware of being scrutinized by hundreds of eyes and thus had to struggle to silence her glee and don a look of casual delight, a look that said "Oh. Hey, yeah, movie stars are always excited to see me." In fact, I was fighting to lessen my smile, when I was swooped off my feet and into a bear hug.

"You look *beautiful*," he said when he set me down.

It was official. I loved him. And so much for lessening my smile, as I now had no choice but to grin like a fool. "Thank you. You're going to this party?"

He glanced at the long line of impatient people, and at the bouncer who simply stared, not entertained, at a trio of guys in suits whose faces were splintered with desperation, their hands moving as they attempted to explain something. "Yeah, yeah," he said. "You too? Come on."

And with that we sailed past the line and straight to the entrance. The bouncer, who'd spotted us coming, not only didn't body slam us to the ground and toss our lifeless carcasses to the back of the line, he practically *leapt* from his stool to open the door for us. *So this is what it's like,* I thought. For a second I allowed my imagination to pluck Matthew from beside me, to lift him from the equation and fling him aside so that *I* was the only one present, so all the fuss had been for *me*. God, what a wonderful— I stopped. The exhilaration, the joy, *the life* drained right out of me.

There, standing at the hostess station just twenty feet away, was the glaring, reflective, shining widow's peak I knew all too well.

My fight-or-flight instinct kicked in and told me to run. *Run! Fly back down the stairs and into Matthew's car and race far, far away from the man who broke your heart.* And I think I might have done just that, except that I caught sight of Wilhelm leaning in and just slightly, just barely, brushing the hostess's hand with his own. They were laughing. He was smiling. And this, I must say, completely altered my instinct. Now I was all fight.

"Pretend you're my boyfriend," I whispered to Matthew.

"Sure, honey."

Without skipping a beat he was in character and holding my hand.

Approaching. Approaching. Getting closer. Almost there. Four feet away I transformed my face into that of shock. I stopped walking, as if I'd just spotted him.

"Wilhelm? Oh my God." I watched as he turned, his eyes widening as he saw me, and then narrowing upon spotting my delicious and successful arm candy.

"Sarah," he said evenly. "Hi. It's good to see you."

Matthew, not one to take any role lightly, had chosen to play the possessive type and now had his arm around me, holding me so close I felt the hard form of his cell phone in his pocket. And yes, I do mean his cell phone.

I tried to look nonchalant. "Nice to see you too. What are you doing here?"

Meanwhile, the hostess, either sensing the skirmish or shamelessly wanting Matthew for herself, came out from behind the station to reveal her ridiculously long legs and equally ridiculous short skirt. She pretended to scan the dining room for something, and I momentarily concentrated my energies on making the gigantic wrought-iron chandelier above her fall.

"I work here," Wilhelm said.

"Really? I thought for sure you'd be in Bangkok or Johannesburg by now. What happened to your journey?"

"Yes, well," Wilhelm mumbled. "Timing, you know."

Matthew, deserving an Oscar for his performance as Sarah's Devoted Boyfriend Who Doesn't Even Look at Sluts with Short Skirts, then took off my coat and tossed it to Wilhelm. "Check this for my girl, will you? Thanks, man."

Before Wilhelm could shriek "I'm not the coat check! I'm the sous-chef! The sous-chef!" Matthew was already leading me away and leaning in to whisper—and kiss my ear at the same time—"Who was that clown?"

Across the room I spotted Holly, sitting at a table with white pillar candles and a single delicate white orchid, an empty seat by her side. I smiled.

"Oh, no one," I said, my skin shivering beneath Matthew's breath. "Just a bizarre metrosexual German sous-chef I once dated."

A week later I was still basking in the glory of the music-industry shindig. The scene was one I'd replayed so many times in my mind that I'd started handing out stage directions to all the minor players: "You there, move to the left when you see us approach. No! Your other left! Camera left! And you in the Armani suit, mouth open in shock, please."

Though I hadn't seen Wilhelm again that evening (and wasn't quite sure why he'd been there in the first place, since he hadn't been dressed as a chef), the evening had just gotten better and better. Not only had I proven to myself that I was truly over the man whose existence was wrapped up in my psychic and psychological downfall, but I'd kissed a man whose laser eyes made my heart snag—and come to the very important decision that my future car was fine with black interior. Hee–hee.

Despite feeling so healthy and happy, habit made my fingers itch to call psychics just for fun, just to see what Wilhelm thought of me, if he was devastated and sad and replaying the scene in his mind as well. *And there's my beautiful ex-girlfriend with a movie star. Oh why, oh why didn't I ask her to marry me? Why did I continually lead her on? She could have been mine. I am a fool.*

I decided to do absolutely nothing for my last Saturday before filming. The whole day I'd do nothing, just relax and maybe take a long bath with the phone on the floor beside me in case Matthew called. Not that I really wanted to get involved with him—well, I did, but only in some alternate universe where the other me had an enormous pain threshold, no expectations beyond the present hour, and absolutely no feelings or emotions, or human qualities at all, for that matter. The fact was he was an actor, and not only was he an actor but he was a famous actor, a detail I knew would lead to endless paranoia and suspicion on my part. Girls literally threw themselves at him. Could I handle that? No. Not at all. In fact, should we get involved, I knew precisely *when* such fear and paranoia would begin, since he'd told me that in just two weeks he would be off to Australia to film his next movie and would be gone *for five months*. For all intents and purposes, I could go ahead and circle the date of his departure on my calendar, scrawl in "Sarah's mental decline begins," and be right on.

Oh, and as if all this weren't warning enough, I'd also recently seen a movie in which he'd played a serial killer. I'd watched him hack a poor trusting young woman into pieces. If I didn't view that as prophetic, I was high.

Still, I had the phone within reach in case he called. I figured if I heard from him then perhaps I'd be slightly justified in calling a psychic just for fun, just to ask their take on what could happen with us, if I'd definitely have Aussie-accented nightmares. Unfortunately, when the phone did ring, trilling the ringtone I'd downloaded—"Que sera, sera! Whatever will be, will be! The future's not ours to see! Que sera, sera!"—my new motto in life and my constant antipsychic reminder, it wasn't Matthew at all, but Gina, who within seconds destroyed all my plans of nothingness.

She needed to find a wedding dress. With the wedding only a year and two months away, she was beginning to panic and had gone into freaky Virgo mode, a mode that involved spreadsheets, printed lists of tasks, and cutout magazine pages of dresses and flowers and cakes that she *laminated* and ordered by subject in a black leather binder. Luckily, one of the dresses she liked was at a boutique in Santa Monica.

"But here's the thing," she said. "We can't just go there. These boutiques are snotty. The girls who work there are hate-filled elitist little snobs who won't give us the time of day if we don't look like we *deserve* it. Seriously, if we go in dressed like we normally are on a Saturday afternoon, they'll take one look at us and assume I have no money. Then they'll *hide* the good dresses, and only bring out the cheap ugly ones."

"*Can* you afford the good dresses?"

"God, no. I'm totally broke. But I still want to try them on, so I can start saving with a goal, you know? I mean, Sarah, this dress is gorgeous. I've been dreaming about it; it's part of the whole vision now. But they won't even look in my direction if they think I'm not buying. So, the plan is to get all glammed up, go there, park a block away so they don't see my car, and then strut around their pathetic little store like we're just killing time before we meet with the actual designers themselves. Okay?"

There went my bath. There went my Saturday. But then again, there also went the distinct possibility that I'd spend the entire day staring at my cell phone, hoping it would ring as much as I hoped it wouldn't. Wanting Matthew was like wanting a hypodermic of sugar water injected straight into a vein— sure, something sweet is always nice, but the whole thing is just really wrong.

"Sarah, you with me? We have only two hours to get ready. Do your nails if they're not done, deep condition your hair, whatever. Then find an outfit that says chic sophistication, like you're old New York money."

The result of such a request was both of us dressed head to toe in black.

"Ah, man," Gina said as I got into her car. "We look like we're coming from a funeral."

"A chic, sophisticated *New York* funeral," I corrected.

Once at the store, surrounded by taunting dresses and snide tiaras that screamed to me, "Try me on! Try me on! Oh, wait, you have no reason. Keep walking there, single girl," I witnessed our rapid collapse. Though we entered with confidence and carefully masked excitement, it was only a matter of time before Gina was thoroughly appalled at all of the ridiculously expensive dresses, and I was fuming from being referred to as "Gina's

Friend" by a bitchy little salesgirl who'd never bothered to ask my name. Throttling the snobby pixie and screaming, "Just because I'm single and not getting married anytime soon doesn't mean I don't get a name! I have a name! I've actually had a name for *years* now, and it's not Gina's Friend!" was an enticing option.

Thankfully I was spared my tirade, as at last Gina emerged from behind the curtain dressed in something that looked as though it belonged on a pimped-out ballerina. She stood before the mirror, her eyes wide and unblinking. I was about to point out that the bowling-ball-size flowers that bloomed on the poofy tulle skirt could most likely be removed, or maybe just trimmed, and actually weren't even that noticeable as the eye went straight to the flashy bodice with sequins shaped into some sort of a heraldic coat of arms, when she turned to me.

"It didn't look like this in the magazine."

"No," I said. "I imagine it didn't."

"Oh, Gina's Friend?" said the snobby salesgirl, Bethany (see, I learned *her* name). "Is that yours?" Her wrist dangled in the direction of my purse. "I'll just move it to Gina's dressing room so people don't trip."

I clamped my mouth shut to squelch a string of words I suspected would be highly unsuitable for brides and their mothers, then quickly turned to Gina and smiled a big, fake, happy grin.

Gina, equally as horrified, was glaring at the salesgirl. When she saw me, she shook her head apologetically, and then turned back to face the mirror. Suddenly her eyes narrowed. "Are those *feathers?*"

"You're just now seeing them?"

She looked at me, her eyes now very wide. "Sarah, listen to me. *It has to come off, and we have to leave. Now*."

Back in the safety of her Jetta we sat in silence, each dwelling in our own special nightmare.

After a while, she spoke. "I'm sorry about that."

"No," I said. "*I'm* sorry about that."

She nodded and started the car.

We decided to take the freeway home, as it was a Saturday and thus might involve use of the gas pedal rather than simple coasting. A couple turns later and we were almost to the freeway entrance, when we saw the ocean, vast and blue and glimmering in the late afternoon light. I don't know why, but it always sort of takes me by surprise that it's there. I guess it's the out-of-sight, out-of-mind thing, but because I rarely *see* the ocean, it always kind of creeps up on me, this gigantic body of water that pops out from behind trees and buildings, suddenly looming on the horizon like, "Hey, look at me, I'm the ocean."

"Want to go to the beach?" Gina asked, an apparently rhetorical question since she was already ignoring the freeway and making a right to head up the coast. "Past Malibu there's this spot with great tide pools. I haven't been there since high school when we got that grant."

I'd heard the tales, Gina and her friends' attempt at padding their college applications by taking part in a grant for the National Science Foundation, something that involved studying the migration of monarch butterflies and was an entirely misguided venture for girls who'd cared nothing about science. "We stuck thermometers up butterflies' butts," she'd once told me, "and then, when none of the scientists were looking, we tried to escape." Still, when lunchtime rolled around on those tedious Saturdays, the whole herd of social misfits—along with Gina and her friends—had crossed the highway and gone tide-pooling. And thus was born Gina's fascination with anemones and sea slugs.

Eventually we pulled to the side of the road, across from the state park where long ago the butterflies had been caught and tagged and released back into their monitored world. Gina paused as she got out of the car and stared cryptically at the eucalyptuses. "Fear not *Danaus plexippus*," she said, "for I am not here for you." Then she turned back toward the water. "Alrighty. Let's go find ourselves some sea creatures."

What we soon discovered was that getting to the sand involved descending a staircase most likely built by California's first settlers, a staircase with wood handrails so ragged and decrepit that even *thinking* about touching them could lead to splinters imbedding in your skin. Arms stiff at our sides, we made our way toward the sand, pausing midway to tell ourselves we could do this, only twelve more horribly slanted and frail stairs to go.

At the bottom we rejoiced—until we took our first step. Our heels sunk deeply into the sand. We struggled to release ourselves, then took another step. Again, there was a struggle to reclaim our feet. This time we stood, wobbling on one leg at a time, and pried off our high-heeled strappy sandals. Then, shoes in hand, we started the long trudge to the water.

It wasn't till we were halfway there that we noticed the surfers. There were at least a dozen of them, on the beach and in the water, and they were staring. Most likely they'd been staring the entire time, confused and watching us—two girls completely decked out in full makeup and head to toe black, carrying high heels in their hands, their purses swinging on their shoulders as they stumbled, as if possessed, to the water. I admit, we didn't exactly look like we belonged. I studied the surfers and then Gina, who gave a little wave, her vintage rhinestone bracelet catching the light, and in my mind the little Sesame Street ditty "One of these things is not like the other, one of these things just isn't the same!" began to chorus.

We charged forth, attempting to both hold our heads high with confidence and watch the sand for chunks of tar and putrid seaweed laced with things we knew instinctively were best left undiscovered. When at last we reached the water, Gina looked confused. She studied the coastline. "*Ah, man. This is* the spot, but the tide's not low. All this water's supposed to be *rocks.*"

Our work would not be for nothing. Determined, we made our way to the nearest rock formation that jutted out into the ocean, and started to climb. Again, we were presented with an activity that proved more difficult than originally anticipated. The jagged and rough rocks were not so friendly to bare, sand–softened, and recently pedicured feet. As I pulled myself up to a higher spot, trying not to drop my shoes and to keep my purse from falling off my shoulder, I immediately scraped the inside of my hand. There on my palm was a little surge of blood smack through my love line. *Fabulous,* I thought, *I just took out my next boyfriend.*

Though I was a mess, I was doing better than Gina, who was swearing under her breath and claiming a shell was now stuck in her foot. Then, ten seconds later, she was squealing with delight and pointing at a little pool of water caught in the rocks. Nothing about us made sense, and I pictured the surfers below, their fun on pause as they continued to observe the two girls who looked as though they'd just left a chic New York funeral to scale a cluster of rocks as though it were Mount Everest, then curse and hobble in pain and stop and squeal and joyfully point at sea snails.

But it was worth it. When we finally made it to the farthest point of the formation, we found the perfect rock to sit on, one softened and rounded by years of water and force, a little bench curved and crafted by time's smoothing hand. Directly below us waves crashed, sending up soft sprays of water, as if we were perched on a giant salty Evian mister—but in a nice way. Gulls dove through the air, white wings sweeping the sky. The ocean, glimmering and tranquil, stretched out into something I could only think of as *forever*.

Gina inspected her left foot, the one pained by what appeared to be a rather invisible shell. "So, what's the latest with Laser Beams?"

"Hasn't called. Which is just as well. It would've been good for my ego, but that's about it. I don't need to get involved with someone who'll be gone for five months."

"An *actor* who will be gone for five months. Double whammy."

"He's just so cute. Did you see him in that last movie? There was a scene where they showed his butt. Let me just say, he has an amazing butt."

"Could've been a butt double."

"No, you can tell he's got a good butt. No double needed. But you know what got me that night? It was feeling wanted. You know? There was someone who cared that I was there, who looked for me when I stepped away."

"Someone else will want you too. The *right* person. Someone who's not a trained liar and who won't be in another country for five months."

This, the issue of the right person or *the one*, was something I'd been grappling with lately. After a lifetime of wrong people, I was no longer holding my breath that the right one was around the corner. I was no longer convinced *the one* even existed. Maybe I had many ones. Maybe they'd come and gone and would continue to come and go. Maybe those words—"the one"—had essentially led me on for years, teasing me, taunting me, forcing me to compare real people with those imagined.

"You know, I'm not sure I believe in *the one* anymore. I mean, *is* there a match for everyone? Maybe there isn't. Plenty of people end up alone. I could be one of them."

Gina shook her head. "No, you'll meet someone. This town just makes it a bit tougher, that's all."

"I might not, though. It's possible I won't, and I can't keep relying on and *living for* some future fantasy person. I need to be happy now. I need to buy curtains."

"Ooh, I'll help you buy curtains."

"Okay. Tomorrow maybe."

Gina smiled. "Yay, curtains. And see, then the next day you start filming. You're the *star* of a movie. Your career is going great. It's all about to happen; it's exciting."

"I know. I'm the happiest career–wise I've ever been."

"Seriously, then, don't mess it up with an actor."

I nodded. The sound of crashing waves encourages silence, and for a while neither of us spoke. I rifled through my purse till I found my piña colada lip balm that smelled wonderful but tasted as pleasant as a cleaning product. It had been expensive and it came in a really cute little art nouveau container, so of course I still used it, but I had to be very careful when I smiled, to prevent even a smidgen from getting on my teeth, as the consequences were severe.

"You know what I miss?" Gina said. "High school. I do. Those stupid boring Saturdays here, thinking about colleges and how amazing life would be. That feeling of having everything in front of you still. All the possibilities."

I offered her the lip balm, which she took, put on, and tasted before I could say anything. For a few seconds she looked like a cat with fur stuck on its tongue.

"Sorry," I said. "I was about to warn you. But how you're remembering high school is in hindsight. When you were *in* high school, all you wanted was for real life to hurry up and start. You didn't appreciate that the world was your oyster and your whole life was still in front of you."

"I can't get rid of that taste. My God that was bad." She paused, regaining her composure. "But yes, I guess that's true. Some woman in her seventies is probably thinking that about us, right? How nice it would be to be back in her thirties. And I know I should appreciate this time in my life; it's a good time, but it's scary."

"At least you'll have a husband to be scared *with*."

"Yeah, well, lotta good he does me at three a.m. when I'm freaking out."

"Why would you be awake at three a.m.?"

She shrugged. "I don't know. I wake up. My mind goes wild. I start to panic about my career—I mean, what should *be* my career, what I'm doing with my life. I love Mark more than anything, but at three a.m. he's sleeping. I don't have him, or any distractions, to take my mind off myself. It's just me." She looked at her hand, at her perfectly painted nails, and started to chip the polish, sending little taupe flecks flying. "I don't know. You're just lucky to be doing what you love."

"I know. Trust me."

Because I did know, and I hoped I'd never forget. I still remembered the first time I'd seen the Hollywood sign, the letters bold and majestic and casting a promise to anyone who looked up at them with longing: "You're here. Anything is possible." That feeling of hope and anticipation, of possibility and wonder, similar to how I felt now, at this time in my life, as if I were pulling a ribbon from a gift and inside could be anything and everything. Of course between then and now had been years of uncertainty, disappointment, anxious waiting, and near misses—but ultimately the town had kept its promise. Success or not, I was doing what I loved. Anything *was* possible.

"Oh," Gina said, "and I'm gonna need your help cake tasting. Mark doesn't like sweets, which, I know, is just really weird. But it would be up to me to eat all that cake and sample flavors and stuff, and I can't do it alone. I need to be on a diet so I can fit into one of those lovely dresses."

I nodded, allowing her to change the subject to sugar and tulle, to frosting and satin. "Sure. I like free cake."

During the time we'd been sitting there, the sky had

noticeably dimmed and then quickly, almost impossibly fast, turned orange—as if God had just then remembered that night needed to come and had gotten up off a chair to flip a switch marked SUNSET. The water was glossy and velvety; the hue deepening and darkening with the setting sun, yet also streaked with reflections of pink. It was beautiful. How had I never realized this before? In my mind the California ocean had been gray and menacing, an ocean of hepatitis and scarily strong fish that had managed to not only survive but to capitalize on the pollution. Yet this whole time I'd been wrong. This whole time it had been right here, hiding behind trees and buildings, looming on the horizon, just waiting for me to notice.

And then there was music. Sly and the Family Stone's "Que sera, sera! Whatever will be, will be! The future's not ours to see! Que sera, sera!" I tore through my purse till I found my cell phone, and saw, with horror, that the screen was lit up with a picture of Matthew—a picture I'd taken that night, his laser eyes half-open, his arm extended in a toast. And there, in the very corner of the screen, was my hand on his shoulder. The picture was supposed to have been of both of us, but I've never been skilled at self-photography and at the time I honestly hadn't cared that I'd missed myself entirely. But now, now seeing all of him and yet just my fingers, just the tips of my fingers curved around his shoulder, I felt differently. The picture annoyed me.

I held the phone to Gina so she could see who was calling, and her eyes widened.

I had seconds to decide whether or not to answer. And you know, I was struck with a vision. In those heartbeats I saw it clearly: me alone, by my phone, ignoring my life as I waited and waited for someone else's words to make me feel better.

I wasn't going to do it. My life was finally heading up. I was sure of myself and determined and confident and finally happy, and I *knew* not to open my heart to this, to something I understood without needing to be told *was not good for me*. I didn't need it, I didn't need him, and I didn't need a reading or a prediction to know this. It was instinct. *My* instinct.

I was still holding the phone when it stopped ringing, when his picture flashed one last time and then was gone.

"I didn't answer," I said to Gina.

She smiled. "Yeah, I got that."

I dumped my phone in my purse and looked up, at the ocean. Below us the surfers appeared to be sailing on flashing, glimmering orange and pink light. No longer were they concerned about us. Maybe they'd accepted that we needed this in the same way they did, the comfort of being a part of something bigger than you can fathom. Finally, at long last, I was looking forward to my future, not because of vows made by others or words craved in the height of despair, but because *I* knew it would be good. Just like that I felt it, just like that I knew.

There I was, sitting beneath a sky that was bright and burning, before an ocean that was immense and eternal—and, now, next to a cell phone that was beeping with a voice mail.

"No," Gina said.

"Not even to check it? I have to check it. Even if I don't call him back, I have to check it."

She shook her head. "Glutton."

Sarah Lassez

I smiled and stood. "If it gets any darker, we'll never see the tar. And I'm thinking I need a bath with my new Zen sea salt. Let's go."

So we did. We made our way down the rocks, jumped back onto the sand, and walked in little zigzags to avoid the dark spots. Soon we were in the car, sand stuck to our feet, and the ocean dark beside us, talking about life and love and all the reasons to avoid an actor with laser blue eyes—even if he *did* leave you a nice message. ☺

About the Authors

SARAH LASSEZ was born on April Fools' Day. Don't ask her the year—she won't tell you. Of French nationality, she was raised in Australia before moving to New York as a teenager. After receiving her BFA from New York University's Tisch School of the Arts, Sarah moved to Hollywood to pursue an acting career. She has starred in more than a dozen independent films, working with directors such as Abel Ferrara, Gregg Araki, and Robert M. Young.

GIAN SARDAR received a B.A. in English from Loyola Marymount University, and is currently working on her second novel.